SHIPS OF THE PORT OF LONDON

twelfth to seventeenth centuries AD

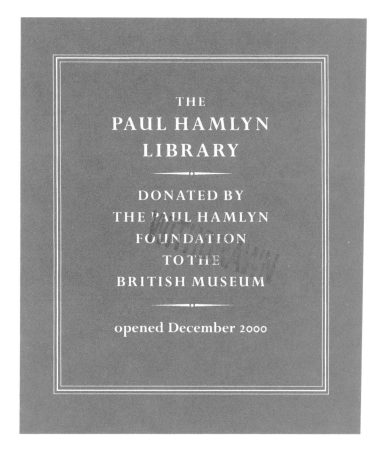

SHIPS OF THE PORT OF LONDON

twelfth to seventeenth centuries AD

Peter Marsden

drawings by Caroline Caldwell

ENGLISH HERITAGE

1996

ARCHAEOLOGICAL REPORT 5

First published 1996 by English Heritage,
23 Savile Row, London W1X 1AB

Printed by Snoeck-Ducaju & Zoon, Belgium
ISBN 1 85074 513 7

A catalogue record for this book is available from
the British Library

Edited by Kate Macdonald
Design and layout by Karen Guffogg, Tracey Croft and Pamela Irving

Contents

List of figures

List of tables

Summary

Three shipwrecks in the River Thames and parts of many broken-up ships and boats, dating from the twelfth to the seventeenth centuries, form the basis of this study. It is a remarkable collection that helps interpret the history and work of the port of London.

The Introduction describes how the timbers were studied, followed by Chapter 1 which summarises the information from the ship and boat fragments and what they indicate about the shipping of medieval and later London, particularly what vessels looked like and how they were built and used. This is supplemented by some medieval documentary records which, in the light of the archaeological finds, give a much broader understanding of medieval shipping and the port. The timbers were all from clinker-built vessels, mostly local river craft, though there are occasional ship timbers, a few of which have Baltic tree-ring patterns. Of particular interest are the small differences in the construction methods of various shipwrights. The chapter ends with a reconstruction of how ships arrived at the medieval port, and shows that the responsibility of the port authority of London, the Corporation of London, extended to the estuary of the River Thames.

Chapter 2 describes and reconstructs the substantial remains of a clinker-built vessel constructed locally about 1160–90, but broken up and reused a century later in a waterfront on the Custom House site, just west of the Tower of London. In Chapter 3 an almost complete sailing barge, Blackfriars ship 3, built about 1400 and sunk about eighty years later, is described and reconstructed. It had the characteristics of a very common type of river craft known as a 'shout'. Also included is a discussion of the remains of a fifteenth-century fishing net that had been caught in the wreck. In Chapter 4 another wreck is considered, Blackfriars ship 4, which lay adjacent to ship 3, possibly suggesting that the two had been in a collision. It is likely that ship 4 was an accidental loss as it still carried a cargo of Kentish ragstone for building purposes. Chapter 5 is a description of a number of river vessel fragments, dating from the twelfth to the early fifteenth centuries, which show that the planks were all built from radially-split oak fastened with iron rivets, and that the local boat timbers were mostly caulked with animal hair. Included with the finds is part of a substantial fifteenth-century anchor found in the River Thames where it presumably marked a mooring site.

Important changes in shipbuilding materials and techniques appear in the sixteenth century, and Chapter 6 reflects this, describing the stern of a boat that had been clinker-built in reverse, the lower planks overlapping the upper outboard. Chapter 7 discusses a clinker-built vessel, Blackfriars ship 2, which sank about 1670 while carrying a cargo of bricks, probably for the rebuilding of London after the Great Fire of 1666. Pieces of coal suggest that the vessel was a lighter to unload moored seagoing ships such as the colliers which had brought coal from Newcastle. The vessel types shown on the River Thames in contemporary illustrations of seventeenth-century London are also studied, in an attempt to define the type of vessel represented by ship 2. Chapter 8 describes many fragments of sixteenth and seventeenth-century vessels found reused in waterfronts and drains. These show that although the clinker shipbuilding in oak continued, there was an increasing use of elm, no doubt because oak was becoming less available. There is also evidence that sawn timber became more widely used than split oak.

A number of specialist appendices follow the main chapters. Appendix 1 discusses the tree-ring dating of plank samples from the ships and boats, and Appendix 2 looks at the timber identification. Appendix 3 examines the types of hair used in the caulking between planks, and Appendix 4 analyses the resin used on plank faces and in the hair caulking. Appendix 5 reproduces for the first time the documentary records of shipbuilding and repair expenses which maintained London Bridge, dating from 1382 to 1398. Appendix 6 is the fourteenth-century record of expenditure on cargoes of stone to maintain London Bridge, 1381–98, and Appendix 7 is an historical account of the lives of three London shipbuilders in the fourteenth century: both published here for the first time. Appendix 8 reproduces the text of a unique and hitherto unpublished thirteenth-century tide table. Appendix 9 is a gazetteer listing the known plank-built ship and boat discoveries in the Thames valley, and Appendix 10 is a report on the radio carbon-14 dating of dugout boats found in the Thames valley. Appendix 11 is a glossary of nautical terms used in this book. The volume ends with a bibliography and an index.

Résumé

Trois épaves retrouvées dans la Tamise et des morceaux de nombreux navires et bateaux, datant du douzième au dix-septième siècles, constituent la base de cette étude. C'est une collection remarquable qui nous permet de fournir une interprétation de l'histoire et de l'activité du port de Londres.

L'introduction décrit la manière dont on a étudié les bois d'oeuvre, puis le chapitre 1 résume les renseignements obtenus à partir des fragments de navires et de bateaux, et s'intéresse à ce qu'ils nous apprennent sur la navigation à Londres à partir du Moyen-Age, et en particulier l'apparence des bateaux et la manière dont ils étaient construits et utilisés. A cela s'ajoutent des documents médiévaux qui, à la lumière des trouvailles archéologiques, nous offrent une vision beaucoup plus étendue de la navigation et du port médiévaux. Tout le bois d'oeuvre provenait de bateaux bordés à clins, surtout de petits bâtiments qui ne naviguaient que dans la région; on a toutefois trouvé quelques bois d'oeuvre dont la répartition des anneaux indiquait qu'ils provenaient de la Baltique. Les petites differences dans les méthodes de construction des divers charpentiers sont particulièrement intéressantes. Le chapitre se termine par une reconstitution de la manière dont les bateaux accédaient au port médiéval, et démontre que la responsabilité des autorités portuaires de Londres, la Corporation de Londres, s'étendait à l'estuaire de la Tamise. Le chapitre 2 décrit et reconstruit les vestiges importants d'un bateau bordé à clins, construit dans la région aux environs de 1160–90, mais démonté et réutilisé un siècle plus tard pour aménager les berges du fleuve sur le site de Custom House, juste à l'ouest de la Tour de Londres. Au chapitre 3 on décrit et reconstruit une gabare presque complète, Blackfriars bateau 2, construite vers 1400 et coulée 80 ans plus tard. Elle possédait les caractéristiques d'un type de bateau fluvial très courant connu sous le nom de 'shout'. Ce chapitre comprend également une étude des restes d'un filet de pêche, datant du quinzième siècle, qui s'était trouvé pris dans l'épave. Au chapitre 4, on s'intéresse à une autre épave, Blackfriars bateau 4, qui gisait à côté du bateau 3, ce qui pourrait suggérer qu'ils étaient entrés en collision. La perte du bateau 4 fut probablement dûe à un accident car il contenait une cargaison de pierre bourrie provenant du Kent et destinée à la construction. Au chapitre 5, on décrit un nombre de fragments provenant de bateaux destinés à la navigation fluviale et datant du douzième au début du quinzième siècles, ils mettent en évidence le fait que les bordages étaient tous fabriqués en chênes fendus dans le sens des rayons et assemblés avec des rivets de fer, et que les bois destinés à la construction navale locale étaient la plupart du temps calfatés avec du poil d'animal. Parmi les trouvailles on compte aussi un vestige d'une ancre, de taille honorable, elle datait du quinzième siècle et a été retrouvée dans la Tamise, où elle indiquait probablement un emplacement pour s'amarrer.

D'importants changements dans les matériaux et les techniques de construction navale apparaissent au seizième siècle, et cela se reflète au chapitre 6, on y décrit la proue d'un bateau qui avait été construit selon la méthode du bordage à clins mais inversée, les bordages inférieurs recouvrent le bord supérieur. Dans le chapitre 7 on examine un bateau bordé à clins, Blackfriars bateau 2, qui sombra vers 1670 alors qu'il transportait une cargaison de briques probablement destinées à la reconstruction de Londres après le Grand Incendie de 1666. Les morceaux de charbon qui ont été découverts nous ont conduits à penser que c'était une allège utilisée pour décharger les navires hauturiers à l'amarrage, par exemple les charbonniers qui livraient du charbon de Newcastle. A partir d'illustrations contemporaines représentant Londres au dix-septième siècle, on étudie également les divers types de bateaux que l'on voit sur la Tamise dans le but d'essayer de définir à quelle sorte de bâtiment appartient le bateau 2. Le chapitre 8 décrit de nombreux fragments de bateaux du seizième et du dix-septième siècles que nous avons découverts réutilisés dans les aménagements des berges et des égouts. On a pu constater que bien qu'on ait continué à construire des bateaux bordés à clins en chêne, on utilisait de plus en plus l'orme, sans doute parce qu'il devenait moins facile de se procurer du chêne. On a aussi des témoignages qui prouvent que, de plus en plus, le chêne fendu était remplacé par du bois scié.

Un nombre d'appendices spécialisés font suite à l'ouvrage principal. Le premier appendice examine la datation des anneaux d'arbres sur des échantillons de bois provenant des navires et des bateaux, et le deuxième s'intéresse à l'identification des bois. L'Appendice 3 examine les types de poils utilisés pour calfater entre les bordages et l'Appendice 4 analyse la résine utilisée sur la surface des bordages et dans le calfatage. L'Appendice 5 reproduit pour la première fois des documents d'archives concernant la construction navale et les frais de réparations pour l'entretien du port de Londres, ils datent de 1382 à 1398. L'Appendice 6 est un document du quatorzième siècle cataloguant les frais des cargaisons de pierre destinée à l'entretien du port de Londres entre 1381 et 1398, et l'Appendice 7 est un compte-rendu historique de la vie de trois constructeurs de navires du quatorzième siècle; tous deux paraissant ici pour la première fois. L'Appendice 8 reproduit le texte d'une table des marées, unique et inédite, datant du treizième. L'Appendice 9 est une liste des découvertes répertoriées de navires et de bateaux construits en bois dans la vallée de la Tamise, et l'Appendice 10 est un compte-rendu de la datation au carbone 14 de canots creusés dans un tronc d'arbre découverts dans la vallée de la Tamise. L'Appendice 11 est un glossaire des termes nautiques utilisés dans cet ouvrage. Le volume se termine par une bibliographie et un index.

Translated by Annie Pritchard

Zusammenfassung

Die Basis dieser Studie bilden drei in der Themse gefundene Wracke und eine größere Anzahl von Boots - und Schiffsfragmenten.

Die Einleitung beschreibt die Untersuchung des Bauholzes, gefolgt von dem ersten Kapitel, das die Informationen über die Schiffsund Bootsfragmente zusammenfaßt. Es weist auf die Bedeutung der gefundenen Fragmente, die sie in der Schiffahrt inne gehabt hatten und besonders auf das Aussehen, die Konstruktion und die Benutzung der Schiffe im mittelalterlichen und spätmittelalterlichen London, hin. Im Lichte dieser archäologischen Funde erlauben diese Informationen, die durch eine Anzahl dokumentierter Eintragungen im Mittelalter unterstützt werden, einen größeren Einblick in die Schiffahrt und in dem Hafen des Mittelalters. Die Planken stammen alle aus klinkergebauten Booten, die auf ein meist örtlich angewandtes Flußhandwerk hinweisen. Jedoch sind einige Schiffplanken darunter, die ein baltisches Baumringmuster aufweisen. Von besonderem Interesse sind die kleinen Unterschiede, die bei den Konstruktionsmethoden verschiedener Schiffbauern auftreten. Das Kapitel endet mit einer Rekonstruktion der einlaufenden Schiffe in einem mitteralterlichen Hafen. Gleichzeitig beweist sie, daß sich der Wirkungsbereich der Londoner Hafenbehörde, 'The Corporation of London', bis zur Möndung der Themse ausdehnte.

Das zweite Kapitel beschreibt und rekonstruiert die Ümfrangreichen Uberreste eines klinkergebauten Holzbootes, welches um 1160–90 hergestellt wurde und das wiederum in Fragmente zerstückelt und ein Jahrhundert später, in einem Hafenviertel des Custom House-Geländes, gerade westlich des Londoner Towers, verwendet wurden. Das dritte Kapitel beschreibt und rekonstruiert ein fast vollständiges Segelfrachtschiff, Blackfriars Nummer 2, das um 1400 gebaut wurde und achtzig Jahre später sank. Es trug die Merkmale einer sehr verbreiteten Bauart. Diese Art von Segelfrachtschiffen war bei den Seeleuten unter den Namen 'shout' bekannt. Weiterhin enthält dieses Kapitel eine Diskussion über die Überreste eines aus dem fünfzehnten Jahrhundert stammenden Fischerbetzes, das sich in diesem Wrack des Blackfriars Nummer 2 verfangen hatte. Das vierte Kapitel wendet sich einem anderen Wrack zu, Blackfriars Nummer 4, das neben dem Schiff Nummer 3 gelegen hatte. Man vermutet, daß die beiden zusammenstoben waren. Es ist auch sehr wahrscheinlich, dab das Schiff Nummer 4 auch durch einen Unfall abhanden gekommen war, da es bei dem Fund, eine Fracht aus der Grafschaft Kent stammenden dunklen Kieselsandstein, der zum Bau verwendet weden sollte, mit sich getragen hatte. Das fünfte Kapitel ist eine Beschreibung einer Anzahl von Flußbootenfragmente, die vom zwölften bis zum frühen fünfzehnten Jahrhundert datieren. Diese beweisen, daß alle Planken aus radialförmig geschnittenen Eichenholz waren und mit Eisennieten befestigt waren. Gleichfalls beweisen sie, daß das örtlich gefundene, für die Wände der Boote benützte Holz vorwiegend mit Tierhaaren verdichtet wurde. Zu diesen Funden zählt man auch einen Teil eines umfangreichen Ankers aus dem fünfzehnten Jahrhundert, der in der Themse gefunden wurde und wahrscheinlich einen Ankerplatz denotierte.

Das sechste Kapitel gibt die im sechzehnten Jahrhundert wichtigen Entwicklungen in Bezug auf Baumaterial und angewandten technischen Methoden im Schiffbau wieder, indem es das Heck eines klinkergebauten Bootes - jedoch in verkehrter Richtung angeordnete Planken, nämlich die unteren Planken überdecken teilweise die oberen - beschreibt. Das siebte Kapitel behandelt ein klinkergebautes Boot, das das um sechzehnhundertsiebzig versunkene Blackfriars Nummer 2. Es trug Ziegel, die wahrscheinlich für den Wiederaufbau Londons, das durch das Großfeuer in 1666 zerstört wurde, gedacht waren.

Kohlenstücke lassen annehmen, daß das Boot ein Schleppschiff war und hochseetüchtige, verankerte Boote wie Kohlenschiffe, die Kohlen aus Newcastle brachten, entladet hatte. Gleichzeitig, in der Absicht die Schiffart zu definieren, die durch die Bauart des Schiffes Nummer 2 verkörpert war, wurden die Schiffsarten, die auf zeitgenössischen Illustrationen im siebzehnten Jahrhundert auf der Themse abgebildet waren, beschrieben. Das achte Kapitel beschreibt viele Fragmente des siebzehnten und achtzehnten Jahrhunderts, die im Hafenviertel und als Rohre in Abflüssen wieder benutzt wurden. Diese Fragmente beweisen, obwohl sich der Bau mit Eichen verfertigten klinkergebauten Booten fortsetzte, daß die Zahl der mit Ulmen verfertigten Boote im Zunehmen war. Ohne Zweifel war dafür der zunehmende Vorratsmangel der Eichen verantwortlich.

Die Spezialisten-Appendizes folgen den Haupkapiteln. Der erste Appendix behandelt die Dendrochronologie der aus Booten und Schiffen stammenden Plankenexemplare. Der zweite Appendix hingegen behandelt die Holzabstammung der Planken. Der dritte Appendix untersucht die Haararten, die bei der Verdichtung zwischen Planken verwendet wurden und der vierte Appendix analysiert das bei den Plankenoberflächen und bei der Verdichtung mit Haaren verwendete Harz. Zum ersten Mal werden die dokumentierten Berichte der Schiffs-und Reparaturkosten, die London Bridge zwischen 1382 und 1398 zu bewältigen hatte, wiedergegeben. Der sechste Appendix ist die Wiedergabe der Kosten der zu tragenden Steinlasten anhand der aus dem siebzehnten Jahrundert stammenden Berichte, die London Bridge zwischen 1381 und 1398 begleichen mußte. Der siebte Appendix ist die historische Wiedergabe des Lebens dreier Schiffbauer im vierzehnten Jahrhundert. Auch diese zwei appendizes werden hier zum ersten Mal veröffentlicht. Der achte Appendix gibt den Text einer einzigartigen und bis jetzt noch nicht veröffentlichen Tabelle über die Zeiten der Ebben und der Fluten wieder. Der neunte Appendix ist eine Aufzeichnung aller Funde der aus Planken gebauten Schiffen und Booten im Tal der Themse. Der zehente Appendix ist ein Bericht über Radiocarbondatierung der im Tale der Themse gefundenen und ausgegrabenen Kanus. Der elfte Appendix ist ein Glossar der in diesen Buch verwendeten, nautischen Fachausdrücken. Am Ende des Bandes befindet sich eine Bibliographie und ein Index.

Translated by Monika Schmid-Jenkinson

Acknowledgements

English Heritage and the Museum of London have jointly funded this study, though the wreck excavations at Blackfriars were carried out by the author as an officer of the former Guildhall Museum of the City of London. The fragments of vessels found in the City of London were recovered by staff of the former Department of Urban Archaeology, and those from Southwark by the former Department of Greater London Archaeology, both of which are now part of the Museum of London Archaeological Service.

Of the various people who have contributed to this study my grateful thanks are primarily due to Caroline Caldwell. She spent much time unpacking, cleaning, and drawing ship timbers, some of which had been in storage for years and were unpleasantly infested with crawling creatures and fungi, and the work was often carried out in cold and wet locations in various parts of central London. Subsequently she prepared the excellent publication drawings used here, and has done so much to help present the information as clearly as possible.

My thanks are also due to those who made a special contribution during the investigation on the sites, particularly on the wrecks found at Blackfriars. They include John Clark, Roger Inman, the late Ralph Merrifield and Hugh Chapman. Also, grateful thanks are due to the following specialists whose researches have greatly broadened the understanding of the boat remains: Ian Tyers who carried out the tree-ring dating and identified the timber samples would like to thank Nigel Nayling and Helen Hibbert who assisted in the analyses, and Cathy Groves and Jennifer Hillam of Sheffield University Dendrochronology Laboratory; Mike Baillie, Dave Brown, and Jon Pilcher of Queen's University Belfast Dendrochronology Laboratory and Niels Bonde of The National Museum who supplied him with data and discussion. Michael L Ryder who identified the hair caulking, John Evans who identified the tar samples, Brian Spencer and Tony Dyson who undertook some important historical studies, and Lyn Blackmore and Ian Betts who reported on dating evidence. Others who have helped include Alan Thompson who kindly checked the records of the Southwark sites, and John Goldman who kindly advised on the use of his naval architecture computer program, Boatcad. Finally, I am grateful to Tony Dyson for his editorial efforts with a complex and specialised text, and to Seán McGrail for his maritime advice, and to Pamela Irving of English Heritage who brought the book to publication.

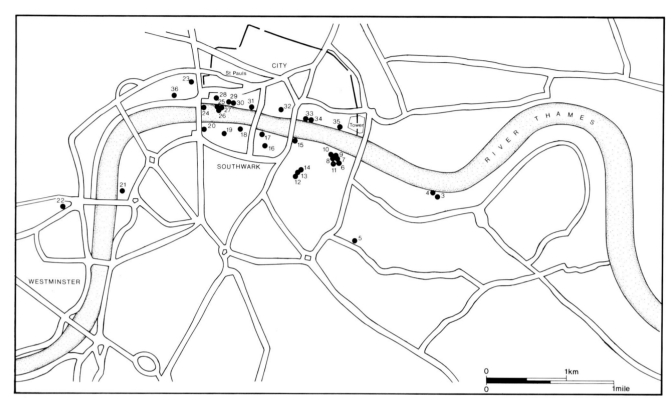

Fig 1 Sites with ship and boat remains in central London (see Appendix 9): Nos 1 and 2 not shown. 3 Cherry Garden Street; 4 National Wharf, Bermondsey Wall East; 5 Southwark Park Road; 6 Abbots Lane; 7 Morgans Lane; 8 Bethel Estate; 9 Gun and Shot Wharf; 10 Butter Factory South; 11 Symonds Wharf; 12 New Guy's House; 13 Maze Pond; 14 Guy's Hospital, Tooley Street; 15 Fennings Wharf; 16 Park Street; 17 5–15 Bankside; 18 37–46 Bankside; 19 Bankside Power Station; 20 245 Blackfriars Road; 21 County Hall; 22 Storey's Gate; 23 9-11 Bridewell Place; 24–27 River Thames, Blackfriars (ships 1–4); 28 Baynards Castle; 29 Upper Thames Street; 30 Trig Lane; 31 Thames Exchange; 32 Thames Street; 33 New Fresh Wharf; 34 Billingsgate; 35 Custom House; 36, City of London Boys School

Introduction

The cumulative discovery in London of parts of ships and boats of the Roman, Saxon, medieval, and later periods is of great importance in maritime archaeology and in the history of London. In no other ancient European port is every major stage of its history represented by the recovered remains of ships and boats, of waterfronts and warehouses, and even of former cargoes. In this book are described the remains of vessels from twenty-one sites(Fig 1), that date from the twelfth to the seventeenth centuries, those from earlier periods having been considered elsewhere (Marsden 1994).

The significance of the collection is illustrated by Seán McGrail's view in 1980 that at that time, for the period before 1500, 'from the British and Irish evidence for wooden boatbuilding ... the corpus of well-recorded and dated wooden boats is minute: twenty or so finds spanning some 3500 years' (McGrail and Denford 1982, 28–30). He listed eleven plank-built finds (four of which were from London) and ten dugout boats (*ibid*). There have only been a few additional important boat finds in the British Isles since 1980, apart from the London discoveries.

Since it is not until the fifteenth century that there exist useful illustrations of the waterfronts and shipping of the port of London (*Front Cover and Fig 70,* see Rowse 1974, 33–4)the archaeological evidence for these is crucial. This seems to show, broadly, that when Roman London was founded, in about AD 50, ships probably berthed at a prepared sloping beach, but that within twenty years timber quays and jetties were introduced, and continued to be used until the Roman waterfront was allowed to decay after about AD 250. The shipping was probably mostly of Celtic type, though a locally-built vessel of Mediterranean-style construction has been found that may have had an official use. The re-establishment of the port on the same site at the end of the ninth century was initially confined to a man-made sloping beach, but by the twelfth century jetties and timber revetments had become normal, and by the fifteenth century the quays were commonly of stone. All known medieval ships and boats from London were clinker built, but after 1500 there were changes in methods of construction and materials which enabled the building of larger, and possibly cheaper, ships.

It is tempting to compare the medieval and later ship and boat finds from London with others found in Europe, but that needs another book to itself. However, it is to be expected that as most of the London fragments described in this volume were apparently from smaller vessels of medieval and later date, they may only represent local shipbuilding practices on the 'inland' waters of the Thames rather than European shipbuilding generally. How distinctive they were will only become apparent when, in due course, they are compared in detail with ship finds from Bergen (Christensen 1985), Dublin (McGrail 1993), the Netherlands, Denmark, and elsewhere.

As an example of the benefits of European-wide comparisons, the large vessel from Woolwich, believed to be Henry VII's *Sovereign*, was a warship of *c* 1500 (*see Chapter 1 and Appendix 9*) and is in a class of its own for the region. It should be compared with other early warships, particularly the *Mary Rose* (1545) in England (Rule 1983) and the *Elefanten* (1564) in Sweden (Ingelman-Sundberg 1985, 946). Even though there is documentary evidence showing that the *Sovereign* was sometimes used in trade (Salzman 1931, 277), there is little archaeological evidence from London of large seagoing merchant ships, medieval or later, though this deficiency could be filled by a broader north-European study taking account of the discovery of seagoing merchant ships of types known to have traded with London. These include the medieval cogs found in Germany and Denmark (Reinders 1985), and at a later period the English East Indiamen that were often built beside the Thames and brought so much wealth to London. They include the discovered wrecks of the *Valentine* which sank off the Channel Islands in 1779, the *Halsewell* sunk off Seacombe, Devon, in 1786, the *Earl of Abergavenny* sunk off Weymouth in 1805, and the *Admiral Gardner,* sunk in the Goodwin Sands in 1809.

It is likely that further study will also clarify some construction methods, and for this reason drawings of as many fragments as possible are published here. They illustrate the quality of the evidence, as well as the forms of ancient shipbuilding, such as the grain of the wood, the patterns of trenails by which the frames were fastened to the planks, the patterns of rivet fastenings holding the planks together, and the forms of damage (eg split planks) and repairs. Much of this information can only be conveyed by illustrations, though further details can be established by consulting the archive records at the Museum of London. Construction details for each piece of planking are given in Tables 6 and 7, and further descriptions of the hair caulking are in Appendix 3, and of the tar dressing in Appendix 4.

It has been difficult to establish the site contexts of many boat fragments since many of the sites themselves have not yet been prepared for publication. Considerable reliance has therefore been

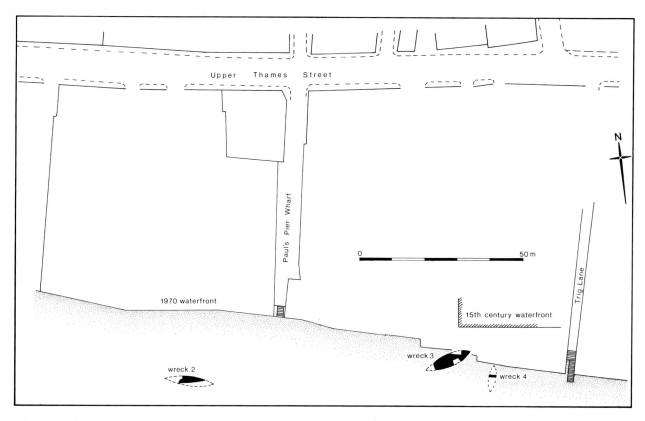

Fig 2 The location of Blackfriars ships 2, seventeenth century and ships 3 and 4 , fifteenth century

placed upon the tree-ring dating carried out by Ian Tyers, which, although it provides a *terminus post quem* date, often does indicate a shipbuilding period. Tree-ring dating can sometimes suggest where two fragments have been cut from the same tree, and may be from the same boat. This has shown that most of the planks were of locally-grown oak, though a few were of oak grown in the Baltic and German regions (*see Appendix 1*).

The ships described in this volume do more than illustrate man's ability to transport himself and his possessions across water. They also reflect his ability to predict complex natural forces, particularly buoyancy, gravity, wind, water resistance, and the tides. Although ancient shipbuilders and mariners may not have understood how these forces worked, they could judge their effect and used them to create safe vessels capable of venturing onto the oceans. The ship and boat finds from London show that almost every major shipbuilding tradition of western and northern Europe was present in the port between the second and the fifteenth century, reflecting its cosmopolitan character. The natural result of this concentration of maritime expertise and experience over time in one port was the domination of world exploration and trade by the merchants and seafarers of London from the sixteenth century onwards.

The objectives of the study of the ship timbers needed clarification at an early stage in the project, and as a result research has been aimed at relating the

fragments, both large and small, to these main characteristics of any ship or boat:

- its construction, which reflects both its cultural shipbuilding tradition as well as its strength
- its shape, and its weight distribution, both of which reflect the stability of the vessel
- its method of propulsion
- its method of steering

Setting the ships into their local working contexts as transporters of people and goods was also felt to be important. The study of former cargoes made it possible to identify likely voyage routes, and the excavation of waterfronts clarified methods of berthing and warehousing. Finally, the lifestyle of the shipbuilders who constructed these vessels, and of the mariners and others who used them was agreed to be significant for understanding the human interaction with these vessels. It is fortunate for the period under review that the documentary information is so numerous, although much still needs collating.

The more than two hundred fragments of vessels from twenty-one sites in central London studied for this book (Fig 1), were found as shipwrecks at Blackfriars (Fig 2) and as salvaged fragments reused mostly in waterfronts. Often the fragments were small samples of much larger remains of vessels found on site, but owing to the difficulties of storing large amounts of ship timbers and the time that their recording would need, the site supervisors had to take a pragmatic view in dealing with them. Although understandable, this approach has led to the loss of much information. Even when parts of vessels were saved, the storage difficulties resulted in some samples being destroyed through decay, and on most planking fragments the finer details, of tool marks for example, had often been lost, even within the plank laps. Moreover, the accumulated volume of timbers was so great that it was not practical to do as much sampling and analysis as was really necessary. Instead, only selective sampling was possible.

The lesson here is that a maritime specialist should deal with ship timbers as soon as they are found. This would not only enable more information to be recovered, but would also allow decisions to be made about the disposal of the pieces. There was some recording of ship remains on the sites, particularly as their reuse in waterfronts was concerned, but their study as parts of vessels needed a more detailed study, only possible by saving all the remains of a vessel and recording them after careful cleaning. Consequently this volume only includes those fragments which were available to the author for study, though more information is available in the site records of finds that have not been kept. In addition the information for this publication had to be selected from what was available; more information can be found in the archive of boat finds preserved at the Museum of London,

Studying these fragments began with tracing the shape of each timber face on film, together with a drawing at full-size scale, which was then reduced by photocopier to a scale of 1:5, the accuracy and straightness of the reduction being checked by the scale. A publication drawing was then prepared at 1:5, for reproduction at 1:10. At least one cross-profile of each timber was also drawn full-size, and usually a section was cut across the timber so that the tree-rings and wood rays could be drawn to show their direction and density.

The salient information for each fragment was recorded on paper. First, the timber was sketched and all significant measurements, such as width and thickness, were noted; these referred to the original size of the timber, and not necessarily only to the piece in its fragmentary state. This recording method showed how the timber was shaped: either tangentially or radially cut; if the grain was straight or knotty, what species of timber was used, and if there were any tool marks. The construction of each fragment was described using these instructions and questions:

- carvel (flush) or clinker (overlapping) planking
- dimensions of the overlap between planks
- the dimensions of any scarfs (with a sketch)
- caulking in the lap or in the scarf, and how it was laid

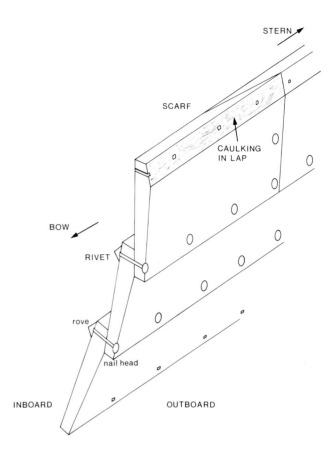

Fig 3 Rules of normal clinker plank construction

- describe and measure the overlap fastenings (usually iron rivets)
- the spacing of the rivets centre to centre
- describe and measure frame fastenings (ie trenails or trenail holes) and their spacing from centre to centre
- describe any surface dressing (normally tar)

Evidence for the use of the vessel, including traces of wear and erosion, damage that might have been repaired, and any damage caused by wood-borers, particularly the *Teredo* ship-worm which would show that the vessel had sailed in salt water, was added to the record. Next, a reconstruction of each fragment was sketched to show the inboard or outboard views, the spacing of the frames (from trenail positions), and any indication of the hull shape. This part was interpretative, including the recorder's view of whether the fragment came from the port or starboard side of its vessel on the basis of surviving plank scarfs.

In interpreting the plank fragments the rules of clinker plank construction were applied (Fig 3):

- that the upper strake or plank generally overlapped the lower outboard
- that the roves or diamond-shaped washers of rivets were placed inboard

- that planks scarfed endways to make a continuous strake were normally overlapped outboard towards the stern (Leather 1987, 86)

Although these rules of interpretation were probably applied by the shipbuilders in most cases it is important to remember that they were not absolute, and in one case (*see Chapter 7*) there is an undoubted example of 'reverse clinker' construction in which the lower strake overlapped the upper. Repairs to planks can also cause some scarf joints to face the bow, so that interpreting a plank with a single scarf cannot be as certain as several articulated planks with a number of scarfs all facing the same direction.

Finally, it was recorded whether or not each fragment was drawn and photographed, and what samples were taken for tree-ring dating, wood identification, hair caulking, or of possible tar dressing of the timber. A note was made of whether or not the samples were sent to a specialist, and the result, and a final note was made concerning the disposal of the timber samples. Photographs were used to record details of construction or tool marks, rather than general views of whole pieces.

It was clear at the outset of the writing of this volume that the interpretation of the London ship and boat remains needed a clear rationale, particularly as medieval documentary records for the port are so rich in maritime detail, and much of it unpublished. It was realised that for the archaeological evidence to make sense it should be related to the documentary records, and that the latter should set the overall context into which the archaeology would fit. However, the archaeology limited the use of the historical records to what seemed relevant, and although a much greater study of the documentary sources was clearly desirable the limitations of time and funding prevented this. For example, it was not possible to examine the historical background of the change from oak to elm in sixteenth-century shipbuilding, and from split oak to sawn-timber planks. It is hoped that the reader will regard any similarly apparent omissions as borne of necessity rather than negligence.

The London ship and boat remains, although mostly of local river craft, included parts of seagoing vessels, some of which were built from timbers from the Baltic region. Consequently, this study of London and its maritime activities includes those regions that were important to the port in the past, and the lower reaches of the river Thames and its estuary. The concentration of evidence, however, is in the ship remains from the London sector of the Thames, though it was mainly by chance that the timbers were found there. As ships and boats were mobile buildings their remains could have been found almost anywhere on the river. For this reason a gazetteer of all known

plank-built ship and boat discoveries in the lower Thames valley is included (*see Appendix 9*), together with a list of dated dugout boats from that river and its tributaries, kindly supplied by Professor McGrail (*see Appendix 10*).

At first it seemed that drawings of only a representative selection of the fragments need be published. But in practice the London timbers would not fit into such a scheme because it was difficult to find 'representative' examples where there were so many constructional variables, and it was considered important to publish the pattern of frame-to-plank fastenings and their spacing, the form and position of repairs, the types of damage by splitting particularly at fastenings, and the types of wood grain, knotty or straight. Illustrating the quality of the evidence was also a consideration.

Ideally, the published drawings should be accompanied by reconstruction views of each fragment, but generally this has not been possible due to time and cost. Instead, the significant information has been converted to a set of tables (Tables 6 and 7) under these headings:

- maximum thickness
- original width
- lap width
- lap caulking (including method of lying in the lap)
- maximum and minimum rivet spacing between centres
- size of rivet shank in cross-section
- scarf length
- pattern and type of scarf fastenings
- spacing of trenails (or other frame fastenings) in the planks, between centres
- trenail diameters
- trenail wood type
- plank wood type
- radial or tangential cutting.

There is some uncertainty about the correct ordering of the site context numbers used for each timber fragment excavated in Southwark. This variation has been retained here, though it seems that the order is not significant as long as the numbers are given. Not all boat fragments or tree-ring sections of planks referred to are illustrated in this volume, and not all drawn tree-ring sections of planks have been dated. When the sites on which the fragments were found are eventually written up and published the significance of the fragments will become clearer.

The written records, and the archive records preserved at the Museum of London, contain much more information, and include notes on repairs:

- were there extra rivets in the laps?

- any extra trenails?
- any patches, and if so what damage were they covering inboard or outboard, and how were they fastened?
- any patch caulking?
- how thick was the patch?
- was there any borer damage or erosion?

Since almost all of the timbers were clinker-built planks (the exceptions were parts of frames) and all were of similar construction, comparisons can be made to establish whether or not the vessels' builders adhered to any shipbuilding rules governing the proportions between parts of the timbers; the maximum plank thickness relative to the original plank width, the plank width relative to the lap width, the lap width relative to the plank thickness, the plank thickness relative to the maximum rivet spacing, and the plank thickness relative to the scarf length. It would seem that that there were no strict rules in the minds of the shipbuilders.

These small fragments of ships and boats have much information to give about the construction of medieval and sixteenth-century vessels in the port of London, but unfortunately they have nothing to say about the size and form of the vessels represented. In contrast Blackfriars ship 3, dating from about 1400, was almost complete and can be reconstructed on paper without much difficulty. Consequently it has been possible to establish its original shape and to calculate the distribution of its weight, so as to assess the vessel for its theoretical stability and performance by means of the naval architecture software program Boatcad (marketed by the Aluminium Boat Company, Trewen Road, Budock Water, Falmouth, Cornwall, TR11 5DY). In this way its unladen draught and its maximum cargo weight have been calculated as if the vessel was a modern craft.

The remains of the vessels described in this book are only part of the many ship finds from the Thames valley which collectively reflect the importance of the river as a highway for over two thousand years (see Appendix 9). The importance of making proper provision for the study of ship timbers in the future is clear, for there will continue to be many similar finds in waterfronts, and occasionally larger pieces will emerge that will allow us to reconstruct the size, shape, and weight distribution of complete vessels. It will be from these that the types of vessels that served the port of London will be reconstructed, and will show better how the quays and docks were used, and how the cargoes of goods were imported.

1 Twelfth to thirteenth-century shipping in the port of London

Summary

As the earliest illustration of the waterfront of London dates from the fifteenth century (*see front cover and Rowse 1974, 33–4*) we have to rely upon a combination of documentary and archaeological evidence to reconstruct what the port, with its ships, boats, quays, and docks, looked like in the medieval period, and how it worked. Tree-ring studies (*Appendix 1*) show that most of the datable boat timbers were local, and their small size suggests that the vessels were probably mostly local river craft. It is estimated that some 31 to 33 craft are represented by the fragments which date from the twelfth to the seventeenth centuries, although these could account for as many as 40 to 50 vessels. However, very few fragments had thick planks, which may indicate that only three or four substantial seagoing ships are represented among the fragments.

The port and its ships

Seventh to eleventh centuries

London's functions as an international port and as a centre of national government were due not only to its location at the lowest bridging point on the River Thames but also to its proximity to the Continent and its situation opposite the mouth of the Rhine, the main northern water highway into the heart of Europe (Fig 4).

The Roman city of *Londinium*, founded by the Romans in *c* AD50, had died at the end of the Roman period, soon after AD 400, and for 200 years the uncertainties of the Dark Ages and the arrival of the Saxons and their kingdoms supplanted the Roman administration (Vince 1990, 4–12). London was re-established in the seventh century when the middle Saxon settlement of *Lundenwic* was developed in the

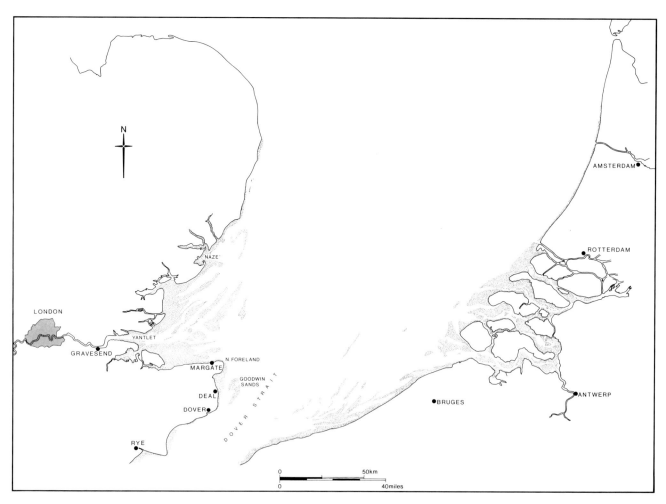

Fig 4 London relative to the southern North Sea, the English Channel, and the mouth of the Rhine

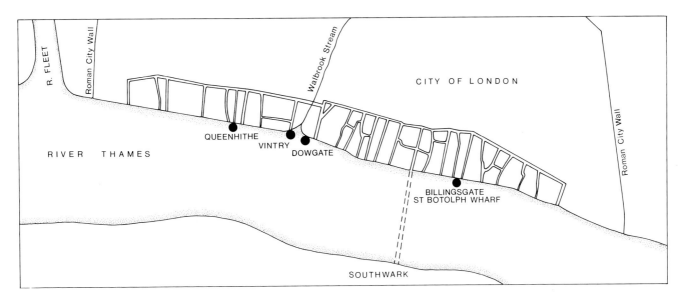

Fig 5 Medieval public berthing places on the London waterfront

Aldwych area about 2 km west of the ruins of the Roman city. But the Viking raids on London which started in 842, persuaded the Saxon inhabitants to move their settlement to comparative safety within the Roman defensive walls. The peace that lasted throughout much of the tenth century allowed the new city to expand under the government of a *portreeve* representing the king. Streets were laid out, houses and churches built, and along the waterfront were established three 'common quays', Aethelredshithe (later Queenhithe), Billingsgate, and St Botolph Wharf (Fig 5), where trading ships berthed and customs duties were collected for the king. It is likely that there were beach markets there for the sale of goods, and at Dowgate and Vintry which were primarily used by German and French merchants (Vince 1990, 93–108).

The archaeological evidence for some of those hithes, the earliest discovered traces of post-Roman berthing, consists of prepared beaches at St Botolph Wharf and Dowgate, and date from the tenth century. There were also indications of timber revetments, and at Botolph Wharf a small man-made inlet with a mooring post which was probably a dock for a boat less than 2m wide (Steedman *et al* 1992, 536).

The earliest-known record of regulations governing the port of London dates from about AD 1000 and is the so-called Law Code IV of Ethelred II (Loyn 1962, 93–4), which lists the berthing tolls at Billingsgate that were due to the king. The code seems to deal with both seagoing trading ships and local river craft carrying agricultural produce from nearby farmsteads. A small ship would pay one half-penny, and a larger ship with sails one penny. A 'keel' (*ceol*) and a 'hulk' (*hulcus*) paid fourpence each. A ship with a cargo of planks paid one plank, and on Sunday, Tuesday, and Thursday only, a toll was payable for cloth. For a merchant coming to

the bridge (presumably London Bridge) with a boat containing fish a half-penny was paid, or one penny for a large ship. Men from Rouen arriving with cargoes of wine or blubber-fish paid six shillings for a large ship and five per cent of the fish. The men of Flanders, Ponthieu, Normandy, and the Isle of France exhibited their goods and paid their toll, as did the men from Huy, Liege, and Nivelles who were passing through London. The men of the Emperor (ie the Germans) were entitled to the same privileges as the local people, though as well as paying the toll they had to pay two lengths of grey and one length of brown cloth, 10lbs of pepper, five pairs of gloves, and two saddle-kegs of vinegar at Christmas and Easter

The bridge mentioned here was of timber, since construction of the stone bridge began only in 1176 (Harben 1918). It seems to have had the effect of a boundary across the river restricting shipping, as is shown by the account of the arrival at London of Godwine in 1052 during his dispute with King Edward the Confessor. The Anglo-Saxon Chronicle relates that:

'Godwine kept on advancing towards London with his fleet, until at last he came to Southwark where he waited some time until the tide came up. In that interval he treated with the citizens so that they nearly all wanted what he wanted. When Godwine had arranged all his expedition the tide came in and they forthwith weighed anchor and proceeded through the bridge always keeping to thc southern bank.'
(Douglas and Greenaway 1953, 126–7)

London capitulated to William the Conqueror in 1066, and, although he confirmed the city's traditional rights, he ensured the compliance of the citizens by building the Tower of London in the south-east corner of the city. It is likely also that he authorised the construction of Baynards Castle at the south-west corner (Harben 1918).

Fragments of ships and boats of the tenth and eleventh centuries have been recovered from waterfront sites at New Fresh Wharf 1974, Billingsgate 1982, and Fennings Wharf 1984, and were, according to tree-ring studies, locally built. They are described in an earlier volume (Marsden 1994; see also Goodburn 1994), but their great interest is that they show that shipbuilding methods were related to traditions current elsewhere in northern Europe. All were clinker built, but some had fastenings of iron rivets as used in Scandinavia, others had wooden pegs as used by the Slavs along the southern Baltic, and another had hooked nails similar to those subsequently used in the medieval 'cogs' of the Low Countries. Constructional features were apparent, particularly in a fragment of a locally-built vessel from the Thames Exchange site in the City (Goodburn 1994), for which there are parallels in the Viking ships of Roskilde, Denmark, suggesting that shipbuilding was taking place during the Viking settlement of south-east England. Another fragment of a vessel had a north German clinker construction and tree-ring pattern.

As only small fragments of vessels of this period have been found in London, they give no information about the shape and size of the original craft. Valuable clues to vessel sizes in this period are the tenth-century Graveney boat (Fenwick 1978a) from north Kent, and two side rudders radiocarbon-dated to the ninth to eleventh centuries, found in the sea off Southwold, Suffolk (Hutchinson 1986). The Graveney boat, believed to have been about 13m long, is thought to have had sides about 1m high amidships and about 1.8m high at the ends (Fenwick 1978a, fig 10.1.1). This compares with the Southwold rudders, 3.91m and 4.36m long, which have tiller positions indicating vessels with sides approximately 2 and 3m high.

Twelfth to fifteenth centuries

Although there are many medieval references to shipping in the port the few contemporary representations very rarely show what the vessels look like. The archaeological evidence, therefore, is crucial for a proper understanding of the documentary and pictorial record (figs 6 and 7).

The remains of ships and boats have been found in two main contexts, as shipwrecks sunk in the bed of the river Thames, and as parts of broken-up hulls reused in waterfront revetments. In some cases large slabs of the bottom planking of vessels were reused (eg at Custom House in 1973 and Abbots Lane in 1987), and in others the pieces were much smaller (eg

Fig 6 Seal of St Bartholomew's Hospital, London, twelfth century, showing a late Saxon-Norman type of ship carrying a church (diam 47 mm, Seal LXVIII.23, reverse. Reproduced by permission of the British Library)

Fig 7 Seal of the Priory of St Bartholomew's, London, style of the thirteenth century but attached to a charter of 1533. The ship is a 'cog' and is shown carrying a church (diam c 56 mm, Harley Charter 83.A.43, reverse. Reproduced by permission of the British Library)

Morgans Lane in 1987). Frequently the excavated pieces were merely 'sampled' by site excavators, and the pieces saved were therefore small and not necessarily representative of the whole piece of timbering as it had survived. In other instances the samples have not all survived and are only known from drawings made soon after their excavation. These have mostly been omitted from this book.

The medieval ship and boat planking can be divided into the following types:

- pieces of clinker boat planking no more than 20mm thick with a local tree-ring pattern, and possibly with borings from the marine mollusc *Teredo* which can only live in saline conditions. Evidence of its borings in the wood of boat remains can indicate that the vessels had been at sea for considerable periods. These fragments are best explained as deriving from local fishing boats (sites ABB 87, 37BS 87; *see Chapter 5 and Chapter 7*).

- fragments of clinker boat planking of about the same thickness, probably parts of river and estuary vessels for their dimensions are probably too small to be from large seagoing cargo ships, and all that have been tree-ring dated are of 'local' oak, indicating a local origin and use.

- fragments of thick planking with substantial fastenings, both trenails and rivets, indicating that they probably derive from seagoing ships.

Archaeological evidence for local vessels

Although the fragments are too small to show the form, size, and purpose of the vessels to which they belonged (*see Chapter 5*), enough of three medieval vessels did remain to suggest their use. The most complete was Blackfriars ship 3, a clinker-built sailing river barge, as it would be termed today, but not in the fifteenth century when it was in use, since 'barges' were then seagoing vessels. Its characteristics closely match one of the most common types of contemporary river vessel, the 'shout' (*see Chapter 3*). It had a broad flat bottom and a plank-like keel suited for sailing in very shallow water. Another vessel with a broad flat bottom was the Custom House boat, dating from the late twelfth century (*see Chapter 2*), which may have had a similar use. Its clinker construction and apparent sharp form at both ends appear to be 'Scandinavian', so it is possible that the original vessel was somewhat like that shown on the twelfth-century seal of St Bartholomew's Hospital, London, but excluding its building (Fig 6).

In contrast, Blackfriars ship 4, probably dating from the fifteenth century, was not so broad and carried a cargo of Kentish ragstone. It may have been a type then termed a *farcost* (*see Chapter 4*), but its small dimensions suggest that it was more likely to be a lighter. This too had a flat bottom and a plank-like keel, but its sides may have been higher than those of Blackfriars ship 3 (1.36m) to carry the heavy stone and avoid being swamped in the Thames and Medway estuaries.

The similarity of construction methods and of materials in the boat fragments helps in interpreting the documentary evidence for medieval shipbuilding in London. The discovery of large parts of the Custom House boat (late twelfth century) and of Blackfriars ship 3 (*c* 1400) enables the sequence of shipbuilding to be reconstructed when following the building of boats through the weekly payments made in the Bridge House accounts (*Appendix 5*). Initially the keel was laid, then the planking was riveted together to make the shell. Then the frames were inserted and fastened by trenails. The basic shipbuilding elements were, therefore, keel, stems, frames, planks, iron rivets, and wooden trenails. It is clear from the fragments that shipwrights, even in the same vessel, did not follow any strict constructional rules based on the proportional relationship between plank width and thickness, the clinker lap size, the maximum spacing of rivet fastenings, and the length of plank scarfs. The proportions used in any one vessel shows considerable variation, within broad limits.

In order to fashion the timber it seems, from occasional tool marks, that three of the most important tools used in boatbuilding were the axe, the auger, and the hammer.

Although radially-cut oak was normally used for ship and boat planking during the medieval period, there were some changes in other materials that help to date the London boat finds. During the tenth and eleventh centuries moss and hair were used as caulking materials, and clinker lap fastenings included iron rivets, pegs of willow or poplar, and, probably, hooked nails. The roves of rivets tended to be fairly small and flat compared with those of, say, the fifteenth century, and by the twelfth to thirteenth centuries hair had become the normal caulking material, with moss very rarely used (it only seems to occur in association with Baltic oak planks). Cattle and goat hair with a little wool were most commonly used, apparently mixed with pine resin (*see Appendices 3 and 4*). The lap fastenings were then exclusively iron rivets, whose roves tended to be larger and perhaps more often domed towards the end of the medieval period. By the fifteenth century the trenails that held the frames and planks together were usually of oak instead of willow or poplar. To what extent these changes in materials reflect their availability or different ideas in shipbuilding is unknown. They could represent variations of a local shipbuilding tradition, and the study of many boat timbers from other ports would in time suggest regional variations. There were different practices between individual shipwrights in London as indicated by the different ways in which the hair caulking was laid in the laps between planks. Some

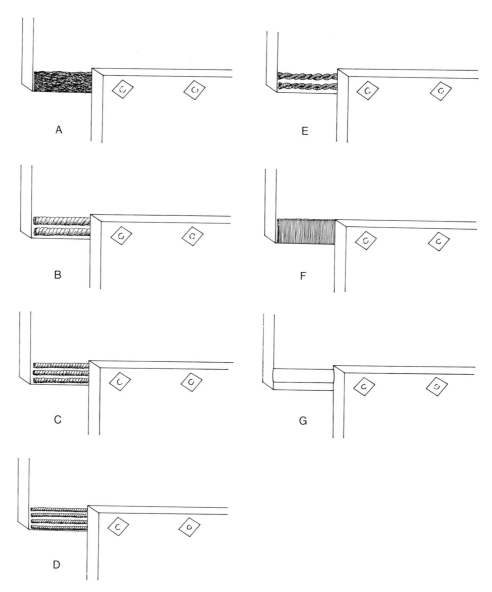

*Fig 8 Various methods of hair caulking in the London boat fragments: A matted; B
2-string; C 3-string; D 4-string; E double twisted; F cross-laid; G a caulking groove*

shipbuilders laid it matted, others twisted it into strings laid along the lap, and others laid the strands of hair across the laps (Fig 8). Also, the fastenings for plank scarfs varied, some having several rivets and others none (Fig 9).

However, when the London boat planking is compared with the planking from Bergen in western Norway, also of the thirteenth to fifteenth centuries (Christensen 1985, 201–3), regional differences seem to appear. The most obvious is that where all the medieval planking from London is of oak, most of the Bergen planks are of pine, with just a few pieces of oak. Less obvious is possibly the spacing of the frame centres in boats as indicated by trenail spacing in planks. In the London remains the trenails mostly lay at 0.31–0.48m, but at Bergen there were clusters at 0.47–0.50m and at 0.63–0.65m. In addition, the Bergen planks have caulking grooves and fine

mouldings at the laps, whereas on the London remains caulking grooves are very rare and no mouldings were found. Although the absence of outboard plank mouldings may be due in part to the erosion of the plank faces in London, the fact that they still occur on the Bergen planks, which were presumably from equally old and worn-out vessels, does suggest that in the London remains they were never there. The contrast between the London and Bergen finds is even more marked when the planking excavated at Wood Quay, Dublin, is considered, for this dates from the tenth to the thirteenth centuries, and although Viking in culture, it follows the London pattern with few caulking grooves, no mouldings, and all were of oak (McGrail 1993).

The London ship and boat fragments do show clear evidence that some vessels continued in use until they were in a very leaky, dangerous condition. Both the Custom House boat (*Chapter 2*) and Blackfriars ship 3 (*Chapter 3*) indicate that they had a working life of about 75 years. No doubt erosion occurred to the fragments reused in waterfronts, and it is difficult to separate this from wear caused by the use of the vessel. Nevertheless, several features were undoubtedly caused by stresses and movement in the vessel whilst afloat, and not from the static reuse in a waterfront (Fig 10). Firstly, planks tended to split where frame trenails passed through them (Figs 11 to 13). Secondly, planks also split along the rivet lines where one plank edge lapped over the next (Figs 12 to 14). And thirdly, the movement in the laps also led to the hair caulking becoming somewhat felted (*see Appendix 3*). Such movements resulted in fastenings working loose and causing leaks, with the result that extra rivets had to be added at the laps and nails at the edges of plank scarfs, as well as patches with caulking fastened to make leaks waterproof. Movements of these types are well-known in clinker-built vessels so it is particularly interesting to be able to examine their effects on a number of different craft. Similar movements were recorded when a reconstruction of a clinker-built Viking ship was sailed from Norway to America in 1893, the master reporting that the hull had considerable elasticity, and that in a heavy sea the

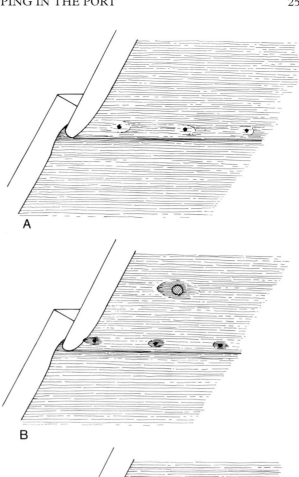

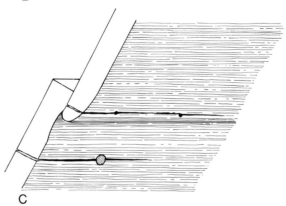

Fig 10 Damage to planks, seen from outboard: A slight eroded hollow below lap, and corner of plank eroded; B eroded hollows around nail and trenail heads, and C splits along rivet line and at trenail position

gunwale would twist up to 0.15m out of line and yet remain watertight (Brogger and Shetelig 1951, 142).

There were other signs of use, particularly in Blackfriars ship 3 which had its bottom patched in such a way as to suggest damage to the laps from grounding. This vessel and many others also bore the effects of water and silt erosion on their outboard plank faces. This was concentrated at two places where eddies formed, beside each lap (Fig 15), and also around nail heads (Figs 10 and 16). The eddies tended to hollow out the planks. A few other planks also had hollows running with the grain, which appeared most likely to be eroded *Teredo* borings (Fig 17).

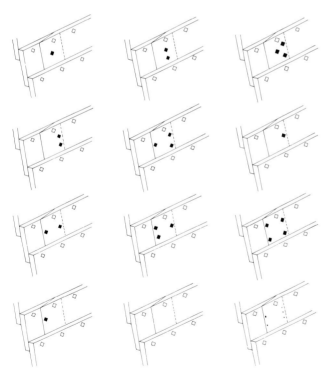

Fig 9 Various methods of fastening scarf joints in planks, seen from inboard: (top l – r) 1-middle; 2-middle; 1-middle, 2-outboard; (line 2, l – r) 2-outboard; 1-inboard, 2-outboard, 1-outboard; (line 3, l – r) 1-inboard, 1-outboard; 2-inboard, 1-outboard; 2-inboard, 2-outboard; (line 4, l – r) 1-inboard; none; tacks at edges in and out

Fig 11 Plank split at the trenails, sixteenth century (MOR 88, context 107/90)

Fig 12 Plank split at a trenail and at lap rivets, sixteenth century (MOR 88, contexts 836/49)

Documentary evidence for local vessels

Some of the many documentary references to medieval ships and boats in London are discussed later, but it is the documentary evidence for medieval shipbuilding, or shipcraft), in London, particularly during the fourteenth and fifteenth centuries, that helps with the interpretation of the archaeological evidence. The archaeology also helps with the interpretation of the documentary sources. For example, the stages by which a boat was built can partly be reconstructed from the shipbuilding purchases and weekly Bridge House payments to the men who were building or repairing boats. This can then be compared with the archaeological evidence for the sequence of shipbuilding.

By the fourteenth century the London shipbuilding industry was centred at the eastern extremity of the waterfront close to the Tower of London. Amongst the shipwrights living there were two who built boats for the Bridge House (*see Appendix 7*). They have been singled out as examples who may be typical of the time because they built a 'shout', which is possibly the type of vessel represented by Blackfriars ship 3 (*see Chapter 3*).Individual shipwrights are often referred to in the Bridge House accounts and are sometimes described as carpenters. This interchange of terms suggests that

Fig 13 Plank split at trenail and at lap rivets, inboard view, fourteenth century (TL 74, context 1382). Note the partly drilled rivet hole and traces of hair caulking

Fig 14 Plank split at lap rivets, sixteenth century (BTH 88, contexts 93/639) (metric scale)

shipwrights turned their hand to other types of carpentry. An example of this can be seen in the large horizontal tie-beams that were used to hold upright the late fourteenth-century waterfront at Trig Lane (Milne and Milne 1982, 22), for almost exactly the same form of beam structure was used to support the decks of merchant ships, particularly 'cogs' (Akerlund 1951, pl 5b, no 25; Ellmers 1979, 8; Christensen 1985, 72–7). In the 1603 edition of his *Survey of London* (1908, I, 137) John Stow commented on a building in London whose construction suggested that it had been built by shipwrights, and not by house carpenters. Its walls were constructed with:

'boordes not exceeding the length of a Clapboord, about an inch thicke, euery Boorde ledging ouer other, as in a Ship or Gallie, nayled with Ship nayles called rugh, and clenche, to wit, rugh nayles with broad round heades, and clenched on the other side with square plates of

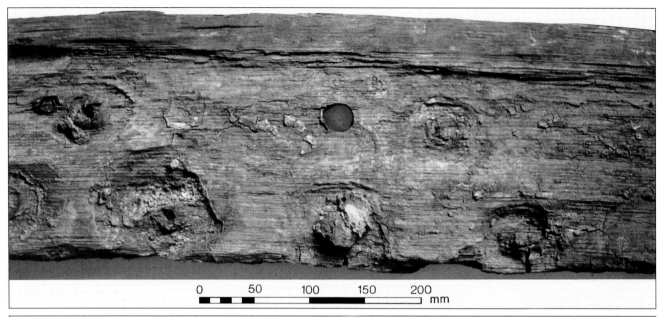

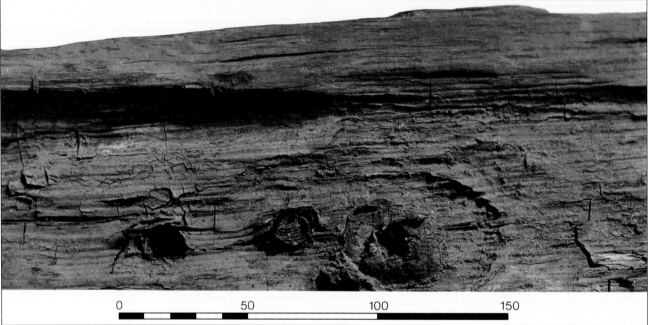

Fig 15 Outboard plank face from ship 3 showing erosion around iron nail heads (above) and beside the lap (below), fifteenth century

iron: the roof of this hall is also wrought of the like boord, and nayled with rugh and clench, and seemeth as it were a Gallie, the Keele turned vpwards.'

The medieval terms used to describe materials in fourteenth and fifteenth-century vessels in London are frequently mentioned in the Bridge House accounts. These have been assembled by Dr Laura Wright in her University of Oxford thesis (1988). Although intended as a study of word origins, her research is of enormous value in understanding shipbuilding at that period. Many of the terms match up with the archaeological evidence and refer to types of timber, such as *wrong* (frame), *wrong nails* (trenails), *shide* (piece of wood split from timber), *shipboard* (plank used in shipbuilding), *stem* or *stempiece* (piece of curved timber used for the stempost), *strake* (planking), *cloveboard* (board split into thin pieces for planking), and *footing* (a curved frame timber).

Other words relate to the waterproofing of boats, such as *caulking* ('3 pounds of tow bought and spent in *calkyng* boats – 3d'), *goathair* ('for 2 earthenware pots for pitch and for goathair bought for the said boat, 3d'), *harpoys* (a resinous mixture), *marple* ('ffor here towe clowtes and mapolte for shipwrites amendyng the cokbote, 2s 4d'), *pitching* (applying pitch), *thrum* (short pieces of woollen or hempen yarn used in caulking), *tow* (unworked fibre used in caulking), and *wiveling* (hair used in caulking).

Also listed are iron fastenings, such as *clench, shipnail, clenchnail, cloutnail, rivet, rove, shoutnail*, and *spiking*. Some of these refer to parts of iron rivets, and there is a reference to a *need*, a metal plate used in riveting. There were many types of rope and cable: *bridle, bucklerope, buoyrope, cord, hawser, keeprope', 'seizing,towrope, warprope*, and *windingrope* (Wright 1988, 179-83). These mostly refer to the uses of the rope, so it is likely that the main difference between them was a matter of size. Of particular interest is the buoyrope, a term dating from a reference in 1373, for this indicates the existence of permanent anchorages in the river marked by buoys.

Equally important are those common terms that do not appear in the archaeological evidence, such as *tallow* and *oil* (applied to waterproof boats), and *canvas* (used in caulking). This last term is particularly interesting for no trace of canvas has been found in any of the hundreds of plank laps, medieval and later, which have been studied. Also, there is frequent mention of tar used in caulking, and yet evidence of this is hardly apparent between the recovered timbers. It would seem to have been used rather sparingly during the medieval period (*see Appendices 3 and 4*), or

simply not to have survived as well as in the post-medieval period, when it is much more in evidence. The accounts show that the Bridge House bought and stored shipbuilding materials wherever was convenient and that sometimes the items were ready-made, such as in 1418–19 when they 'paid for 1 small mast 1 rudder and 1 oar bought from Paddeslee's wife', and in 1471–2 'for 2 rudders bought and kept in the brew house called the Cock at the end of Ivy Lane, 4s' (Wright 1988, 165).

The medieval documentary records also refer to many different types of vessel, with varying purposes, such as the Billingsgate to Gravesend ferry, known as the 'Long Ferry', which had been in use since the late thirteenth century (Broodbank 1921, II, 396). The records of the Corporation of London and the Bridge House during the fourteenth and fifteenth centuries also refer to such types as: *barge, bark, chalkboat, cock/cockboat, crayer, dungboat, farcost, ferryboat, flune, float, galley, hulk, keel, lighter, rushboat*, and *shout* (Wright 1988, 144-58). Some of these, like the *barge* and *hulk*, were clearly seagoing, but to what extent these and each of the various names of fishing boats represent vessels with distinct and individual shapes and methods of construction is unknown. It is possible that many were of similar shape and construction, and that the differences lay mainly in their use. Certainly, the similarity of construction in the fragments does

Fig 16 Outboard face of planking showing generally eroded face except fore and aft of iron nail heads, probably due to grounding; fourteenth century (SYM 88, context 196/120)

Fig 17 Eroded hollows in an outboard plank face, possibly due to Teredo *borings, late fifteenth to sixteenth centuries (37 BS 87, context 200/199) (metric scale)*

indicate that all medieval river vessels had the same basic clinker construction, although it is possible that the remains of carvel-built vessels were present as well, albeit unrecognised.

Medieval seagoing ships

Archaeological evidence

The waterfront excavations have disclosed fragments of substantial planking that were presumably derived from larger, seagoing, ships. These are from Gun and Shot Wharf 1988 and Symonds Wharf 1988 (*see Chapter 3*), both late fourteenth century. These ship fragments are of Baltic oak (*see Appendix 1*), but it is not known whether they were built there or elsewhere. The Hanseatic League did import into England great quantities of planking from the Baltic as early as 1275 when *bord de Alemain* was brought for work at Westminster (Salzman 1967, 245), so it is quite possible that the vessels from which the fragments derive were built in England. Although nothing is known about the types of ship from which any of these fragments came, it is clear that they were all clinker built, as were most medieval ships in northern Europe at this time.

Documentary evidence

Fortunately, there are many medieval records available for the port of London which refer to types of seagoing cargo ships. These include the *hulc* and *keel*, and *cogs*, such as the *Marie Cog* of Greenwich used in the wine trade between London and Sluys in 1338–9, and the *Le Cog John, Le Cog Thomas de la Tour*, both in 1350–4, and *Rodecog de la Tour*, in 1414, which carried wine from Bordeaux to London (James 1971, 151–3). A distorted view of a *hulc* is shown on the seal of New Shoreham, but little is otherwise known about this type of seagoing ship. In contrast the cog is commonly represented on medieval seals, and examples of this type of vessel have been found at Bremen, Germany (Ellmers 1979), and in the Netherlands and Denmark (Crumlin-Pedersen 1979; Reinders 1985). In London a *cog* is shown on the seal of the Priory of St Bartholomew, Smithfield, and is of thirteenth-century style (Fig 7).

References to the quantity of cargoes are a useful indication of the size of the larger ships used around south-east England. For example, during the reign of Edward I (1272–1307) the king had the right of first choice of wine from ships arriving in the port of London with cargoes of ten tuns, nineteen tuns, twenty tuns, one hundred tuns, and two hundred tuns (*Liber Albus* 1861, 217). These tuns are presumably roughly equivalent to modern tonnes and the largest must represent very large ships indeed, especially as by comparison it is calculated that Blackfriars ship 3 could carry a maximum of only seven tonnes (*see Chapter 3*). Another clue to earlier medieval ship sizes is a side rudder found in the sea off Rye, East Sussex, that is dated to the late twelfth to early thirteenth century (Marsden forthcoming). It is slightly over 6.7m long, and was for a ship with a side nearly 6m high.

Post-medieval ships of London

Changes in many aspects of shipbuilding, in England and further afield in northern Europe, had ocurred by the sixteenth century. About 1500 further development was encouraged by Henry VII's creation of England's first permanent navy, of which the 1487 carrack *Sovereign*, apparently found at Woolwich in 1912, was a part (Clowes 1959, 45), and by Henry VIII who enlarged the navy and encouraged the art of shipbuilding (Salzman 1931, 450).

The sixteenth-century ship fragments from London show that important changes were also taking place amongst the smaller vessels, particularly in the type of materials being used. The most obvious was the use of elm planking as well as oak, and that much of the planking was by then being tangentially cut by saw. Even in the many cases where radially-split oak was used for planks, the tree-rings show that the timber had grown much faster than was general in the earlier Middle Ages, probably indicating changes in the density of forests and also the decline in the availability of very old trees (*see Appendix 1*). In fact, the timber generally used for building ships and boats tended to be more knotty and less straight-grained.

It could be said that the sixteenth century saw a decline in the quality of building of smaller vessels. For example, the roves of rivets were sometimes held not by riveting, but merely by hooking the nail point over the rove. Also, the sixteenth-century planking was much more thickly coated with tar as a waterproofing than was the case earlier, as if the joining of timber faces was not so well made. Another feature of change, but not of skill, is the spacing of frame centres in boats; in the medieval planking the trenails marking the centres of frames were mostly spaced at 0.31m–0.48m, whereas in the sixteenth century the spacing was mostly 0.50–0.61m. This may not be particularly significant, though this slight widening of the spacing between frames would have reduced the number of frame timbers required

Changes in shipbuilding methods were also occurring. A late sixteenth-century boat from Morgans Lane was built in 'reverse clinker', and for this was probably built upside-down from the gunwale to the keel (*see Chapter 6*). Such a construction was rare, though no doubt the shipbuilder had good reason to do this, perhaps because the vessel could be cleaned out more easily (Leather 1987, 102–3), but the fact that apparently there was a break with tradition seems consistent with other changes in shipbuilding of the latter half of the sixteenth century.

The major hull change, however, was in the largest ships and apparently dates from about 1509 when Henry VIII introduced carvel edge-to-edge planking into naval ships. Carvel construction was much stronger than clinker and could accommodate gun ports, so when the *Mary Rose* was built in 1509 it was apparently built carvelwise. The Woolwich ship, probably Henry VII's warship *Sovereign*, had it's clinker planking removed, and if correctly identified this occured in 1509 when the stepped or joggled face of each frame smoothed down (though still leaving traces of the steps) for carvel planking to be attached (Salisbury 1961). The larger merchant ships followed this change, and by the seventeenth century carvel construction was normal. This is the significance of the two reused sixteenth to seventeenth-century ship's frames from NAT 90 which apparently come from a carvel-built ship.

The change from clinker to carvel was no superficial matter, for it involved a fundamental change in the way the whole hull was built. Clinker ships were shell-built, the shell of planks being constructed first and the frames added later, and carvel ships were normally skeleton-built, the planks being fastened to a pre-erected skeleton of frames. However, many types of Thames river craft still continued to be built in the traditional manner, as is shown by Blackfriars ship 2 which sank probably about 1670 (*see Chapter 7*), and by the vessels shown in the many illustrations of the port of London dating from the latter half of the sixteenth century. Even in modern times the metal lighters or dumb barges towed by tugs in the Pool of London follow the shape of the traditional wooden barges of the seventeenth century (Carr 1989, 19).

Medieval and later use of the port of London

The voyage

Having considered some types of vessel in the port, what they looked like and how they were built, we must look at how they were used, particularly in relation to the waterfronts and cargoes, for this has an important bearing on the interpretation of the archaeological evidence. From the twelfth century onwards there is an increasing amount of documentary evidence to throw light on the port and the three

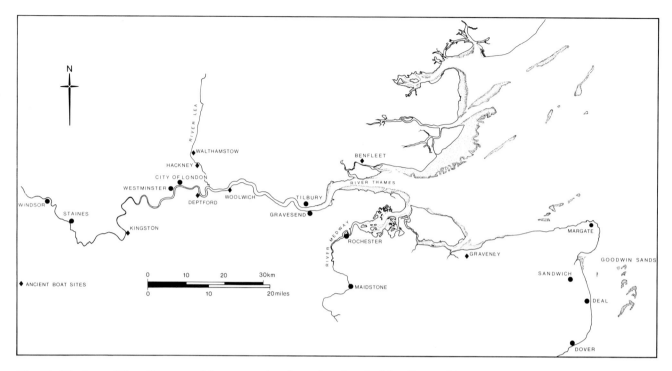

Fig 18 The lower River Thames with some ancient boat sites (marked by diamonds)

professions, the merchant, the banker, and the shipper that controlled its day-to-day activities. From this it is possible to reconstruct a typical voyage and the arrival of a large merchant ship in London during the period from the twelfth to the sixteenth centuries, and to incorporate the archaeological data into this.

Trading voyages to and from London in the medieval period were normally governed by agreements between the merchant who chartered a ship, and the master who commanded it. The merchant might well borrow money from someone else, the banker, to finance a trading voyage; though the master of the ship might not be necessarily the owner of the vessel, but might be only a part-owner. Consequently, agreements were sometimes fairly complex, though they generally dealt with the cargo, the freight charge, the destination, and the payment of various costs such as pilotage and port customs. Normally the charterer gave the master full responsibility for the voyage, at the end of which, usually within six to twenty-four days, the master would receive full payment (James 1971, 133–7). The profits for merchants and bankers could be considerable.

The Goodwins and the estuary

Since voyages into and out of the port of London involved navigation through considerable hazards it is not surprising that from the twelfth century onwards the City of London acquired an increasing responsibility for the port and its river approaches, over an area extending upstream to Staines and downstream to Yantlet Creek in the estuary near the mouth of the River Medway, and even including part of that river itself (Kemp 1976, 661). In 1857 the Thames Conservancy took over that responsibility, and this was superseded in 1909 by the Port of London Authority whose territory now reaches out to a more distant imaginary line across the estuary from the North Foreland, at the north-east corner of Kent, to the Naze in Essex (Broodbank 1921, I, 33–5). This responsibility enabled the port authority to control hazards to shipping and trade in the approaches, particularly seaward. There were great dangers to be avoided by sailing ships, particularly sandbanks and wrecks, and until comparatively recent times there were also pirates. Smuggling goods ashore to avoid customs charges was another source of concern to the authorities at all periods.

All ships that sailed across the English Channel from France and Spain to London had to avoid the notorious Goodwin Sands off the east coast of Kent (Fig 18), and, at least by the fifteenth and sixteenth centuries, for this they would employ a pilot, often collected at Dover. In 1527 the King of Spain complained to Henry VIII that certain London merchants had freighted a Spanish ship in the Bay of Cadiz for the City of London, but that when it arrived off Dover it took on board a pilot lodesman who 'did bryng the ship a grounde vpon the banke of Thamyse

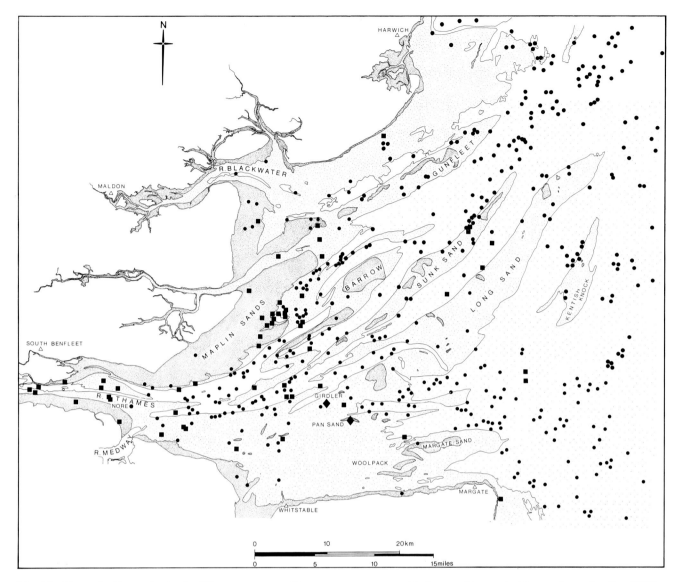

Fig 19 Charted shipwrecks in the Thames estuary. Dots represent reasonably intact ships probably mostly sunk after 1850, squares represent 'obstructions' that may be older wrecks that are decayed or buried in the seabed, and diamonds represent identified early wrecks at Pudding Pan Sand (Roman) and Girdler Sand (sixteenth century)

and there she was broken and lost' (Harris 1969, 100–101). At least 1081 shipping losses have been historically recorded in the Goodwin Sands region between 1483 and 1971, 131 having occurred before the end of the seventeenth century (Larn 1979). Shakespeare in the sixteenth century (The Merchant of Venice, Act 3, scene 1) called the Goodwins 'a very dangerous flat, and fatal, where the carcasses of many a tall ship lie buried'. How many wrecks still remain is not known, but many have been charted, and fishermen routinely trawl up objects as early as Roman in date, showing that the sands have long been a hazard (Nautical Archaeology Society 1983).

Round the north-east corner of Kent and within the Thames estuary between the Kent and Essex coasts, there are long tongues of sand reaching out towards the North Sea. These could catch unwary seafarers, for even as far out as 30 to 40 miles from the shore (48–64km) large areas of sand were, and still are, exposed at low water. Channels weaved through the banks, sometimes deep but ending in cul-de-sacs, and at other times providing a route through to a main channel. But always they were changing their courses, as the masters of Trinity House reported in 1570:

'many sands, shallows and flatts reach many miles into the main sea, lying from thence dispersed up to the estuarie or fote of the Thames, commonly changing the usuall channell .... pilots dare not adventure to crosse or come nigh to them without conduct of beacons.'

(Harris 1969, 155)

In view of the importance of the port of London it is perhaps not surprising to find that the earliest surviving English maritime chart dates from the sixteenth century and details the sandbanks of the Thames estuary (Taylor 1956, 193). Running aground was common, and the dangers did not arise only from rough seas. A fourteenth century record describes how a trading ship, the *Little Edward* of London under the command of John Brand, a citizen and merchant of London, was attacked by the French while she was lying aground off Margate in 1315. Apparently the French thought that she was a Flemish vessel, possibly because she was carrying a cargo of 120 half-sacks of wool, valued at £1200, from London to Antwerp on behalf of three Hanse merchants (Broodbank 1921, I, 47).

Although the few small fragments of medieval and sixteenth century seagoing ships found in London are valuable indications of construction methods, their significance will be better understood in the light of more complete discoveries. The dangers of the Thames estuary and the potential archaeological wealth of historic shipwrecks lying there are indicated by Admiralty Chart no 1183 which shows 353 wrecks identifiable as ships (Fig 19), most of which probably sank after 1850. The number of wrecks lost during the previous two thousand years must be considerable, as is suggested by the 66 'obstructions', which are probably older wrecks that have collapsed down to the seabed and are liable to snag fishing nets or anchors. A great deal of hull structure may survive buried, as was the case with the *Mary Rose* which sank in the Solent in 1545, and which when first found during the nineteenth century, was noted as a 'net fastening' (Rule 1983, 42–6). Although the actual age of the Thames estuary obstructions can only be judged by future underwater investigation, there is no doubt that important historic shipwrecks lie there, for a sixteenth-century wreck, probably of an armed merchant ship, has already been found on the Girdler Sand, off Whitstable, from which were recovered iron guns, 2700 lead ingots, tin ingots, and a doublet (J British Archaeol Assoc **1**, 1846). Close by is Pudding Pan Sand, which from as early as the eighteenth century has been known to be the site of a Roman wreck of the second century AD, sunk with a cargo of samian ware from Gaul. Its exact location is unknown but the sand dries at low water springs, and it seems likely that the Roman merchantman was bound for London and was damaged perhaps in a storm while aground on the sandbank (Pownall 1779, 282–90; Findlay 1885, 62–7). The Roman, medieval, and seventeenth-century wrecks found in the Thames at London, therefore, are not merely isolated archaeological discoveries but are part of a much broader picture of shipping losses associated with this port. They are merely amongst the first to be described in detail.

Seamarks

The value of seamarks, features on the shore, cannot be overestimated in enabling ships to navigate their way through the perilous channels to London. Consequently, ships often sailed within sight of the shore and chanced running aground, particularly off the north coast of Kent. One such seamark was described by the writer Blaeu who warned ship masters sailing into the Thames not to:

'leese sight of the spyre of the steeple of Margat [Margate] behind the land, for then you should come too neere it. But if you keepe so far from the shore, that you can see that foresaid steeple aboue the high land, or keep it even in your sight, then you cannot take hurt of the south grounds.'

(Blaeu 1612, ii, 103)

A little closer to London were the towers of the medieval church at Reculver near modern Herne Bay, on the north coast of Kent. Of these William Camden wrote:

'the steeples whereof shooting vp their lofty spires stand the mariners in good stead as markes whereby they avoid certaine sands and shelues in the mouth of the Tames.'

(Camden 1610, 335)

Pilots

Although the earliest surviving documentary records of the use of pilots on the Thames and its estuary are late medieval, the need was so great that they must have existed much earlier, possibly even during the Roman period. In 1597 a Spanish official reported the problem: 'From the cape at North Foreland to the river at Rochester, where the Queen's fleet lies, and then on to London, it is necessary to take on pilots from the same country, since the shoals are shifting' (Loomie 1963, 299). For square-rigged medieval merchant ships it must have been particularly difficult to negotiate these sandbanks and channels, as the route to London was westwards against the prevailing wind. The importance of the work of pilots (or *lodeman*), even before the sixteenth century, is shown by the Laws of Oleron, a set of maritime regulations used in England probably since the reign of Edward I in the late thirteenth century. These detailed drastic penalties for neglect.

'It is established for a custom of the sea that yf a shyp is lost by defaulte of the lodeman the maryners may, if they please, bring the lodeman to the windlass or any place and cut off his head withoute the maryners being bounde to answer before any judge, because the lodeman has committed high treasone against his undertakynge of the pilotage'. However, a majority decision of the crew was needed.'

(Harris 1969, 101–2)

The establishment of Trinity House in 1517, by Henry VIII, and prior to that the establishment of the Fellowship of Lodemanage, an organisation of pilots of the Cinque Ports, were undoubtedly important factors influencing the expansion of London during the sixteenth century, for they enabled larger and larger ships and their valuable cargoes access to and from London safely. The Fellowship ended its existence as recently as 1854 (*ibid*, 262), though Trinity House still continues to operate and has its headquarters in the City of London. It is only from the sixteenth century onwards that records of shipping losses began to be documented with some regularity. The Master of Trinity House, in an Admiralty Court case in 1561, declared that he:

'in his tyme hathe knowen meny shippes to have perisshid vnder pilottes of this Ryver.'

(*ibid*, 101–2)

The route over the shallows off the north Kent coast was also followed by outwardbound ships, such as the *Pellican*, 400 tons and 12 ft (3.65m) draught in ballast, which set sail in March 1561 from Blackwall for Spain, under the command of Peter Mayre, who was also part owner. He carried a pilot, William Holland of Ratcliff, who directed the ship along a channel off the church of Reculver, but this was not followed by other ships, and

'Peter Mayre spake and askid if he would not followe the course which the other shippes kept. Who seid he woulde kepe that course whiche he had be gon, ffor the other as he seid would be by an by on grownde. And with that the seid *Pellican* strake on grownde vppon the Wollpacker or the Last'.

(*ibid*, 102–6).

The *Pellican* was a total loss, and when her mainmast collapsed the ship's boy was killed. In a court case Holland was acquitted of responsibility for reasons that are unclear. He seems in other respects to have been a rather irresponsible person against whom the Crown appears to have started proceedings in 1569 for dealing in goods stolen by pirates at the Isle of Wight. The term *lodemanage* or *loadmanage* was frequently used instead of pilot, and is derived from the two words *load*, meaning way, journey, carriage, etc (as also used in lodestone), and *manage*, meaning to handle a ship or boat (Murray 1908, 105, 367–8). References occur as early as *c* 1386 (Chaucer, Prologue 403), but the use of pilots in other ports as well as in London is particularly well demonstrated by the Bridge House accounts. These list, for example, the charges of one ship carrying stone from Caen to London in 1429 which included another 10s for lothmanage, or the pilot's fee, from Caen to the sea, and another 10s for *lothmanage* from Sandwich to London (Salzman 1967, 136).

The Thames

Once a ship entered the lower reaches of the River Thames at the Nore, by the mouth of the River Medway, it would have difficulty in sailing upstream on the winding route to London against both the river current and the prevailing wind from the south-west. Progress upstream depended upon the skill of the master in using the wind to tack across the river when possible, and upon using the tidal flow so that he could be carried upriver on rising tides while anchoring during the ebbs. With two tides a day it was possible for a ship to be carried upstream 20 to 40 miles (Broodbank 1921, II, 371). Being able to predict when high tide would occur at London Bridge was important not only to mariners but also to shipping owners and merchants, particularly as there were considerable restrictions on ships arriving at the port at night during the medieval period, presumably for reasons of safety and security.

The importance of tides to the success of the port of London since Roman times cannot be overestimated, for they brought a useful depth of water at high tide, and the ebb and flow enabled vessels to arrive and depart even though the port was a long way from the mouth of the river. The traditional method of predicting the tides is shown by nineteenth-century advice to mariners which works this out relative to the phases of the moon.

'In the River Thames the time of flowing and the perpendicular rising of the first tide after the full and change of the moon [ie new moon] are nearly as follows: at London Bridge, the time is 2h 15m; at the docks, 2h 10m; at Blackwall and Woolwich 2h 5m; at Purfleet, 1h 45m; at Gravesend 1h 30m; at Hole Haven, 12h 45m, and at the Nore 12h 30m. At London spring tides rise from 17 to 20ft 8in [5.2m-6.3m]. Allowance must, however, be made for the wind, which frequently affects the tide considerably. It appears, therefore, that the tide flows at the Nore about one and three quarter hours before it is high water at London Bridge.'

(Findlay 1885, 13–14)

the water 1

Fig 20 A boating casualty after passing through London Bridge, view by John Norden, 1597

So important were the tides to the port that it is not surprising that the world's earliest-known record of high tide calculation relates to London Bridge. This important document, originating before the mid thirteenth century (*see Appendix 8*), shows that the arrival of 'fflod at London brigge' at full moon (ie on the fifteenth day of the moon's age) would occur at 3pm, and that the moon would then shine for 12 hours. It is an academic rather than strictly a practical table for it does not take account of tidal variations, but as a rough guide, and with a time adjustment, it is still valid.Nowadays high water occurs at London Bridge between one and one and a half hours earlier than in the thirteenth century, but in 1870 it was only about one hour earlier (Whittakers Almanack 1870). High tide there has therefore been becoming gradually earlier over the past seven centuries. These differences in time are primarily due to the sinking of south-east England relative to sea level, and the consequent movement of the tidal limit further upstream, beyond the bridge. Therefore the peak of each daily tidal surge, beginning in the estuary and moving upstream, which arrived at London Bridge at 3pm in the thirteenth century, has nowadays already reached the bridge and moved on further west to Teddington by that time.The construction of Teddington Lock has placed an artificial limit on the tides, though high water occurs there on average about one hour later than at London Bridge (Information from Hydrographic Dept, Port of London Authority).

Hazards

There were many hazards facing the larger ships on the Thames: shoals, wrecks, fishing structures, and even pirates and smugglers. As late as 1526 pirates were still able to operate there, for in that year two ships were 'taken awaye, robbed, and dispoyled on the Ryver of Tamyse by certeyn pyrotts' (Salzman 1931, 268). Two years later there was a running fight between a French warship and a Flemish vessel which ran all the way up to Tower Wharf (Harris 1969, 89). Another major hazard was London Bridge which so impeded the tides between its narrow arches that there could be a difference of over one metre in the river level between one side of the bridge and the other. Vessels that chanced the journey at times of maximum flow and ebb were often wrecked or swamped, as shown in John Norden's view of the bridge published in 1597 (Fig 20).

The wrecks of Blackfriars ships 3 and 4 during the fifteenth century, at points close to the contemporary waterfront, must have caused problems, though both wrecks were apparently soon buried in alluvium (*see Chapters 3 and 4*). It is not known why there was a concentration of four wrecks in the Blackfriars area, one Roman, two medieval, and one seventeenth-

century, but it may have been partly due to the configuration of the meandering river at that point. Moreover, it may seem surprising that neither wreck was removed or broken up, though until the beginning of the sixteenth century no provision seems to have been made for this in London. The clearing of obstructions in the river, particularly *kiddles* (ie fish weirs), had long been the responsibility of the Water Bailiff to the Corporation of London (*Liber Albus* 1861, 440; Salzman 1931, 210-11), but in 1502 Geffrey Moreton, Water Bailiff, applied to the Lord Mayor and Aldermen for authority to tackle wrecks.

> 'That where often tymes hereafore diverse Showt[es] Barg[es] and Bot[es] hath lien drowned and sonkyn in the seid water of Thamyse. And some other like vessell[es] and other thyng[es] as wood Tymber and ores have driven and flette upon the same water withoute any persone or ruler in or aboute them to grete hurte and stoppyng of the fairewey and jeopardie of passyngers therby. It may therefore pleas your good lordeship and maistershippes in eschuyng and reformacion of the premisses to graunt unto your seid servant the forefaiture of all such vesselle and other the premisses with all other dryftes [ie floating remains of wrecked ships] and drenches [ie submerged shipwrecks that are a hazard to shipping] the which in the seid water in tyme to come shalbe found so drowned or dryven and full auctorite and power to sease them to his own proper use and behove and your said seraunt shall daily pray to God for the preservacion of your good Lordship and Maisterships.'
>
> (City of London Record Office)

This was agreed by the City of London on Thursday 21 June, 1502.

As the sea level had been rising relative to the land level of south-east England at least since the twelfth century there was continued alluvial deposition on the river bed, which probably explains why Blackfriars wrecks 3 and 4 were so quickly buried. As a result it was necessary to embank low-lying land, though the flooding of the marshlands was an ever-present threat to shipping and to buildings. This was shown by the effects of a major flood, probably in 1294, revealed by excavations at Toppings Wharf in Southwark, just east of London Bridge. Not only had the walls of a large stone building of the twelfth to thirteenth century been washed away, but so had the once buried remains of the Roman settlement. There are documentary records of many commissions for the repair of riverside embankments in 1298, 1303, 1309, 1311, 1320, and 1325 (Sheldon 1974, 3–5, 25, 30), and so on, but flooding has still continued into living memory.

Arrival at London

Port regulations

On arrival at the port a ship would have to pay various tolls, particularly for berthing, and also customs duty for importing goods. In the eleventh century the shipping of London was mainly associated with the Scandinavian world and with northern Europe, but, although that trade remained important in the twelfth and thirteenth centuries, the main centre of trade gradually moved southwards to Germany, Flanders, Normandy, and the rest of France. Major exports from London included wool and cloth which were shipped to markets as far away as Spain and Italy. Important imports included French wines, particularly from Bordeaux and Poitou. A great deal of this trade was undertaken by foreign merchants, especially Scandinavian, German, and northern French, who had settled in London, and of these the Cologne and Danish traders had their headquarters close to the major hithe of Dowgate where archaeological finds include large quantities of eleventh to twelfth-century red-painted pottery from the Low Countries (Dunning *et al* 1959; Dyson 1985, 20).

In 1191 the City achieved a degree of self-government independent from the king in line with other cities in Europe, and thereafter the City of London increasingly administered the port according to arrangements which sometimes dated back to time out of mind. These were set out in various documents that were transcribed by Richard Whittington and John Carpenter in 1419 into the *Liber Albus*. An earlier collection, apparently dating from the reign of King John (*c* 1210), includes a text which may date from as early as *c* 1130 (Bateson 1902, 495–502), and is known as *The law of the merchants of Lower Lotharingia*, in Germany. It describes their procedure for entering the port of London: they must first raise their ensign and sing *Kyrie eleison*, and then may reach London Bridge, according to old law. Having passed under the bridge they reach a hithe, presumably Dowgate, and there must wait two ebbs and one flood-tide (ie about one day) during which the sheriff and king's chamberlain could visit the ship and take certain items on behalf of the king, with payment to be made in two weeks. Nobody was permitted to enter the ship to trade under penalty of 40 shillings to the king, though the first barrel of wine might be broached and wine sold at a penny a stoop. If neither the sheriff nor the chamberlain arrived then the merchant might sell his goods without forfeiture.

Even though it was possible for ships to pass under London Bridge on a flood tide, there is a suggestion here that it, or a place downstream, may have served as an administrative barrier at that time.

The requirement for German ships to fly their ensign and sing a prayer before passing the bridge suggests a pause in the voyage before berthing so that the entry of the alien ship to the port could be recorded. This is also suggested by the story of Tristan by the French poet Thomas about 1160 who described how the hero's friend Caerdin sailed into the port of London.

'He sails up-river with his merchandise and within the mouth, outside the entry to the port, has anchored his ship in a haven. Then, in his boat, he goes straight up to London beneath the bridge, and there displays his wares, unfolds and spreads his silks'
(Brooke 1975, 158–9)

The method of berthing and offloading cargoes varied according to the size of the ship. Some had to moor in the stream and offload into lighters, but smaller ships could berth at a quayside for unloading. The method of unloading very large ships at the time of Edward I (1272–1307) is described:

'And if a great ship that comes with wine has to unload into boats before it arrives [at the wharf], and then follows the boats, with the remaining wines, unto the wharf, the Chamberlain ought to take for ship and boats only a single prisage', [ie the king's right of first choice before the cargo was sold].
(*Liber Albus* 1861, 217)

The broken anchor found associated with fifteenth-century objects off the modern Custom House building is indicative of the mooring position of one of the larger ships (*see Chapter 5*). However, there were strict regulations concerning the berthing of ships at medieval London. Anchoring in the stream could present some difficulties, particularly near London Bridge where the tides rushed through the arches with great turbulence, and in 1417 the Common Council of the City enacted

'that no ship lying at Fresh wharf nor in other places on the east side of the bridge lay nor cast no Anker in the said "Goleis" [?gullies or openings in the bridge] nor upon the "Stadelynges" [?starlings of London Bridge] nor near unto the same by the space of 20 fathom.'[ie within 36.5m of the bridge]
(Sharpe 1899–1912, I, fo 200)

It was likely that ships moored there impeded access to the bridge, and their anchors could hole vessels taking the ground at low water.

By the fifteenth century the Corporation of London regulations ruled:

'That no ship or boat shall anchor at night, or moor, between sunset and sunrise, except at Queen-Hythe and Byllynggesgate; nor shall at night remain upon the bank-side of Suthewerk, under pain of loss of vessel and imprisonment of body. ... That ships and boats which come by Thames with victuals, shall lie one day in peace without selling aught.'

(*Liber Albus* 1861, 498)

Similar regulations were in operation as early as the thirteenth century and were apparently to stop thieves on the river as much as to restrict the use of the brothels in Southwark.

'No boatman shall have his boat moored and standing over the water after sunset; but they shall have all their boats moored on this [ie the north] side of the water, that so thieves or other misdoers may not be carried by them, under pain of imprisonment: nor may they carry any man or woman, either denizens or strangers, unto the stews [ie brothels], except in the day-time, under pain of imprisonment.'

(*ibid*, 242)

Some of the regulations might seem petty, such as the Fishmongers' statute which in the thirteenth century prescribed that:

'No one shall buy fish in any vessel afloat, until ropes are brought on shore.'

(*ibid*, 324–5)

Once the vessels had arrived they had to sell their catch quickly, no doubt while it was still fresh.

'And that no boat that brings oysters, whelks, mussels, or soles, shall remain longer upon sale than one high tide and two ebbs. And whosoever shall lie a longer time, as for his oysters, whelks, or mussels, let them be forfeited.'

(*ibid*, 214)

Complicated payments were due for mooring in the river, going aground, and for offloading cargoes. For example, probably from about 1300, it was decreed that:

'for every vessel with bulwarks [ie a high-sided ship] that anchors in the Thames the Sheriff takes two pence'

(*ibid*, 201)

For those vessels that berthed at the public quay of Billingsgate in the thirteenth century, the customs provided that:

'every vessel that grounds shall pay two pence for strandage. For a small vessel with oarlocks that grounds, one penny. For a boat that grounds, one halfpenny.'

There followed the charges for many types of imported goods such as, corn, sea-coal, ale, fish, butter, leather, nuts, honey, lead, iron, wine, onions, garlic, clay, and potter's earth 'imported and exported'. There were boards called *weynscotte* and *ryghholt*, and flax, feathers, and litmus. Also:

'for pottery imported, that is to say tureens, pipkins, patens, earthen pots, the said bailiff shall take nothing.'

(*ibid*, 208–9)

Although the regulations were primarily aimed at securing for the king a customs income from the use of the port, the effect was also to reduce the risk of plunder of cargoes. The public quays restricted the landing of goods, so that customs could be levied, but there is some evidence that attempts to avoid the charges occurred as early as the fourteenth century. But it was not until 1559 that the first legislation was enacted that governed the discharge of cargoes at London and tackled the loss of revenue due to 'greedy persons' (Broodbank 1921, II, 401). This had little effect, and by the late eighteenth century the problem had reached epidemic proportions and was instrumental in the creation of the enclosed docklands downstream from the City of London (*ibid*, I, 83). The regulations were also designed to stop smuggling which was evidently taking place at least as early as the fifteenth century, for the Corporation of London had decreed that

'no merchant shall go to meet merchandise coming unto the City, by land, or by water.' That no one shall go upon the Thames for such purpose, nor shall go on board ship to buy, before such merchandise shall have come to land.'

(*Liber Albus*, 570)

Many of these controls were necessary as the river was undoubtedly busy with traffic. This is suggested by hints at other boating activities, such as in 1404–12

'for the tugging of 1 boat with board from Billingsgate to the Bridgehouse, 3d', or cleaning boats by Sponging.'

(Wright 1988, 188–9)

Fig 21 Quayside of the East Watergate, fourteenth century, excavated near Blackfriars in 1973. The oak rubbing posts, to protect moored boats, were fastened to the top of the stone quay, which was later partly robbed. The contemporary quayside surface lies just above the level of the posts

Also, there are constant references to the hazards on the river, and sometimes to the loss of life, as on a Sunday in 1413, when William, the son of Richard Bulke, master of the ship *Kok Johan* of Bristol, moored in the Thames at Greenwich

> 'being on board the ship and willing to go out of the port thereof into a boat called a "cokbote", because of the motion of the ship did in so going fall into the river and was drowned.'
> (*Calendar Close Rolls* 25 Feb 1413)

Unloading

The royal butler's accounts over the period *c* 1270–1370 show that wine arriving at the port of London from France was either hoisted out of the ship berthed at the quay, for which a charge of 2d a ton or 1d a pipe was made, or if the ship was moored in the stream and had to offload into a boat which took the barrels of wine ashore, a *batellage* charge of 2d a ton was imposed. Once on the quayside the barrels were rolled into cellars, which at the Vintry in London were by the waterfront, at a charge of 3d a ton. But if the wine was left on the quayside until sold or carried away, it was necessary to hire boys to safeguard the goods at 2d a day or 3d a day and night (James 1971, 138–9).

Excavations at Billingsgate have shown that, in the eleventh and twelfth centuries at least, part of the waterfront took the form of a sloping artificial beach, possibly for vessels to run ashore. There were also timber revetments and a man-made inlet or dock for a small boat (Steedman *et al* 1992, 53–6).

But by the fourteenth and fifteenth centuries much of the waterfront of London comprised timber and stone quays (Milne and Milne 1982), in which parts of broken-up ships and boats were sometimes reused (eg at Custom House 1973, Trig Lane 1974, and Billingsgate 1982). The reuse of an old boat for a dock revetment is apparently recorded in the Bridge House weekly payments for 1418–19: 'And paid for timber bought from one old boat for the dock' (Wright 1988, 70).

The only excavated late medieval public quay is the East Watergate, dating from the fourteenth century (Fig 21). This public landing place, near the south-west corner of the walled medieval city upstream from London Bridge, was found in 1972–3 (Marsden forthcoming). Private stone quays on either side formed a narrow inlet, like a modern dock, with rectangular wooden rubbing posts to protect boats. The public landing place lay at the inner end of the inlet, at the foot of St Andrews Hill. The dock itself was used by river transport rather than by seagoing ships, for it was recorded in 1343 that a new stone wharf had encroached onto the East Watergate to the nuisance of ships (*navium*), shouts (*shoutarum*) and boats (*batellorum*) (Chew and Kellaway 1973, 453). The discovery of this dock inlet is very significant, since from the sixteenth century onwards docks became increasingly important to the work of the port of London. Ultimately in the nineteenth century docks provided tideless secure havens for ships trading with the rest of the maritime world, making London one of the world's most important commercial centres, a role the City of London still holds, though its ancient port has now died.

2 The twelfth-century Custom House boats, City of London, 1973

Summary

Large pieces of the bottom and fragments of the sides and gunwale of clinker-built barge-like vessels were found in 1973, reused in a river waterfront. The main vessel had been locally built c 1160–90, and its minimum size was probably 3.5m wide and 9.75m long.

Discovery

Excavations in 1973 on the Old Custom House site, Lower Thames Street, City of London, under the direction of Tim Tatton-Brown, revealed a medieval waterfront in which substantial parts of a boat had been reused (Tatton-Brown 1974, 128–32). The construction of this revetment is dated to the late thirteenth or fourteenth centuries (*ibid*, 128), but the construction of the boat itself is tree-ring dated to c 1160–90 (*see Appendix 1*).

Two large slabs of articulated clinker-built boat planking were found laid on edge in the waterfront, with the outboard side facing the river, and with many smaller pieces of broken planking laid above (Figs 22, 23, and 24). Since the construction of all the pieces was similar it is clear that they were parts of the same vessel (Boat 1). The riverfront revetment was supported by a series of vertical posts and raking struts on its southern or river face, and one post was a reused part of a boat frame. As its size and trenail spacings were different from those in the planks, it was evidently from another vessel (Boat 2).

The boat planking was recorded *in situ* and then numbered for later study, but unfortunately it was left unsupported on the site and soon collapsed into many fragments. These were carefully recovered and numbered before being removed to a water storage tank. In 1973–4, they were cleaned, reconstructed, and drawn with the help of J Weeks, H Pell, and P Broady. The inboard face was most easily recorded (Fig 25) since it had been drawn on site and was protected from

Fig 22 Inboard face of a waterfront in which part of a late twelfth-century clinker-built boat has been reused. Note the scarf joints which show that the stern lay to the right (centimetre scale)

erosion by facing inshore, but the outboard side had been eroded while exposed to the medieval river (Fig 26). The drawings of the two faces, therefore, are not of equal quality and ideally need further study, though the significant constructional features are clear. The timbers were then returned to the wet store where they remained until 1991 when they were further recorded and sampled.

Boat 1

Materials and woodworking

Planks

The planks were of oak, generally radially-cut from the tree (Fig 27), only the heartwood being used, though the edge of sapwood was recognised in one plank. Three tree-ring sections (nos 13, 136, and 153) seem to be more tangential, though it is possible that they were cut from large radial wedges of timber, perhaps because it was intended to fashion a twist in the plank shape, curving it horizontally. The exposed surfaces of the timber were all eroded, but traces of an edged tool, probably an axe, were noted in some lap and scarf joints, but there was no indication of the width of the blade (Fig 28). Augers had been used to drill holes in the planks for the trenails that fastened the planks and frames together, and their bit diameters were about 23mm and 27mm. It seems that a much narrower auger with a bit diameter of about 4mm was used to drill holes for the rivet nails, as was the usual practice in more recent times, since there was no compression or distortion of the wood around the rivets, as might have occurred had the rivets been driven into place. Drilling a hole admitted the rivet nail relatively easily, and also stopped the plank edge from splitting away.

Rivets

These were of wrought iron.

Caulking

The hair caulking (cattle hair and some wool) was twisted in strands and laid in the laps between the planks.

Trenails

One of the trenails holding the frames to the planks was identified as of willow or poplar.

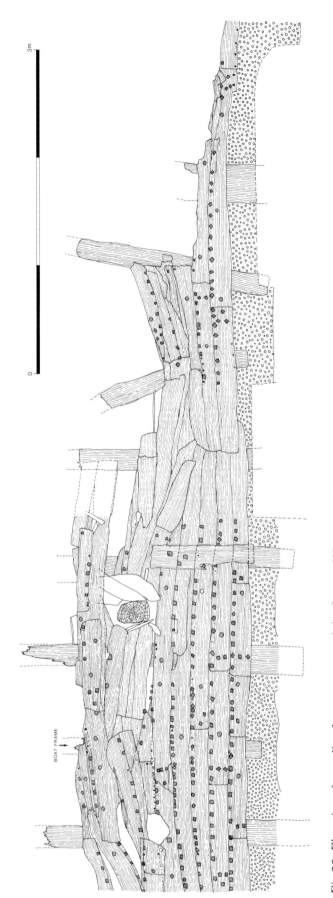

Fig 23 Elevation of a medieval revetment containing late-twelfth-century boat timbers found at Custom House, 1973 (after Tatton-Brown 1974). This is the protected inshore side looking south towards the river

Fig 24 Inboard face of a waterfront in which part of a late twelfth-century clinker-built boat has been reused. Note the scarf joints which show that the stern lay to the right. Custom House 1973 (centimetre scale)

Construction

A careful study of the two large articulated slabs of planking shows that they had the same construction and frame spacing as each other, one was from the port side of a vessel, and the other was from the starboard side. The frame spacing was indicated by holes for trenails that had once held frames to the strakes, and it is their spacing that enable the positions of the two slabs to be established relative to each other (Figs 25 and 26). Together they gave a surviving hull length of 4.3m. Not all fragments were saved undamaged, which probably accounts for the absence of a record of some trenail holes in the bottom at frames 8 (S3, S5), 11 (S4), 13 (S4), 14 (S5), and 15 (S4).

Bottom strakes

Parts of three strakes of oak had survived on the port side (strakes P1, P2, and P3), and parts of five strakes, also of oak, on the starboard side (strakes S1, S2, S3, S4, and S5). Both P1 and S1 were fairly straight, though as the other strakes were curved, the greatest

extent of that curve indicated the widest part of the boat originally. The curves of the planks also indicate that they were from the bottom of the vessel. At their broadest point each strake was about 0.27m wide, though the outboard faces of the planking had been eroded from about 18–21mm in thickness, judging from the thickness of the rivets, to about 14–16mm.

The strakes overlapped each other clinkerwise by about 0.040–0.048m, and the laps were fastened by iron rivets whose centres were mostly spaced between 0.090m and 0.130m apart (Figs 28 and 29). Each rivet was of iron, its shank 5 × 5mm and 7 × 7mm square with a flat head about 22–24mm in diameter. The roves were almost flat, and diamond-shaped, though some were almost square. Sizes varied, but roves measuring about 0.021 × 0.030m and 0.019 × 0.023m were fairly average. The end of each iron nail had been hammered out over the rove. Since little deformation of the planks had been caused by the insertion of the nails, it is assumed that holes about 4mm in diameter had been drilled through the planks before the rivet nails were hammered into place.

Each lap between the strakes was made watertight with a caulking of hair, generally laid as three strands each loosely twisted to resemble knitting wool. When the laps were opened each flattened row of hair was found to be about 10mm wide. There was no obvious trace of pitch or tar, though analysis showed that the hair had been coated with tar.

The plank faces at the laps were not angled or bevelled to any great extent but instead followed the line of the plank faces so as to make a flat bottom. This evidence is important in reconstructing the shape of this part of the vessel.

Each strake comprised a number of planks scarfed endways (Table 1). The scarf joints were simple overlaps mostly held by two rivets at the outboard end, and by either no rivets at all or just one at the inboard end. These were in addition to the rivets in the strake laps. The scarfs were made watertight with a caulking of matted hair laid evenly between the overlapping plank ends. The length of each scarf relative to the plank thickness is particular interesting since it is considered nowadays that a length of 12 times the plank thickness (ie *c* 8%) is good practice (Leather 1987, 86–7). Six of the scarf joints in the bottom strakes were examined in detail and it was found that they had gradients which ranged from 6.53–10.35 (ie 15–10%).

The proximity of the scarfs to each other in the planking shows that although most were staggered so that none was close to another, there were two immediately adjacent to each other in strakes S1 and S2 next to frame 10. Such closeness of scarfs is considered to be poor practice in clinker boatbuilding because it places two potentially weak points next to each other. Indeed 1.82m (6 feet) and three planks between is considered to be the right length to separate two scarfs on the same side of a boat in the same vertical line (Leather 1987, 86). The scarf in strake S1 may have been a repair, particularly as it is at one end of a plank only 1m long.

Bottom frames

We can presume that the trenails and trenail holes in the strakes marked the approximate centres of the missing frames, giving these spacings between frame centres:

Table 1   Custom House Boat 1 strakes

strake		scarfs	strake		scarfs
S1	–	4	P1	–	2
S2	–	4	P2	–	1
S3	–	1	P3	–	1
S4	–	0			
S5	–	1			

0.44m (frames 6–7)
0.45m (frames 7–8)
0.40m (frames 8–9)
0.45m (frames 9–10)
0.45m (frames 10–11)
0.43m (frames 11–12)
0.41m (frames 12–13)
0.46m (frames 13–14)
0.44m (frames 14–15)

The trenails, about 23mm in diameter, had pierced the planks so that each frame was fastened to alternate strakes. One trenail was identified as having been made from willow or poplar and the remainder appeared to be of the same wood. There was a tendency for the outboard heads of the trenails to be larger than the hole in the plank, so that it resembled the shape of a champagne cork projecting out of the plank by as much as 6mm (in strake S1). One trenail hole just forward of frame 7 in strake S5 was in an unexpected place, between the regular frame positions, and may have marked the lower end of a side frame, or, less likely because the frame trenail should not lie in that strake, it could suggest that frame 7 was not straight.

Sideplanks

Among the broken planking in the revetment, lying above the slabs of articulated bottom planking from the starboard side, were various pieces whose original position in the once intact boat cannot now be established. As these included part of the gunwale, it seems likely that many were from the sides of the boat.

One of these fragments (Fig 29, no 103), from a plank more than 180mm wide, had a curved edge, indicating that it came from the bottom of the vessel near one end. A scarf joint shows that this was probably from the port side. Another piece of planking, originally more than 190mm wide, also had a scarf joint which showed that it too was probably from the port side. The strake lap was slightly bevelled, indicating that it probably came from the curving side of the vessel, rather than from its flat bottom.

Fragments show that one strake, presumed to be from the side, was 177mm wide, 30mm thick, and with a lap of 42mm, and another was 240mm wide and 20mm thick with a lap 30mm wide. Rivets were spaced at 89–106mm centres (Fig 29, no 19). Generally, the rivets had nail shanks 5×5mm square, and rather flat roves of varying sizes, 22×28mm, 23×18mm, 23×23mm, and 22×21mm were typical. In general it seems that the side strakes were about the same width as those on the bottom. One plank fragment had a scarf with a rivet at both outboard and inboard ends (Fig 29, no 103), and another had two

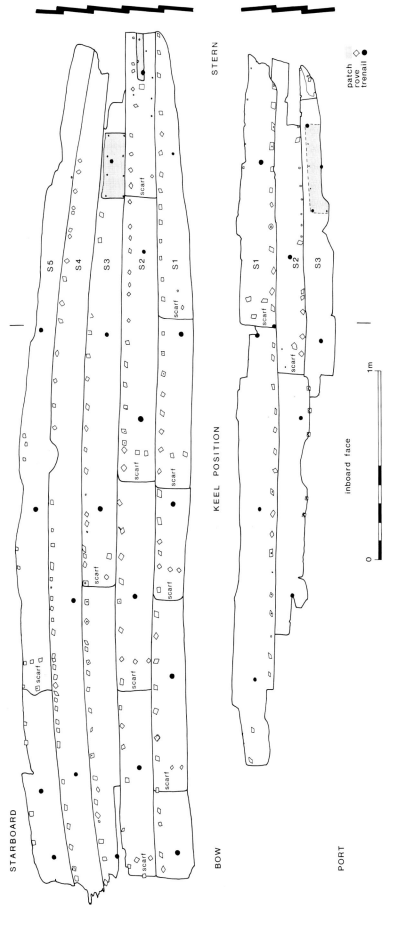

Fig 25 Inboard plan of the two clinker boat fragments correctly related to each other (Custom House Boat 1)

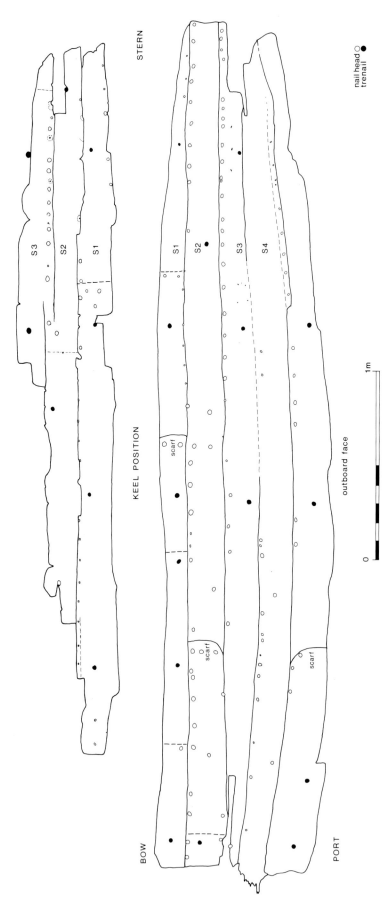

Fig 26 Outboard plan of the boat fragments (Custom House Boat 1)

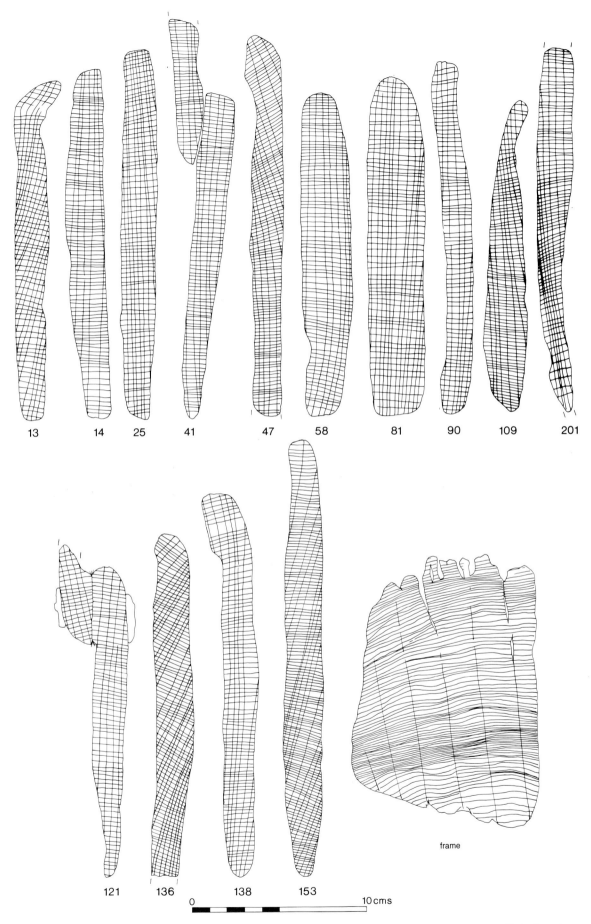

Fig 27 Samples of tree-rings in the Custom House boat 1 planks showing that most are radial, though numbers 136 and 153 seem to be more tangential. A section of the frame is included

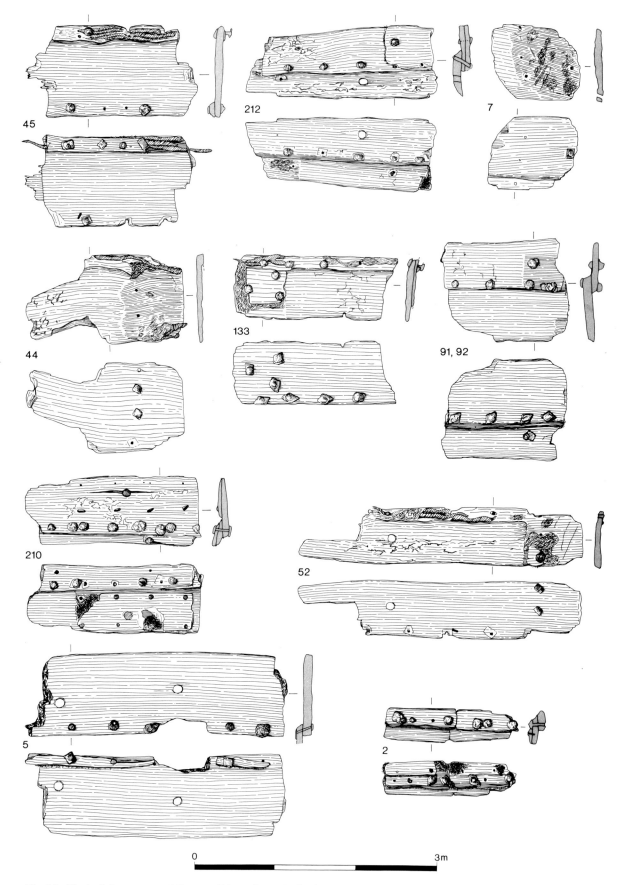

Fig 28 Typical fragments of Custom House boat 1 planking showing outboard (top) and inboard (bottom) views for each piece

rivets at its outboard end and one at its inboard end (Fig 28, no 7), as had most scarf joints in the bottom planking.

Gunwale

0.78m of the gunwale had survived amongst the fragments (Fig 28, no 5). It was an oak plank 0.238m wide and 0.027m thick, with a rounded upper edge with no trace of fittings or fastenings. Its lower edge was fastened with a row of normal iron rivets, spaced 0.109–0.133m apart, which held the gunwale to the next strake. The lap on the gunwale was 34mm wide, and contained a caulking of hair laid in several twisted lines. An intact rivet and pieces of the adjacent planking showed that the next strake was 18mm thick at that point. Also, the rivets passed through the gunwale at a slight angle, as if to suggest that the side of the boat flared at that point.

Side-frames

The gunwale fragment was pierced by two trenail holes whose centres were 0.36m apart, and these presumably mark the spacing between two frames at that level. The holes were 23mm and 27mm in diameter. Another fragment of planking, possibly also from the port side, had two trenails whose centres were 0.317m apart. They were 24mm and 27mm in diameter. These indicate that there was a shorter spacing between the frames at the side than between the frames in the bottom, suggesting that the bottom and the side may have had different sets of frames. This may account for the extra trenail in strake S5 just forward of frame 7.

Damage and repairs

The outboard surfaces of the strakes were generally water-eroded to a depth of about 3mm, judging from nail heads and laps which indicate the original plank thicknesses. There was also a slight tendency for the outboard plank faces beside the strake laps to be a little more deeply hollowed by erosion, presumably due to eddies caused by the clinker lap as the water flowed by. Many of the plank faces also had small winding channels, about 1mm wide, which may have been formed by small organisms.

Several repair patches to the strakes were noted, mostly around trenail fastenings where the planks had been split, presumably because the movement of the timbers had stressed the wood. Rectangular oak patches 4–10mm thick were fastened over the damaged planks with iron nails, sometimes, but not always, with a layer of matted cattle hair caulking (*see Appendix 3*) between the patch and the plank. These nails had flat heads and square shanks, and usually had their pointed ends bent over. One plank (Fig 29, no 19) had two splits each covered by a patch outboard, whereas inboard there was a single large wooden patch. Two of the patches had no hair caulking, but one outboard patch, covering a split along the rivet line, was caulked with hair.

Another repair, on the inboard face of strake S3 (Fig 28, no 210), was a patch 0.36m × 0.111m, and up to 10mm thick. It covered a split in the plank 0.22m long and up to 9mm wide running from a trenail hole. A layer of matted hair caulking lay between the patch and the plank face. The strake S2 had been similarly split at a trenail hole, and this too had been repaired inboard by a wooden patch 7mm thick nailed in place. Hair caulking lay underneath. A trenail hole in the gunwale (Fig 28, no 5) also had a split running from it, but there was no patch, presumably because it was small and lay above the waterline.

Another type of repair was the strengthening of lap joints which had evidently become leaky. Such repairs were made by adding more rivets, and these occurred in the bottom of the boat in strakes P2 and S4, in strakes S2/S3 (Fig 28, no 210), and probably in the side (Fig 28, no 45).

Reconstruction

Just enough of this vessel had survived to suggest its original minimum size and shape, but as only part of the bottom and fragments of the sides and perhaps the ends were recovered, there remains considerable uncertainty. Nevertheless it is still possible to attempt to draw a minimum reconstruction of a substantial part of the vessel (Fig 30).

The form of the bottom planks suggests the general shape of the entire vessel, even though the keel, stems, and frames were missing . It appears to have been sharp at both ends with its greatest width in the middle. Since only the articulated planking from the flat bottom was reused, it is likely that the parts of the hull cut away and reused as small pieces were from the curving ends and the sides. Of particular importance are the scarf joints, all of which faced the same direction and show which end was the bow, according to the normal rules of clinker boatbuilding (*see Introduction*).

Reconstructing the width of the hull bottom depends upon correctly interpreting the strakes. The strake pattern best survives on the starboard side where the outer edges of strakes S2-S5 were all curved in plan, in contrast to the outer edge of S1 which was straight. This pattern indicates that S1 was probably the garboard strake running beside the keel, as occurred in Blackfriars wreck 3 (*see Chapter 3*), and would explain why it was broken off along the edge

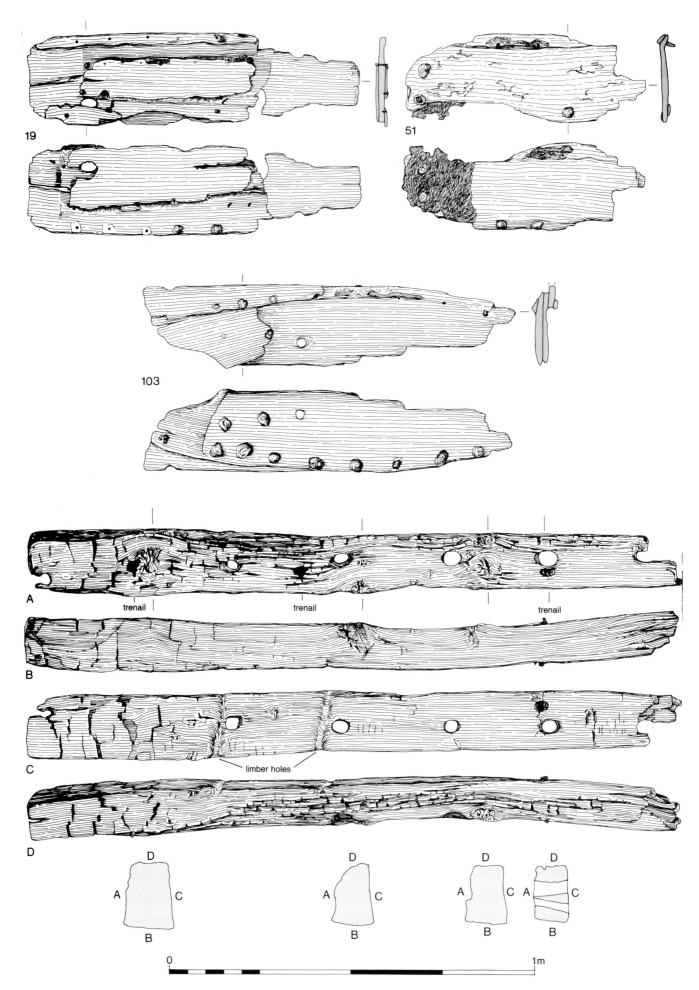

Fig 29 Typical fragments of Custom House boat 1 planking, and the frame of boat 2

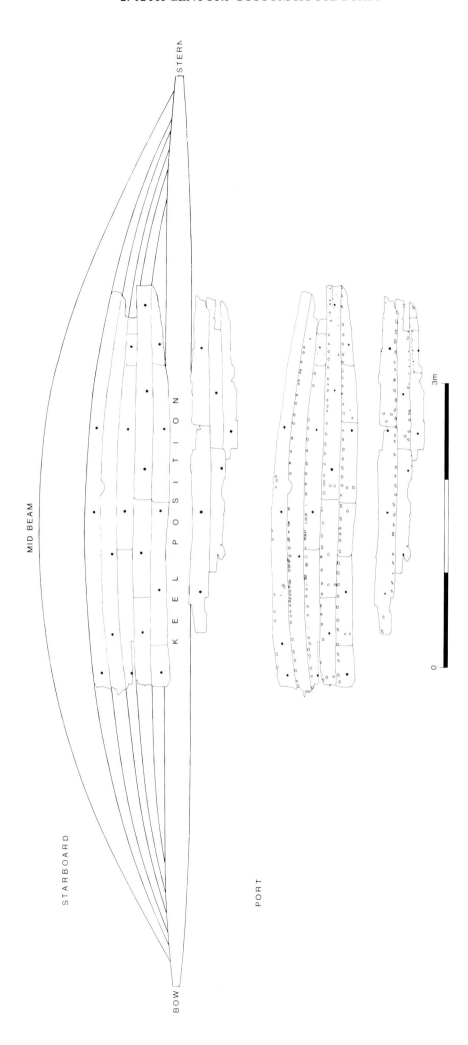

Fig 30 Suggested minimum reconstruction of the Custom House boat 1

nearest to the keel. This interpretation is also suggested by the less complete strake P1, and by the fact that the trenail pattern in both strakes S1 and P1 was the same.

There is no clue to the original width of the keel, so, for the purpose of this reconstruction, it is assumed to have had a minimum width similar to that of the strakes, about 0.20m, though judging from the Blackfriars wreck 3 (*see Chapter 3*) and the Graveney boat (Fenwick 1978) the keel could have been twice that width. The greatest width of the flat bottom of the boat, on this basis, was at least 2.2m, at frame 10.

As the fragments of planking presumed to be from the sides and ends had a similar width to the bottom planks, and the laps were bevelled, it seems clear that the bottom of the boat curved up to form the sides. There is no reason to believe that the sides met the bottom to form a sharp angle or chine to give a box-shaped vessel. Moreover, the slanted angle of the rivets in the gunwale may indicate that the upper part of the sides were slightly flared. There is no clue to the height of the sides, and none can be suggested on the present evidence. In order to determine a minimum width for the vessel it is possible to use the curving sides of both the Graveney boat and Blackfriars ship 3 as parallels to establish how tight the turn of the bilge could have been. The comparison suggests that at least 0.70m should be added for each side, giving a total minimum width of 3.5m for the vessel. The curving form in plan of the bottom strakes indicates that the boat was sharp at both ends, and that its minimum overall length was about 9.75m.

Conclusions

The form and size of the vessel is consistent with what is known of the ships and boats in northern Europe at that time. This form is suggested by the late Saxon boat from Graveney, Kent, and by the thirteenth-century port seals of Dunwich, Hythe, Pevensey, Poole, Southampton, Sandwich, Faversham, Portsmouth, and Yarmouth (Brindley 1938, nos 2, 5, 12, 13, 15, 16, 19, 20, and 21) and other contemporary illustrations (Fliedner 1969, 111–15). These show vessels that were pointed at both ends, with a mast placed almost amidships where it supported a square sail, and steering was by a side rudder usually fastened to the hull on the starboard side. There is no evidence for the forms of propulsion and steering in the Custom House boat, but its size would not preclude it from carrying a sail, and steering was almost certainly by side rudder or steering oar (McGrail 1987, 241–51).

The shipbuilder undoubtedly had some building rules in mind when fastening the vessel together, just as modern shipwrights using wood have rules of safe proportions between the components of a vessel. The planks from the Custom House boat varied in width from 177 to 269mm, and their maximum thickness was 17–32mm, though most were 19–23mm thick. The ratio or plank thickness to width was from 1:5.9 to 1:13.45, but some of this variation may well be due to outboard surface erosion. The laps between the strakes were 30–51mm wide, though most were in the region of 40–45mm, showing that lap widths were between one and a half and three times the maximum thickness of the individual planks, but averaging about 2.2 times the maximum thickness.

Although the width of planks narrowed towards the ends of the vessel, it is possible that the shipbuilder used a relationship between the lap width and the maximum plank width. The maximum proportion was 1:5.85. Also, although there was considerable variation in the spacing of rivets along the laps, showing that they were positioned roughly by eye, there may have been a relationship between the maximum spacing of lap rivets and the maximum thickness of the planks, though at the laps themselves the planks were usually thinner. The ratio of maximum plank thickness to maximum rivet spacing was from 1:1.85 to 1:3.91, averaging at 1:2.86. The rivet shanks themselves varied from 5×5mm to 8×8mm square, averaging at 6×6mm or 7×7mm square. The ratio of maximum plank thickness to scarf length ranged from 1:4.53 to 1:10.35, but mostly averaged at about 1:8.93. The significance of these ratios will become apparent below.

Features that might reflect the work of individual shipwrights include methods of caulking. In this case the caulking in the laps is particularly distinctive, consisting of three twisted strands of hair, rather like knitting wool, laid side by side along a seam (Fig 28, no 52), whereas in the plank scarfs the hair caulking is made of matted hair. The method of fastening the plank scarfs includes the following rivet patterns: two rivets at the outboard end and none at the inboard end, one rivet at the inboard end and one at the outboard end, and two rivets at the outboard end and one in the middle of the scarf. These variations might suggest the hand of more than one shipwright, or perhaps some were repairs.

The hull form and construction follows that of the Scandinavian shipbuilding tradition represented by Saxon and Viking ships and boats (Brogger and Shetelig 1951; Olsen and Crumlin-Pedersen 1967), but few ship and boat finds of the thirteenth century from northern Europe have yet been published in sufficient detail to allow a close comparison to be made. The late Saxon boat from Graveney is particularly striking as a parallel to the Custom House boat, for it had the same basic form, and had trenails of willow or poplar that fastened frames to alternate strakes, while the caulking was likewise of wool impregnated with wood tar, and the strakes were similarly fastened by iron rivets. There were also several differences, including the absence of a caulking groove, or hollow, cut in the face of a plank at the strake lap in the Custom House boat. The caulking was twisted as a single broad strand in the Graveney boat rather than as three narrow strands of cattle hair (sometimes with a little wool) in the Custom House boat, while some iron rivets in the plank laps of the Graveney boat were driven through pegs, unlike the iron rivets in the Custom House boat.

The plank scarf arrangement in the Graveney boat was slightly different from that in the Custom House boat; in the former there was a single rivet in the middle of each scarf, and in the latter the scarf rivets were placed at the outboard end of the scarf. Since the purpose of these fastenings was to stop the erosion of the lap by the water, the best position for scarf rivets was near the outboard end. The reason for the central position of the rivet in the Graveney scarfs was probably because the scarfs were only between 0.093m and 0.133m long and thus were much shorter than those in the Custom House boat. This is reflected by some of the scarfs in the oak planks of the Graveney boat which had length-to-plank thickness proportions of 33.3%, 28.5%, 20%, 20%, 18.3%, 18.1%, 17.5%, 16.6%, and 16.6%, (Fenwick 1978a). In the Custom House boat the proportions were mostly between 11.7% and 8.7%. This contrasts with the medieval ship planks from Bergen, Norway, dating from the twelfth century and later, whose scarfs were even shorter than those in the Graveney boat (Christensen 1985, 93-7), The Bergen scarfs, having the proportions 38.4% (pine), 35.7% (pine), 31.2% (?wood type), 29.2% (?pine), 26.6% (pine), 26.6% (oak), 25% (pine), 25% (?pine), 21.7% (?pine), and 19.2% (pine). At Dublin scarf gradients were from 21%-37% in an eleventh-century vessel, from 8%–17% in two twelfth-century vessels, and from 8%–16% in a thirteenth-century vessel. In the case of Skuldelev ship 3 (oak planks) the scarfs had a similar short dimension, though exact figures cannot be calculated from the report (Olsen and Crumlin-Pedersen 1967, 122-3).

It is apparent from these figures and the findings that although there are differences in detail between the Custom House boat and other vessels of a similar period, these are probably no more than might be expected between one boatbuilder and another.

Sequence of construction

All the planks were of oak, and several fragments were sectioned to record how they had been fashioned from the tree. All show that the oak was of a fairly narrow straight grain, and that generally the planks had been formed from radially-cut sections of the tree. Presumably this means that the logs had been split into wedge-shaped segments, and that the planks had then been fashioned from them. Also, although only the heartwood was used some sapwood was noted at the edge of one plank.

There is every reason to suppose that the Custom House boat was constructed like other clinker-built vessels, first with the keel being laid, and then with the garboard strakes being fastened to it. The other strakes were attached next by iron rivets, but just before each plank was fastened the outboard edge of the plank already in position was carefully worked, sometimes with a bevel, to give the hull its shape. For each rivet to be inserted a small hole about 4mm in diameter was drilled through the two overlapping planks, so that the rivet nail could be driven from outboard and its end clenched (spread by hammering) over a diamond-shaped rove. Immediately before the rivets were driven in place the caulking of hair coated with tar was placed on the lap, and the rivet nails were driven through that. The scarf joints show that the planks of each strake had been fastened from the stern forward, so that the outboard end of the simple scarf lap faced the stern (ie away from the flow of water past the hull).

Although nothing can be said about the stem and sternposts, the one missing group of structures for which there is some evidence are the frames. Their positions are marked by trenail holes which had been drilled through both frames and planks, and they had been fastened by trenails of willow or poplar whose champagne–cork shaped heads show that they were driven from outboard. It is clear that the frames had been fastened after the shell of planks had been constructed, since the frames must originally have overlaid rivets which otherwise could not have been fastened with the frames in position. The boat, therefore, was shell-built.

Date and place of construction

The size of the vessel and its tree-ring study shows that it was built locally for use on the inland waters of the River Thames and its tributaries, between 1160 and 1190 (see Appendix 1).

The vessel was quite small, with scantlings and frame spacings a little less than those of the Graveney boat. Since the Graveney boat has been reconstructed as about 12.3m long, 4m in the beam, and about 1m deep amidships (length:beam ratio of 3.0:1), proportionally this fits the Custom House boat which has been independently reconstructed at at least 9.75m long, and with a beam of at least 3.5m (length to beam ratio of 2.8:1). Thus the Graveney boat provides a useful check on the Custom House boat reconstruction. A vessel of such a size is rather small for work at sea, and it is most likely that it was a river craft. This is also suggested by its considerable beam relative to its length, which would enable it to carry a cargo in shallow waters. These proportions are usefully contrasted with the Skuldelev, Denmark, ships, of the eleventh-century AD, most of which were warships: Skuldelev ship 1 (3.5:1), ship 2 (6:1), ship 3 (4.2:1), ship 5 (7:1) and ship 6 (5:1) (Olsen and Crumlin-Pedersen 1967). It is thought that ship 1 was a merchant ship, and that the longer, narrower vessels were warships. Thus it seems that the Custom House boat was a small broad flat-bottomed barge for river use.

The outboard face of the planks was quite deeply eroded by up to 3mm, judging from uneroded areas around nails and the laps. This erosion may partly have occurred after the planks had been reused in the waterfront, since the outboard face of the boat faced the river. The erosion may also have destroyed any trace of tar waterproofing.

Repairs did take place, however, showing that the vessel was well used, the repairs being intended to stop leaks. In some places extra rivets had been fastened in laps between strakes, and in others oak patches had been fastened over splits in the planking. In the fragments studied these patches were fastened by small iron nails both inboard and outboard, more commonly the latter, and in most instances there was some hair caulking under the patch. The damage that required the repair was splits in the planks along the wood-grain around the trenails. The patches were rather roughly made and suggest that they were made by the owner, rather than carefully by a shipwright, and as most were inboard they could have been fastened without beaching the vessel on stocks to allow access outboard.

The date of the reuse of the boat timbers in the quay revetment is not clear, though it seems to have occurred between the late thirteenth and mid fourteenth centuries (Tatton-Brown 1974, 132–5). If correct this means that the Custom House boat was about a hundred years old before it was broken up.

Boat 2

Part of an oak frame from another boat (Fig 29) was also found reused in the same waterfront at first it was supposed that it derived from the same vessel, further study, however, proved this view untenable.

The frame was recorded after it had dried so that its dimensions were originally slightly larger than given here, except longitudinally, since shrinkage along the grain is negligible. It was 1.80m long, 0.11m deep, and about 0.14m wide. One end had definitely been cut, presumably sawn, for reuse, and although

the other end was decayed it is clear that originally the frame was longer. At intervals along the frame were holes for trenails that once held the frame to the planks, and in one was an oak trenail that had not been wedged on the inboard face. These holes were oval shaped, the minimum diameter being about 24–32mm. They were spaced generally at centres of 0.244–0.295m, but there were additional holes which show that the frame had been re-trenailed. The frame therefore derives from a repaired boat. There were also two trenail holes which had been only partly drilled through the frame, from inboard, and it seems likely that these may have been for fastening internal timbers such as a stringer or keelson. One of these holes lay in the centre of a gap of 0.494m between the main trenail holes.

The underside of the frame is identified by two limber holes cut in that face. These had an almost flat shallow V-shape profile, and were 18–30mm wide, and 2–10mm high. The limber holes crossed the frame diagonally and had centres 0.280m apart. These show that this frame was from the bottom of a flat-bottomed vessel, and their diagonal angle to the frame faces probably indicates that they came from near one end of a boat, for in intact vessels such drainage holes normally followed the alignment of the strake edges. One end of the frame was beginning to curve upwards and perhaps reflects the bottom of the turn of the bilge.

The spacing of the trenail and limber holes indicates that each strake was originally about 0.25–0.28m wide at this point. Since it was normal for frames not to be fastened to the keel in clinker-built boats, and as there is a gap in the trenail spacing of 0.494m, it is likely that this part of the frame crossed the keel. At the centre of the gap is one of the partly drilled holes, which in this position is most likely to have held a keelson or mast-step timber, as was found in Blackfriars ship 3 (*see Chapter 3*).

This frame was not stepped for overlapping planks and there is otherwise no evidence that the vessel was clinker-built. Furthermore, there were no insets cut into the underside of the frame to accommodate the inboard ends of rivets. It is possible, then, that this frame could have derived from a vessel with flush laid bottom planking. This is far from certain, however, since most of the lowest frames of the Graveney boat had also not been stepped over its clinker planking, and there were no rivet insets cut in their undersides.

As the Custom House frame does not match the trenail spacing in the planking of boat 1, it is clear that it was from another boat with a flat bottom which, at this position near one end, was more than 1.44m wide. Such a vessel would have been well over 3m wide and may have been a barge.

3 Blackfriars ship 3, *c* 1400, City of London, 1970

Summary

An almost complete river barge, possibly of the shout type, found in the bed of the Thames, where it had sunk most likely during 1480–1500, (Fig 31) but was locally-built, probably between 1380 and 1415. It was about 14.64m long, 4.3m wide and 0.88m high amidships, of oak, clinker-built and sharp at both ends. A mast situated amidships probably carried a square sail, and it probably had a steering oar. A hydrostatic analysis indicates that the vessel could carry a cargo of about 7.5 tonnes at a waterline of 0.4m.

Fig 31 Bow of ship 3 during excavation, with the floor-timbers still in position, port side stringer top right

Discovery

The wreck of a sailing vessel dating from about 1400 was found on 25 November, 1970, during excavations within a coffer-dam sunk into the bed of the River Thames, just west of the foot of Trig Lane, near Blackfriars in the City of London(Fig 32). The coffer-dam was one of several that had been constructed to enable sections of a new embankment wall to be built by the Corporation of London. Most of this vessel, here called Blackfriars ship 3, had survived, though much of its bow was destroyed during the contractor's excavation prior to the discovery. Also, a portion of the port side near amidships was destroyed by the mechanical grab, and a portion of the starboard side near amidships lay outside the coffer-dam, and, as far as can be judged, still remains *in situ*.

The term ship rather than boat is used here for convenience so as to differentiate this vessel from three other wrecks found nearby at Blackfriars.

Investigation

Once the discovery was reported to the Guildhall Museum the author was given three days in which to excavate and record the vessel. This was not enough time for a detailed excavation, so to make the best use of it long hours were worked on site with the help of museum colleagues and volunteers, in particular Hugh Chapman and John Clark from the Museum, and Valerie Fenwick who had worked on the late Saxon boat from Graveney, north Kent. The archaeological work was not funded, and those working on the excavation relied upon the good-will of the contractors and others.

Fig 32 General view of ship 3, looking aft, after removal of the floor-timbers, the mast-step timber, and the stringer

Fig 33 View from the port side of ship 3 after removal of the floor-timbers. Labels mark the forward edges of the frames

The method of excavation was to use a grab to clear away most of the alluvium above the vessel, and then, starting at the lowest end of the vessel (the bow), to remove the remaining gravel between the frames using a hosed jet of water. Since each bottom frame or floor-timber acted as a dam across the vessel the position of the forward face was marked with nails and labels on both the keel and the planking, before the frame was removed.

The aim was to make a basic record of the vessel *in situ* by drawing a profile along the keel and then two cross-profiles, one near amidships and one near the stern. It was clear that there would be no time in which to make a detailed record of the vessel *in situ*, so as much of the vessel as possible was removed, particularly its structure of frames, keel, stempost, sternpost, mast-step timber, and stringer, in addition to as much of the planking as could be stored. The objective was to record the framework after the excavation, and, with the record of the vessel *in situ*, which included very detailed photographic coverage, to produce drawings of the vessel (Figs 32 and 33).

The dismantled timbers were wrapped in polythene (Figs 34 and 35) and transported to a National Maritime Museum store which had been set aside as a working area (Fig 36). As soon as the

Fig 34 Cutting the keel with a chain-saw proved difficult, a drill bit was more successful

excavation was finished the rest of the vessel was abandoned, though the workmen were reluctant to destroy it and tried to raise the rest of the hull by sliding wires below so as to lift it by crane (Fig 37). Unfortunately the planking simply collapsed. The process of cutting the keel into manageable lengths was difficult, for the hard black waterlogged oak heartwood broke several chain-saws, and a series of adjacent holes had to be drilled to separate the lengths.

Recording the ship timbers

Recording the timbers at the National Maritime Museum took the author some months, during which time the timbers were drawn to a scale of 1/10 in to 2cm. This scale was used because only imperial graph paper was available at the time. Ideally, all faces of each frame and both outboard and inboard faces of the planking should have been recorded, but as time was extremely limited, and since there was no provision then to publish the vessel the recording only identified the evidence that would at a future date enable the hull shape to be reconstructed, and show how the vessel was built.

The inboard face of each piece of planking was recorded as follows: a length of fine string was stretched between the ends, and offset measurements were taken from this to all features. The inboard and forward faces of each frame were drawn similarly, and, in order to save time, those features which existed on the outboard face were drawn with dashed lines on the plan of the inboard face. Such features included the steps (joggling) for the overlapping planking, limber holes, recesses for planking lap rivets, and also rust marks made by iron rivets. Drawings made in 1970 of significant timbers are included below (Figs 39, 40, 42, 46–58, and 63), together with a small selection of frames (Fig 58) that were recorded in 1992 while still wet, to show the grain of the wood. The recently recorded timbers do show that there had been some deterioration during the intervening twenty years. Other drawings of timbers can be consulted in the site archive at the Museum of London.

Many of the timbers deteriorated as they dried, especially after they were moved to a store in the warmth of the seventeenth-century brick vaults under the Queen's House at Greenwich. Some, including the keel, contracted dry rot there, and had to be destroyed. This was a far from an ideal place in which to finish the recording, but the Corporation of London could provide no alternative, and the author was extremely grateful for all the help given by the National Maritime Museum. A few timber samples were retained in a tank of water in the City, and during the next twenty years were moved from one temporary wet store to another in the hope that one day it would be possible to work on them for publication (Marsden 1972). The other timbers, which had dried, took up much-needed storage accommodation at the National Maritime Museum. By 1982 this space was required for other purposes but there was not enough storage space in the Museum of London, the institution which had

succeeded the Guildhall Museum, and although a few typical examples were retained it seemed that the bulk of them had to be disposed of. It was decided to give them to the Nautical Museums Trust, a registered charity established by the author to save the timbers and create a museum of nautical archaeology. The timbers were moved to yet another temporary store, in a vacant City office building due for demolition, until such time as funds were raised and a museum could be built in which to preserve them. In 1986 they were transferred to the Shipwreck Heritage Centre, which had then opened at Hastings.

Working on the records of the ship became feasible in 1991 when the publication of the vessel became part of a research project funded by English Heritage and the Museum of London. By that time many more facilities were available than had existed previously to extract information from the timbers, particularly by tree-ring dating, and by identification of the hair caulking. Also, there were now other published examples of medieval ships from northern Europe for comparison. Computer technology had advanced to the point at which it was possible to undertake a theoretical hydrostatic analysis of the hull to examine its stability, load carrying, draught, and speed. Although dried and shrunken, damaged, and reduced in quantity, the many surviving timbers still represented the most complete medieval sailing vessel yet found in Britain, and it was important that the timbers should remain available for further study.

The vessel

The timbers have been coded as follows: the strakes are numbered from 1 to 12 outwards from the keel, with the prefix P for the port side and S for the starboard side. The frames are numbered from 1 nearest the bow, to 22 at the stern, a sequence that does not reflect the original total since there was an additional frame at the bow that had been destroyed prior to the excavation. The bottom frames or floor-timbers are prefixed FT, and the side-frames, which only survived on the port side, bear the same numbers and are prefixed SF. Thus FT 14 and SF 14 comprise components of the same frame and were originally fastened together.

When found the vessel was distorted (Fig 38), the stern in particular having been pushed over a little to the south or port side, probably because the river bed sloped down in that direction towards the centre of the river. The bottom of the vessel had sagged on either side of the keel, but in general the shape of the craft was much as in its original form.

Fig 35 Wrapping frames of ship 3 in polythene for removal from site

Fig 36 Lifting the wrapped timbers. The absence of protective padding resulted in damage

Fig 37 Lifting boat timbers from the coffer-dam, Southwark Bridge in the distance

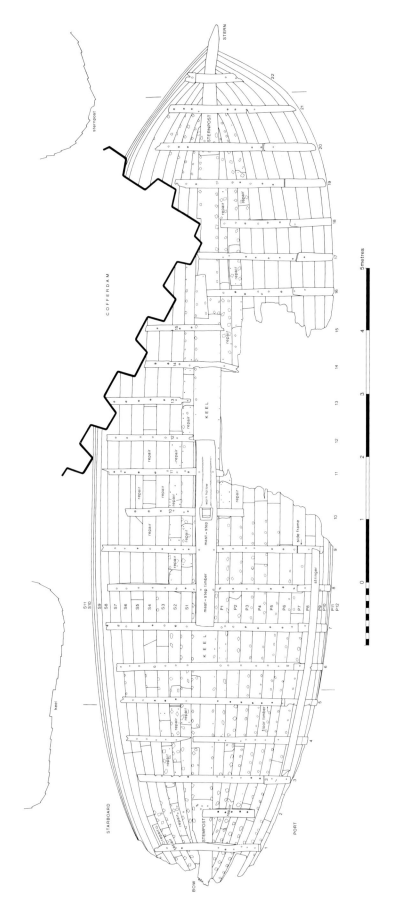

Fig 38   Plan and cross-profiles of ship 3 in situ (see also Fig 65 a fold-out)

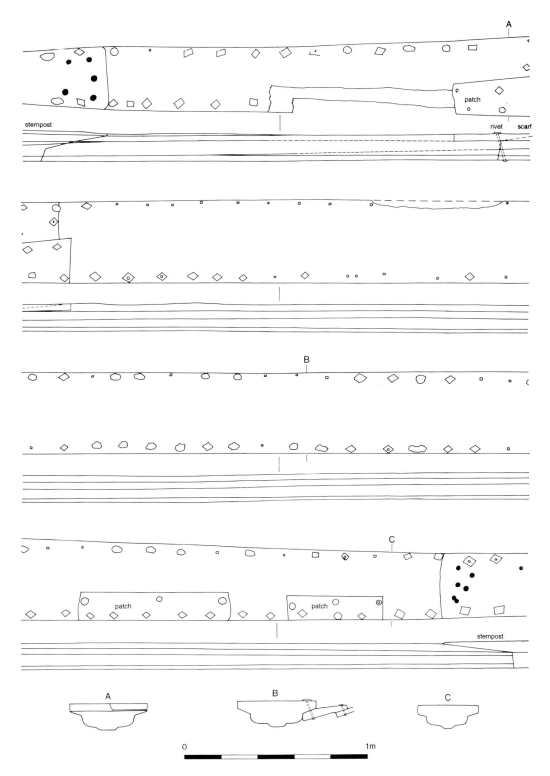

Fig 39 The keel of ship 3 in plan and side elevation, with sections recorded in 1971

Bow and stern

There are three clues to show which end of the vessel was the bow: the position of the mast-step, the direction of the scarf joints in the hull planking, and the shape of the hull. In a ship with a single square sail the mast is usually stepped at the centre of the vessel or somewhat forward of it, and, in the case of Blackfriars ship 3, this was towards the west end, which should therefore be the bow. The direction of the scarf joints between planks making up each strake or run of planks confirms that the bow was at the west end as they were overlapped outboard towards the east end, enabling the water to flow eastwards towards the stern with the minimum of erosion of the scarfs. The east end of the vessel was fuller in form than the west as if allowing more space for steering and control of the sail. Thus the port side lay to the south, and the starboard to the north.

Construction of the ship

Materials

All of the main timbers, keel, frames, planks, and repair patches, were of oak. Trenails that held the frames to the planks were of willow or poplar The planks had been radially cut, as had the repair patches. Caulking between the planks and in the repair patches was of matted goat hair (*see Appendix 3*), and the rivets holding the plank laps together were of wrought iron.

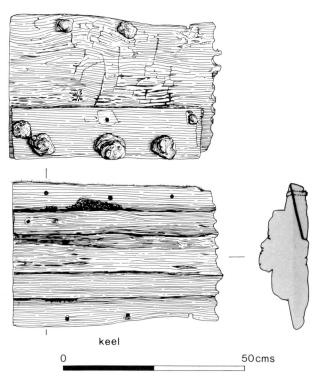

keel

0   50cms

Fig 40 Fragment of the keel recorded in 1991 to show the grain of the wood, with some distortion due to shrinkage

Keel

The keel consisted of two oak timbers joined endways with an overlap scarf to give a total length of 10.77m. The separate timbers were 8.42m and 2.69m long. At the ends of the keel were scarfed joints to the stempost and the sternpost. The keel had been cut tangentially from a log, with the pith position above the centre of the top of the keel. This enabled the rounded part of the log to help form the slightly rounded lower part of the keel.

The keel was straight with no sign of 'rocker' or vertical curve, and was 0.43m wide amidships narrowing to 0.34m at the ends, and was 0.14m deep (Figs 39 and 40). It was therefore of the plank keel type in which width was greater than depth (McGrail 1987, 113), with a depth-to-width ratio of about 0.32:1. It had a flat top, but the underside was elaborately shaped (Fig 41). On each side was a rabbet 0.06m deep to contain the garboard strakes which were attached by iron rivets, and between these the lower part of the keel was rounded with the centre projecting about 0.02m downwards. The angle of the rabbet in the keel was about 22° from horizontal, but the angle of the outboard face of the garboard strake was 18°, the difference having been caused by the angle of bevel of the garboard strake and the keel. The purpose of the longitudinal downward projection in the centre of the otherwise flat bottom of the keel was presumably to help the vessel oppose leeway (drifting sideways downwind).

The horizontal scarf holding the two lengths of keel together was 0.34m long and lay near the stern, between frames 15 and 17. It was diagonally-cut across the keel with the outboard end facing the stern, to allow water to flow past without eroding into the scarf. The ends of the keel were then fastened together with six long iron nails and rivets. On the starboard side inboard was a piece of oak timber up to 0.7m long, 0.24m wide and 0.04m thick, that had been inset into the scarf and then nailed in place. It seems likely that this was a repair, since there were two other

Fig 41 The underside of the keel of ship 3 with its central ridge, and a scarfed garboard strake. Note the erosion hollows around the iron rivet heads (metric scale)

similar patches that were probably repairs on the same side of the keel further forward. One of these other patches lay beneath frame 5, and was 0.15m wide, 0.8m long, and about 0.04m thick. The third patch, 0.13m wide and 0.53m long, lay beneath frame 3. The last two patches were fastened to the keel by the rivets which also held the garboard strake, and in addition there were nails with flat heads. There was some matted hair caulking under the patches. These patches had repaired the upper face of the keel where the rivet fastenings lay, and it is likely that they repaired the holes for the rivet fastenings in the edge of the keel which had presumably been damaged, perhaps by running aground on obstructions on the river bed. This is suggested by the very localised area of repair.

Sternpost

The sternpost comprised two primary pieces of timber, the lowest curving up from the keel, and the other extending the post further upwards (Fig 42). A third small piece of timber roughly filled in a hollow on the inboard face of the lower timber (Fig 43).

The sternpost was horizontally scarfed onto the after end of the keel with a diagonal lap 0.36m long, sloping downwards aft at an angle of about 13.° The lower half of the scarf had an almost vertical butt joint. The scarf lap was fastened with five iron nails driven in place from inboard. It is likely that the scarf was caulked with hair, but this could not be checked.

The after end of the garboard strakes P1 and S1 extended across the keel-sternpost scarf to the lower end of the sternpost, thus strengthening the scarf, and were held by rivets, but strakes above that had bevelled ends which were nailed to a rabbet on each side of the sternpost. This means that as the sternpost curved upwards the width of the rabbet narrowed and its depth increased so as to become a slight bevel about 0.012m wide. The upper end of the lower sternpost timber had become deeper (0.28m) than it was wide (0.19m).

The timber that extended the shape of the sternpost upwards was fastened to the lower curved sternpost timber with a vertical lap scarf 0.12m wide and 0.22m long, and was held there by one central nail and by three further nails near its lower edge.

Fig 42 The stern of ship 3 after the removal of all bottom frames except FT 22 (metric scale)

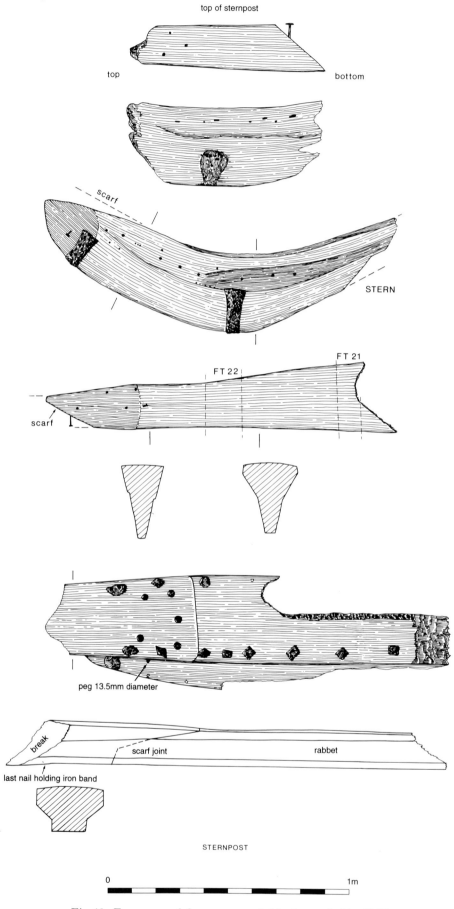

Fig 43 Fragments of the sternpost of ship 3 recorded in 1971

On the inboard face at the top of the lower timber of the sternpost was the beginning of a horizontal scarf which had been filled with a rough piece of timber nailed in position (Fig 44). This is best explained as the position of a third sternpost timber that was originally horizontally scarfed in position, but had been replaced by the present upper timber.

The outer edge of the sternpost had been protected from wear by a thin band of iron 0.04m wide and about 3mm thick. This extended from a point about 0.20m aft of the scarf with the keel to at least as far as the highest surviving part of the edge of the sternpost. It was held in position by iron nails driven through the strip into the sternpost, and by three iron brackets each about 0.06m wide.

Stempost

Although only the lowest 1.2m of one half of the stempost had survived, enough remained to show that its shape and scarf with the keel was the same as that at the sternpost (Fig 45). It was originally about 0.29m wide at the scarf, the scarf itself being 0.4m long and diagonally cut horizontally to fit the forward end of the keel where it was fastened by several iron nails driven from inboard (Fig 46). About 1.14m forward of the bottom of the stempost its width had increased to about 0.33m, and the rivet construction that held the garboard strakes to the keel extended across the rabbets of the scarf itself, as at the stern, to give the scarf greater strength. Forward of this the planks were nailed to the rabbets in the side of the stempost.

Planks

Of the twelve strakes on each side of the vessel six were on the flat bottom, three were at the turn of the bilge, and three were on the side (including the gunwale). Parts of all of these had survived and were of oak, and in the middle of the vessel were between 0.23m and 0.27m wide, but averaged 0.25m. They were 0.025–0.05m thick, but averaged about 0.035m. They had all been fashioned from radially-cut oak heartwood timber, though the edge of the sapwood could just be seen occasionally.

The strakes were laid clinkerwise with the laps generally ranging from 0.06–0.09m wide, most being about 0.07–0.08m wide (Figs 47 and 48). This means that the laps were roughly two to three times the thickness of the plank, and accord with a modern rule-of-thumb that overlaps should be twice the thickness of the planks (McGrail 1987, 128). It is important to note that both upper and lower lap faces had been bevelled according to the position of the plank in the boat, though in general the shipwright had shaped the upper lap of the strake before offering up the lower lap of the next strake to be fastened by rivets.

Fig 44 The upper part of the sternpost of ship 3 with the roughly filled-in scarf

Fig 45   The bow of ship 3, with the lower end of the stempost

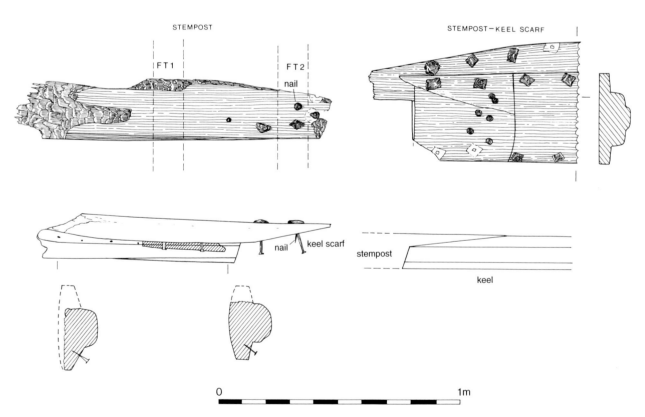

Fig 46   Fragments of the stempost of ship 3 recorded in 1971

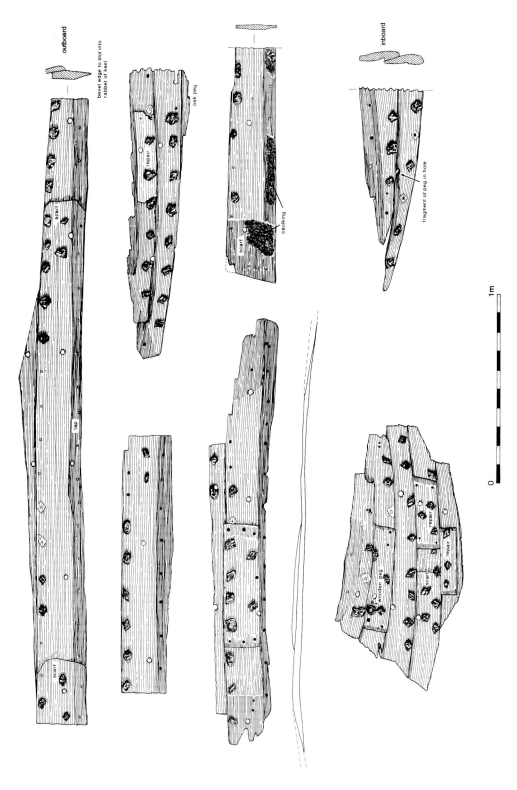

Fig 47 Typical examples of planking, inboard view, recorded in 1971, showing scarfs and repair patches

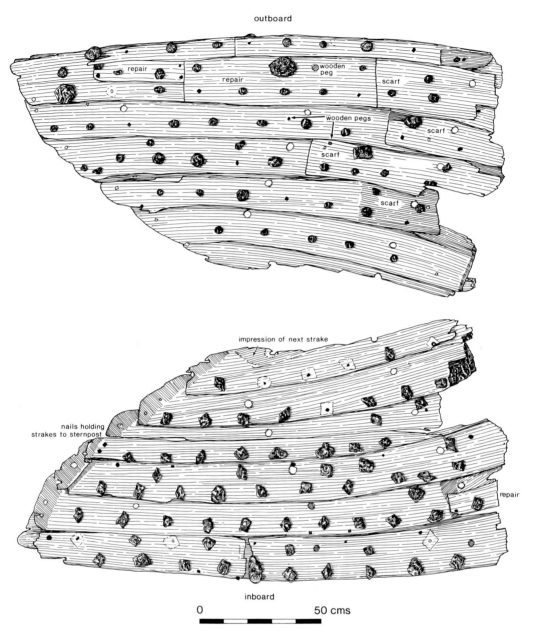

Fig 48 Outboard (top) and inboard (bottom) views of stern planking on the starboard side of ship 3, showing the pattern of nail attachment to the sternpost

The plank faces at the laps were flat, and had no groove to contain the caulking that made the joints watertight. The caulking itself was of matted goat hair impregnated with tar spread over the whole lap area.

Iron rivets, with centres spaced at intervals generally of about 0.11–0.20m, but averaging 0.15–0.17m, fastened the strakes together. Each rivet comprised an iron nail with a flat head outboard and square shank about 7mm square passing through the planking. As the planking had not been deformed by the rivets it seems clear that a hole had first been drilled with a diameter slightly less than that of the nail shank. On the inboard face there was a fairly flat diamond-shaped iron rove about 30–40mm × 30–45mm.

Each strake was formed from several planks scarfed together endways, most of the scarfs being simple overlaps with the outboard end facing the stern. The ends of the scarfed planks were mostly feathered off to a wedge-shape inboard when seen in long section, and were generally fixed together by an iron rivet fastened at the inboard end, and another at the outboard end of the scarf, in addition to the normal lap rivets between strakes. Occasionally scarf joints were squared off leaving a butt end about 5mm thick. This tended to occur at the outboard end, with the end of the scarf sunk into a corresponding recess in the next plank. The feathered and butt-ended scarfs suggest the handiwork of at least two shipwrights, one perhaps carrying out repairs. The scarf joints generally ranged from 0.28–0.44m long, with the majority between 0.30m and 0.34m. The ratio of scarf length to plank thickness ranged from 5.6:1 to 8.8:1, but averaged about 7.2:1. This is much shorter than the modern practice which favours a ratio of 12:1 (Leather 1987, 86). Also, scarfs were sometimes placed very close together in adjacent strakes, even though this could cause a weakness in the hull structure.

The garboard strakes ran parallel to the side of the keel, except at its ends where the remaining strakes were slightly curved to give the vessel its shape. Where they curved into rabbets in the sternpost the strakes were held by two iron nails, driven through the upper and lower laps, with a caulking of hair. Occasionally there were extra nails in the breadth of the plank end that evidently strengthened the attachment and stopped leakage

Plank repairs

There were many repairs to the planking, and these took two forms, replacements and patches.

Plank replacements

A few of the scarf joints faced the bow and did not follow the general rule which determines that they should face aft to avoid erosion. It is assumed, therefore, that they result from repairs in which a length of planking had been replaced. To do this it was necessary to remove many iron rivets and some frames to reach the damaged timber.

Plank patches

There were many patches fastened to both inboard and outboard faces of the planking, though not all could be recorded. A random few were taken apart in the hope of identifying the damage in question. For example, at floor-timbers 1 and 2 there was a repair patch in strake S3 which was 0.54m long and 0.12m wide, at the full width of the plank at that point. In order to make this repair it was necessary to remove floor-timber 2 and to remove five rivets which fastened strake S3 to S4. The inboard surface of the strake S3 was then shaved away so reducing its thickness. The oak patch was then placed in position inboard with a layer of matted hair caulking between it and the plank.

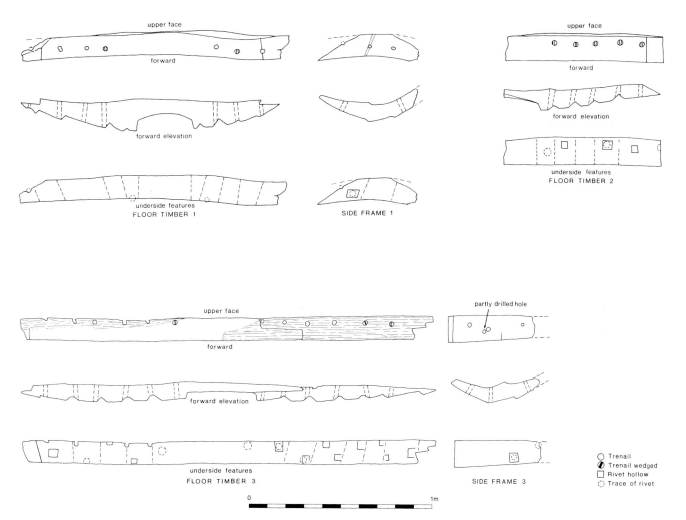

Fig 49 Frames 1–3 of ship 3, recorded in 1971. The underside features of each frame are as viewed from above

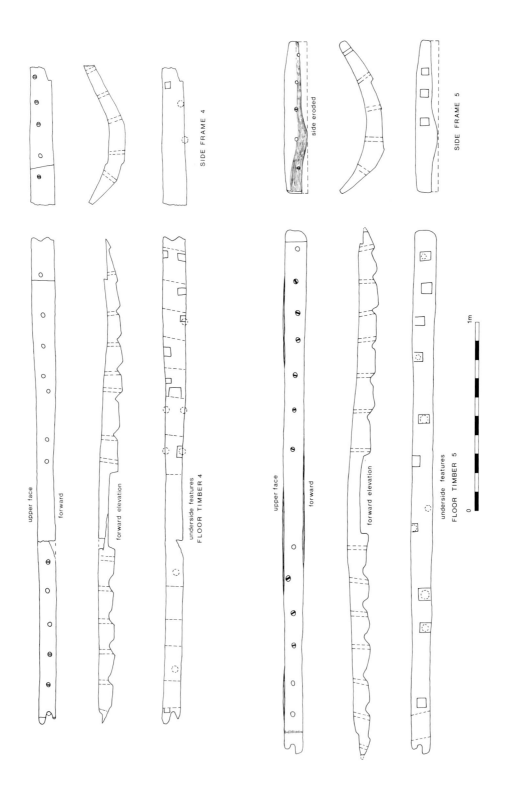

Fig 50 Frames 4–5 of ship 3

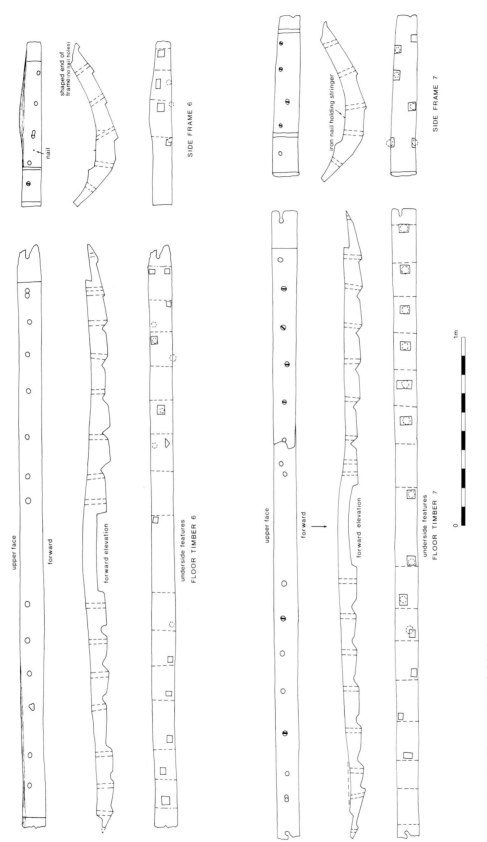

Fig 51 Frames 6–7 of ship 3

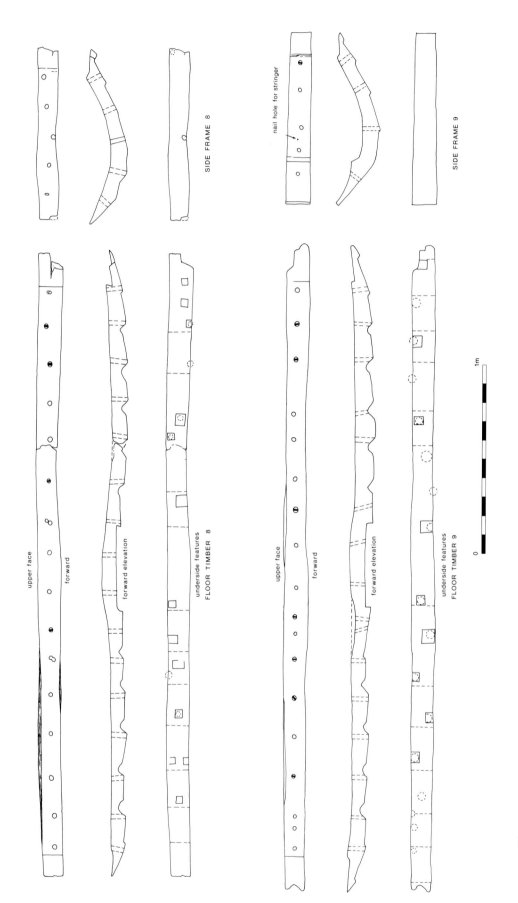

SIDE FRAME 8

nail hole for stringer

SIDE FRAME 9

upper face

forward

forward elevation

underside features
FLOOR TIMBER 8

upper face

forward

forward elevation

underside features
FLOOR TIMBER 9

1m

0

Fig 52 Frames 8–9 of ship 3

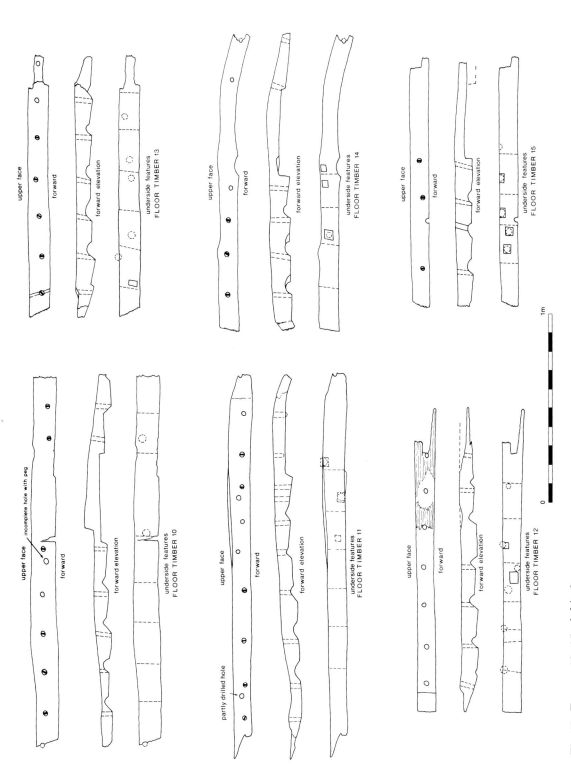

Fig 53 Frames 12–15 of ship 3

The three rivets were then replaced together with two additional rivets close to the edge of strake S2, and four nails held the ends of the patch. The replacement of the frame meant that a new hole for a trenail had to be drilled through the patch.

Two further patches lay nearby on strakes S5 and S6. The patch on S5 was 0.37m long and 0.12m wide, covering the visible width of the plank. Again, the inboard plank surface below the patch must have been removed as the patch had been fastened by replacing two existing lap rivets and adding another in the centre of the patch. Also a nail had been driven from inboard into each corner of the patch, and a hole had been drilled through the patch for the frame trenail. The patch in strake S6 was smaller and was held by three rivets only.

There are several possible reasons why these and other inboard patches had been added, including the need to hold together a split plank, to make certain that rivet and trenail fittings were watertight, to replace rotten wood, to replace worn plank surfaces, and to strengthen existing scarfs. Wherever a patch could be removed there was no split apparent in the plank below. However, as the patches incorporated new laps and rivets, and often were at trenail positions, it would seem that the usual problems were leaks caused by the fastenings working loose, perhaps due to frequent grounding. Several patches were also noted inboard over plank scarfs, indicating that scarf fastenings too were a source of leakage.

Frames

Each frame comprised a floor-timber with a side-frame fastened by a trenail to each end. The floor-timbers were used only on the flat bottom of the vessel, and therefore were cut from reasonably straight-grained oak. In contrast, the side-frames were cut from naturally curving timbers to give the best shape to the side of the vessel. The shape of each frame was carefully recorded soon after excavation (Figs 49 to 57), and examples were recorded recently to show the grain (Fig 58), though they had deteriorated in the intervening twenty years despite being stored under water.

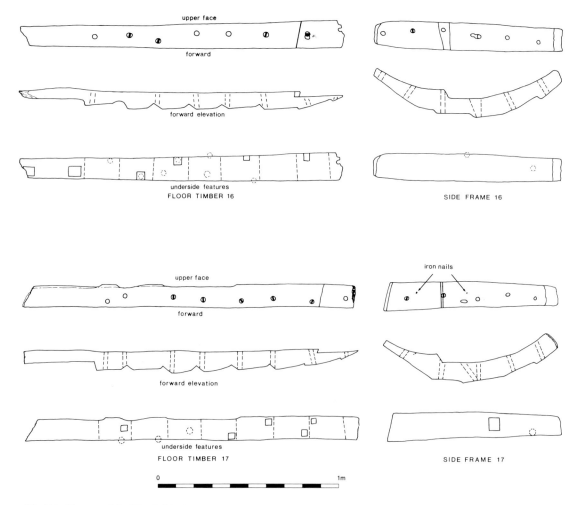

Fig 54 Frames 16–17 of ship 3

Opposite: Fig 55 Frames 18–19 of ship 3
Fig 56 Frames 20–21 of ship 3

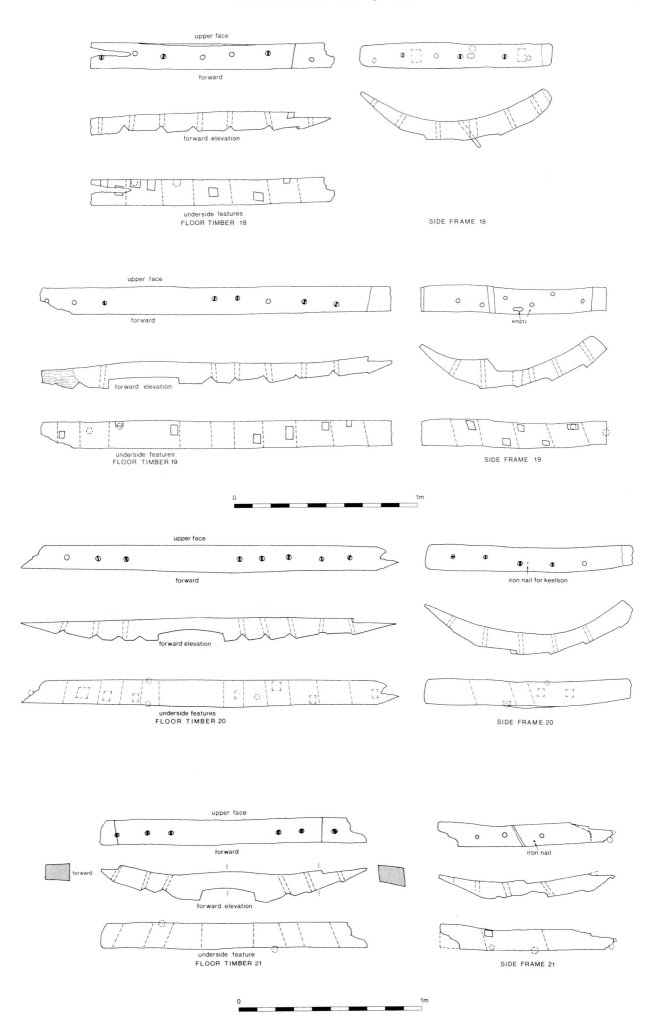

upper face

forward

forward elevation

empty

underside features
FLOOR TIMBER 18

SIDE FRAME 18

upper face

forward

forward elevation

underside features
FLOOR TIMBER 19

SIDE FRAME 19

0   1m

upper face

forward

forward elevation

iron nail for keelson

underside features
FLOOR TIMBER 20

SIDE FRAME 20

upper face

forward

forward

forward elevation

iron nail

underside feature
FLOOR TIMBER 21

SIDE FRAME 21

0   1m

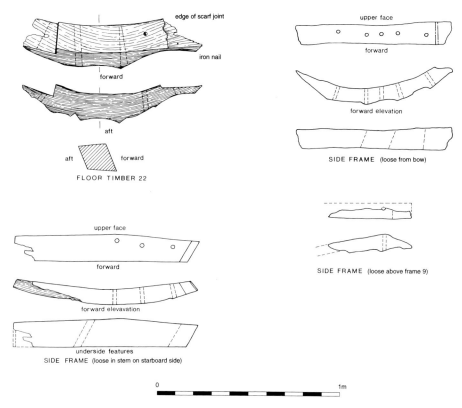

Fig 57 FT22, and three loose side-frames of ship 3

The frames were spaced apart at intervals of 0.405–0.565m, but averaged 0.468m, throughout the bottom of the vessel, and each floor-timber was between 0.09 and 0.17m thick (moulded), averaging 0.115m, and 0.09–0.14m wide (sided), averaging 0.12m. They were joggled, or stepped, on their undersides to take the overlapping strakes, and square hollows (Fig 59) were cut in the undersides to accommodate the roves of the planking rivets. Five arched limber holes, each about 0.06m wide and 0.02m high, were also cut in the underside of each floor-timber on either side of the keel, and each of these coincided with the first five strake laps beyond the garboard strakes. The undersides of the floor-timbers were recessed as they passed over the keel, and at that point the timbers were between 0.05m and 0.08m thick. Thus the floor-timbers were rather weak, though they preserved in their shapes a great deal of information about the form of the vessel and its construction. The floor-timbers were not fastened to the keel, but instead were attached to each strake by a trenail about 0.13m in diameter, a sample of which was identified as willow or poplar. A hole had been drilled through both the frame and the plank below and the trenail had been inserted from outboard, since only the inboard end of the trenail was wedged, and was of smaller dimension than the outboard end (Fig 60). The wedge was of oak and had been driven across the grain of the frame to avoid splitting the frame. Not all trenails were wedged, however, indicating that refastening had occurred. The method of fastening was shown by partly drilled holes for trenails in the top of some frames (eg in floor-timbers 7, 8, 9, 10, and 11), showing that it was from inboard that the trenail holes had been drilled for fastening to the strakes. Furthermore, in some frames it is clear that trenail holes had been drilled twice (eg floor-timbers 6 and 16) and even three times (eg floor-timber 6) on about the same spot, presumably due to the refastening of frames following repairs.

The lower end of each side-frame was fastened to the outer end of each floor-timber by a trenail which also fastened these frames to the plank below (Table 2).

Table 2 Spacing between forward faces of frames over keel

between frames	measurement	between frames	measurement
FT 1–2	0. 53	11–12	0. 56
2–3	0. 545	12–13	0. 60
3–4	0. 68	13–14	0. 57
4–5	0. 59	14–15	0. 57
5–6	0. 555	15–16	0. 575
6–7	0. 62	16–17	0. 595
7–8	0. 64	17–18	0. 515
8–9	0. 61	18–19	0. 585
9–10	0. 59	19–20	0. 59
10–11	0. 61	20–21	0. 56
		21–22	0. 495

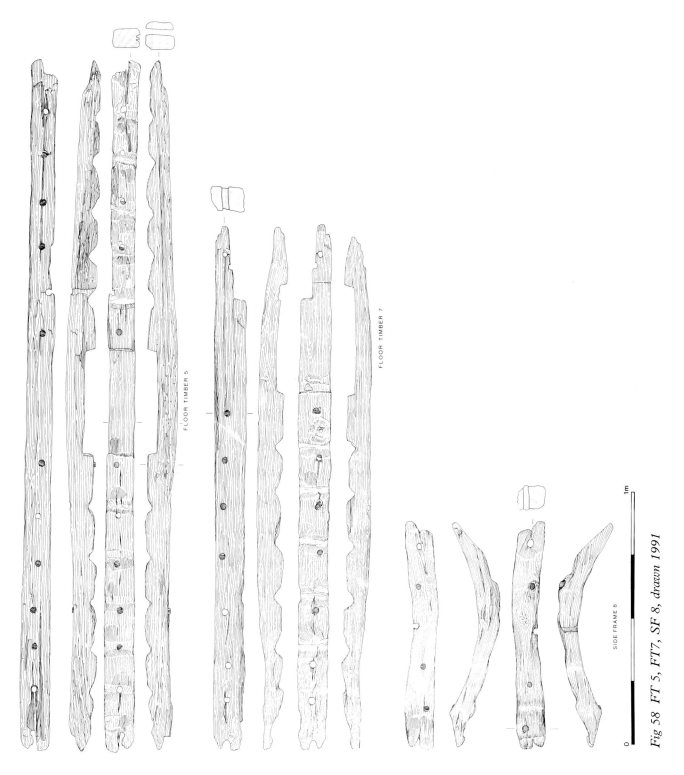

Fig 58 FT 5, FT7, SF 8, drawn 1991

Although the trenail hole had been driven from inboard, the trenail itself had clearly been driven from outboard, for in many cases its inboard end had been wedged across the grain of the frames. Not all had been wedged, however, the differing techniques again possibly reflecting the varying handiwork of the shipwrights who had repaired the vessel. The side-frames were 0.10m to 0.14m wide (sided) and 0.08m to 0.10m thick (moulded), and had been stepped for the clinker planking. Also, shallow recesses, about 0.05m square, had been cut in the side-frame undersides facing the planking so as to accommodate the roves of the iron rivets in the planking. These allowed the frames to rest on the inboard plank surfaces. A small ledge had been cut in the inboard face of each side-frame at the turn of the bilge (Fig 61) to accommodate a stringer extending along the length of the vessel.

Fig 59 Hollow cut in the underside of a floor-timber of ship 3 to take a rove projecting above the planking (centimetre scale)

Fig 60 A wedged trenail from FT 7, the wedge was driven from inboard (scale 1:1)

As this vessel was shell-built with edge-fastened planking, in theory there could have been planking above the side-frames. Consequently the upper ends of the surviving side-frames were carefully examined in case there were further fastenings, perhaps to attach a wash-strake, but as none was found it is clear that the upper limit of the side was represented.

At the stern the upper and lower faces of the frames were bevelled as they passed across the sloping sternpost so that their fore and aft sides stood roughly vertical across the stern.

Mast-step timber

The mast-step timber (Fig 62) was a rectangular block of oak 2.93m long, 0.195m high, and 0.365m wide at its base (Fig 63). The top was slightly narrower. It was fastened to the tops of floor-timbers 8–11 over the keel by trenails 25mm in diameter, and although the forward end, which just edged over the top of floor-timber 7, appeared to be broken the absence in that frame of any trenail fastenings over the keel indicates that the mast-step timber was at about its full length.

The mast-step socket lay over floor-timber 10, near the midship position, so that the full weight of the mast was properly supported. The socket was 0.08m deep, and had a central recess 0.127 by 0.121m square, the lowest part of which had largely rotted away to expose

Fig 61 Port side of ship 3 looking aft with the side-framess in position. The uppermost strake, the gunwale, beside the nearest frame has iron fastenings (metric scale)

the top of the floor-timber below. On three sides around this at a slightly higher level the step was larger, with a ledge about 0.04m wide, above which the sides of the hollow sloped upwards and outwards. It would seem that the step followed the shape of the foot of the mast, and that the base of the mast itself was 0.18m by 0.20m square, with a tenon 0.03m deep and 0.127–0.121m square set to the after side of the centre. The shape of the step presumably ensured that the mast was stepped in the correct position. In the top of the mast-step timber, and extending aft from the step, was a slight hollow with rounded sides, about 20mm deep and about the width of the inferred tenon. There is little doubt that this hollow was worn as a result of lowering the mast frequently by lifting it out of the step and sliding it aft.

Stringer

Fastened to small ledges cut in the side-frames from SF 3 to 9 on the port side at the turn of the bilge was part of an oak stringer, roughly triangular in section (Fig 63). It had a flat top about 0.12m wide and a vertical face 0.12m high facing the keel (Fig 64). A third face lay in the recess cut in the sloping side-frames, to which it was fastened by one trenail 27mm in diameter. This ledge was traced from SF 1 to 21. No particular wear was noted to suggest that the stringer

Fig 62 Mast-step timber looking forward. Note worn hollow running aft from step (metric scale)

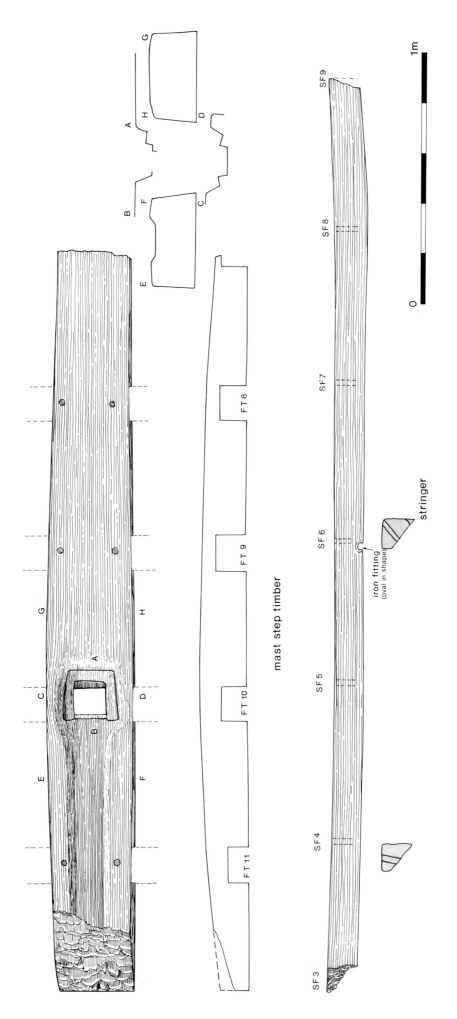

Fig 63 The mast-step timber and the port side stringer of ship 3

Fig 64 The stringer in situ *on the port side of ship 3. The small loose piece of planking over the floor-timbers was presumably driftwood (metric scale)*

had been used for tying ropes, though above SF 6 there was noted a small unidentifiable corroded iron fitting, oval in shape. No doubt there was originally a similar stringer on the starboard side, whose frames were lost, and both stringers evidently gave additional longitudinal strength to the entire vessel.

Reconstruction of the ship

Reconstructing the former appearance of this vessel and the method of its construction is made easy by its excellent state of survival. Most of its bottom, sides, stern, and the lower part of the bow remained to give its overall length, beam, and gunwale height. The only difficulty concerns the exact shape of the upper part of the bow, though the shape of the lower part of the stempost and the run of planks towards that end limit the range of possibilities. The specific objectives in reconstructing the vessel were to define its construction, its form, and the distribution of its

weight. Of these its construction reflects its strength, and its form and weight reflect its stability. Clues to the methods of propulsion and steering were considered, followed by a hydrostatic analysis to establish the ship's theoretical stability and performance.

How reconstruction was achieved

The first step was to establish the original shape of the ship, using the asumption that the discovered form of its timbers was original unless there was reason to believe that some distortion had occurred. This follows the principle that, in correcting distortion, the minimum of modification should be made to the surviving shape of a vessel. A particularly useful guide is to assume that the vessel was originally symmetrical about the keel or middle line. Therefore, as the sternpost of Blackfriars ship 3 was found to be leaning a little to port and as the sides at the stern were not of the same shape, it had clearly suffered some distortion. It was also necessary to make a slight adjustment to the cross-profile of the vessel near amidships for the hull had sagged downwards on either side of the keel.

Shape of hull bottom

The downward sagging planks on both sides of the keel were not in their original shape as indicated by the fact that the frames and their wood grain curved up and over the keel (Fig 65). The curve of the grain shows that they had been bent and not cut to that shape. Also, the rabbet in the sides of the keel for the attachment of the garboard strakes showed that the bottom planking should lie almost horizontal. That the keel itself should project down below the level of the planking is indicated by its central downward projecting ridge whose purpose must have been to oppose leeway as well as to add some longitudinal strength. The original extent of the flat bottom is shown by the limber holes cut in the underside of the floor-timbers; these permitted the flow of bilge water and would have lain at the lowest part of the hull.

As a result, the section of the hull bottom at each discovered frame was reconstructed with the floor-timber redrawn straightened and horizontal (Figs 66 and 67). In effect this meant 'lifting' the bottom planking and each floor-timber on either side of the keel by only about 0.06m.

Shape of hull sides

The side-frames on the port side were found still attached to the ends of the floor-timbers, but because they were standing largely vertical they did not seem to have been distorted by overlying pressure, except

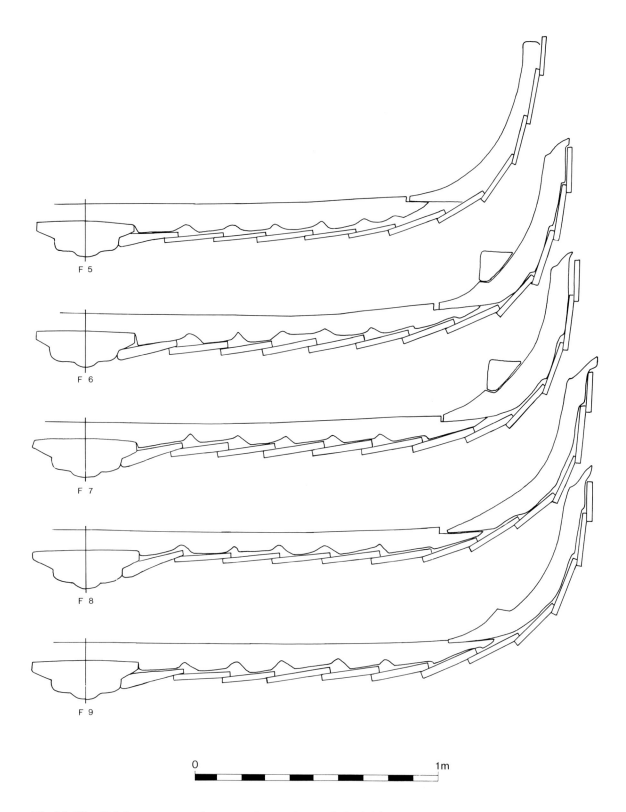

Fig 66 *The slightly reconstructed cross-sections at frames 5–9 of ship 3*

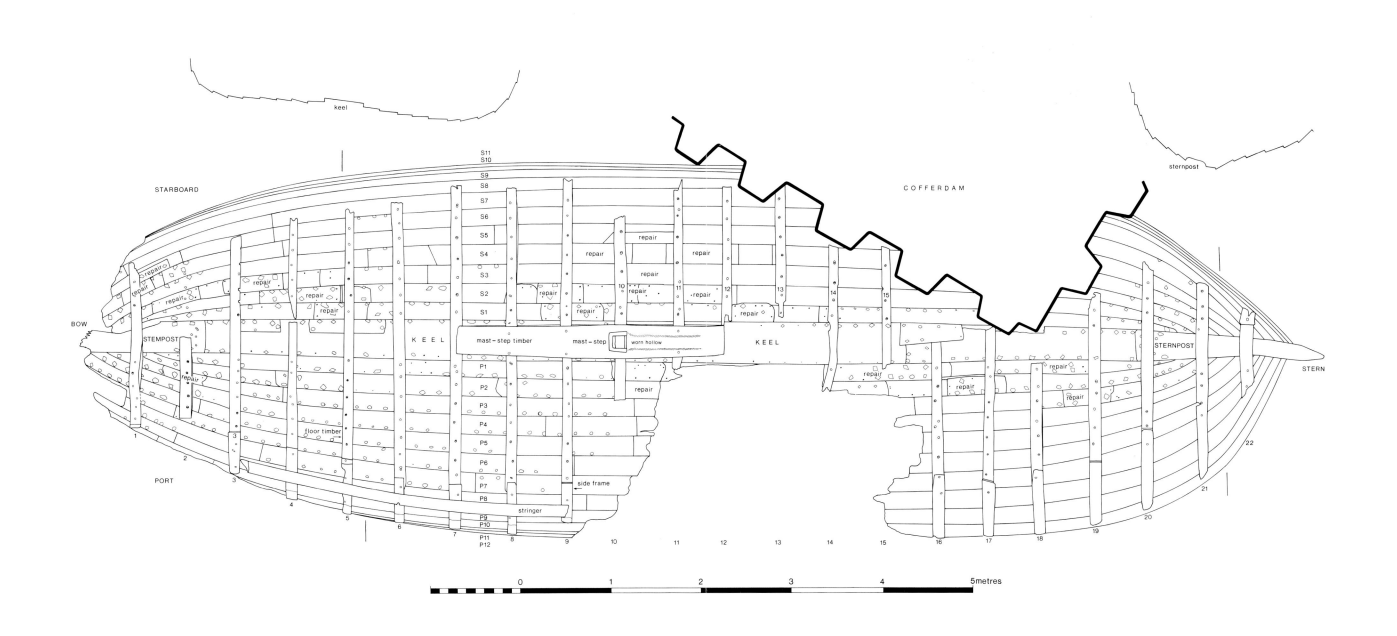

keel

sternpost

S11
S10
S9
S8
S7
S6
S5
S4
S3
S2
S1

STARBOARD

COFFERDAM

repair

repair

repair

repair

repair

repair

10

repair

11

12

13

14

15

repair

repair

repair

BOW

STEMPOST

KEEL

mast-step timber

mast-step

worn hollow

KEEL

STERNPOST

STERN

repair

repair

repair

repair

P1

P2

P3

P4

P5

P6

P7

P8

P9
P10
P11
P12

floor timber

side frame

stringer

PORT

1

2

3

4

5

6

7

8

9

10

11

12

13

14

15

16

17

18

19

20

21

22

0   1   2   3   4   5 metres

Fig 65a Plan and cross profiles of ship 3 in situ

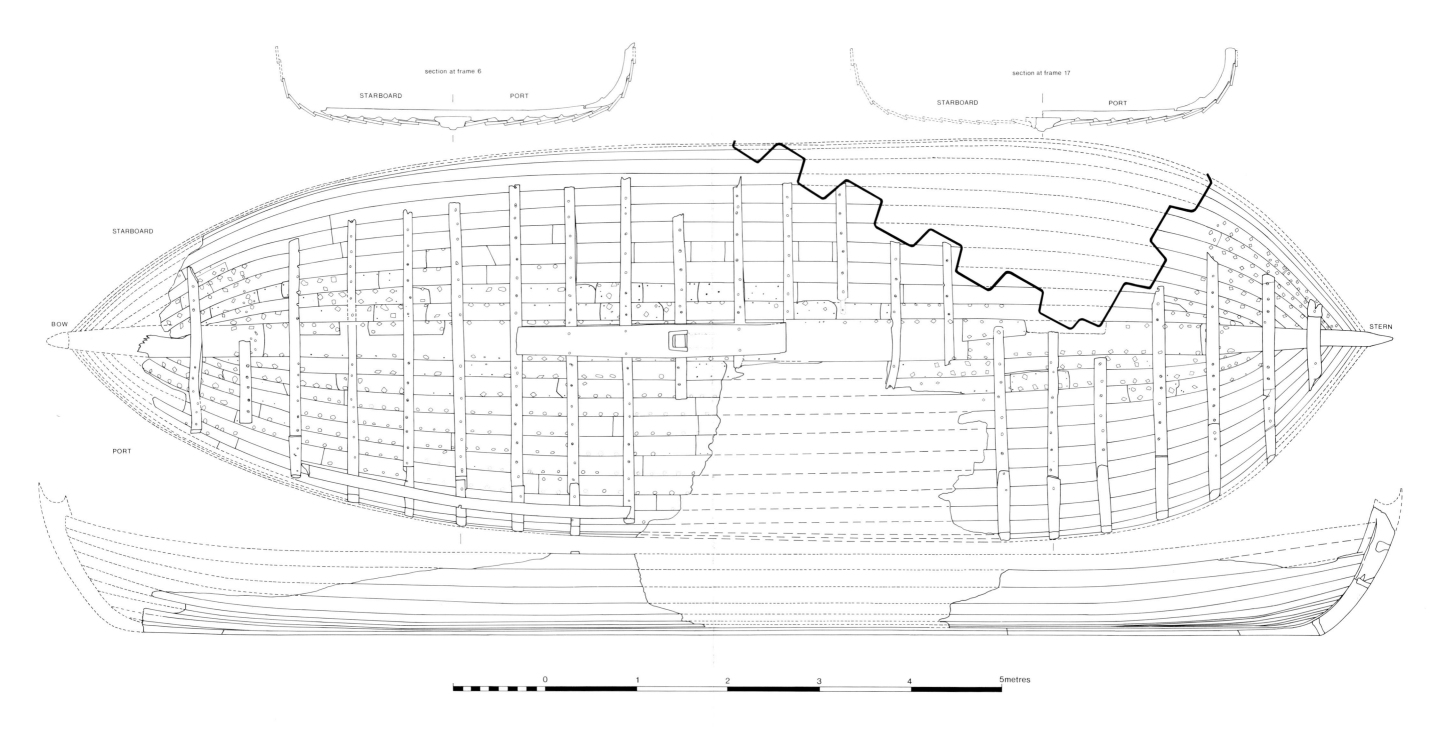

section at frame 6

STARBOARD PORT

section at frame 17

STARBOARD PORT

STARBOARD

BOW

PORT

STERN

0 1 2 3 4 5metres

Fig 65b Ship 3 with its stern straightened to follow the keel line

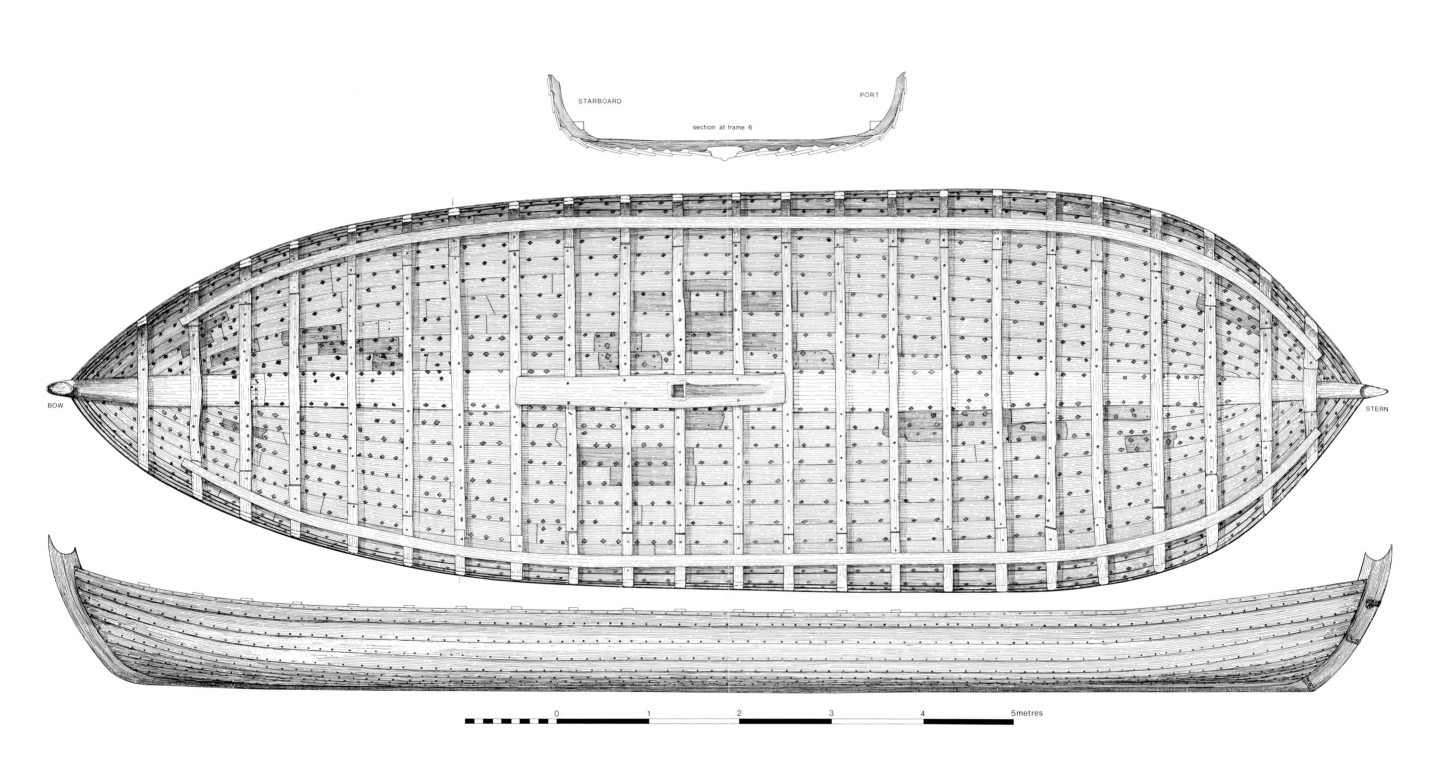

STARBOARD

PORT

section at frame 6

BOW

STERN

0   1   2   3   4   5metres

Fig 71 Complete reconstruction drawing of the hull of ship 3

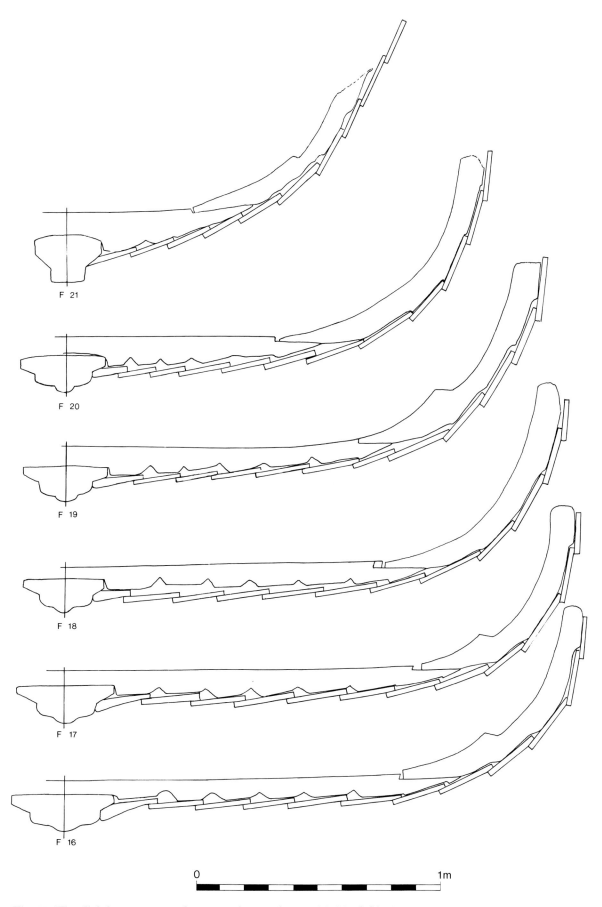

Fig 67 The slightly reconstructed cross-sections at frames 16–21 of ship 3

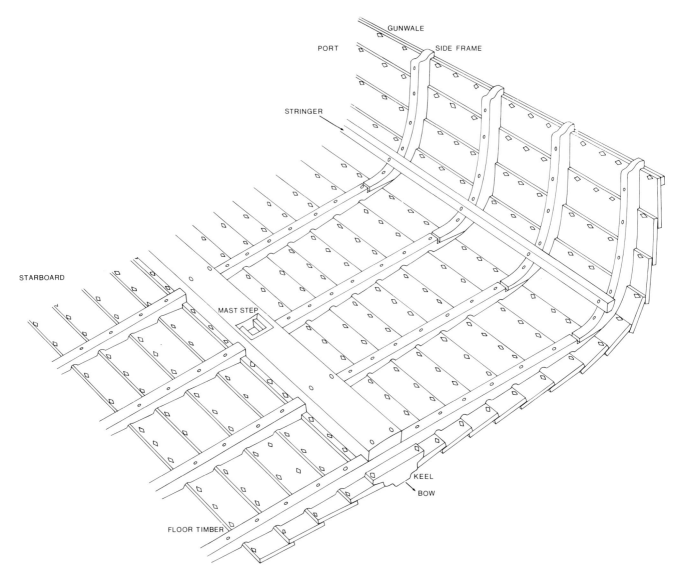

Fig 68 The reconstruction of ship 3. The form of the wooden rail attached to the outboard side of the gunwale is the only uncertainty

perhaps at the stern. By placing the side-frames as discovered onto the ends of the slightly re-shaped floor-timbers, they themselves completed the form of the hull, which amidships gave a vertical side at gunwale level. In the after part of the vessel the side-frames were of a slightly different shape, and it seems that the sides there had a little flare and gave the stern area more of a spoon-like shape.

The exact width of each side strake is given by the steps and rivet hollows cut in the outboard face of the side-frames, to which an overlap allowance has been added to give the full breadth of each strake. Part of the gunwale, strake 12, had been preserved between SF 7 and 9, but because of the great pressure of work on site this was unfortunately not investigated in detail. Instead its inboard face was photographed and shows three iron fastenings, resembling corroded rivets, along its top between SF 8 and 9. SF 6 and 8 also had

evidence of this uppermost row of fastenings, a rust mark left by an iron fastening was found on SF 8, and on SF 6 was a cut hollow to accommodate a rove. Judging from photographs and from the outboard overhang of the top of the side-frames, the gunwale strake was only about 0.02–0.03m thick, like the lower strakes, but it seems that the iron fastenings along the top of the gunwale held an additional strengthening timber or rail against the outboard face acting perhaps as a rubbing strake (Fig 68). It is possible that this timber was the bottom of a wash-strake, but as such a strake would have been unsupported by any frames it would have been vulnerable to damage as cargoes were loaded and unloaded. Consequently, it is probable that such a strake did not exist.

The carefully shaped top of SF 6–9 appear not to have been extended aft to SF 16–19 at the stern, which instead were thicker and slightly rounded. The

Fig 69 The end of some lower strakes on the starboard side outboard of ship 3, where they were fastened to the sternpost. This shows holes for the nail fastenings to the sternpost driven through the middle of each plank and through each lap. Note also the erosion hollows around the iron nail heads (metric scale)

reason for this is not clear, particularly as no side-frame in the vessel included any fastenings which might suggest that other timbers, perhaps for a covered awning, were once fastened on top of the sides. Alternatively, there may have been a higher strake to enable

the stern to carry a greater load, though this could cause problems with the trim of the vesel. It would seem, therefore, that the shaped top of SF 6–9 was merely decorative, and it is perhaps possible that the absence of such shaping in the stern side-frames was due to their being replacements of earlier timbers that had been so shape

Bow and stern

The stern planking was intact up to strake 11, but the nails that fastened the overlap between strakes 11 and 12 and the top of strake 12 were found in the side of the sternpost, thus giving the original position of the planking at the stern (Fig 69). Unfortunately the surviving top of the sternpost, which stood above the top of the planking, was rather eroded so that its original shape is a matter for conjecture. However, two paintings of the fourteenth and fifteenth centuries, depicting the Tower of London, may be helpful for they include views of several river vessels on the Thames (Fig 70 and Front cover*)*: Rowse 1974, 33–4). In each case the stem and sternposts terminated in a crescent, a form which, if in general use, may have been used in Blackfriars ship 3.

Although the bow had been destroyed, the lower end of the stempost had survived together with the beginning of its upward curve, and the run of the bottom and side planking towards the bow enabled the shape of the bow to be reconstructed with considerable confidence. This shows that it was similar to the stern, though with a slightly longer and sharper entry into the water (Fig 71).

Propulsion

The mast was missing, but its step or socket had survived just forward of the midships position of the vessel. It measured 0.18m by 0.20m square, and had a smaller lower socket measuring 0.121m by 0.127m, as if for a rectangular tenon at the foot of the mast. This shows that the foot of the mast was square, but above that it was presumably round in cross-section, so as to reduce aerodynamic turbulence and drag, with a diameter of 0.18m.

Fig 70 White Tower, London Bridge in background, from manuscript of poems of Charles D'Orléans, captured at Agincourt (1415), imprisoned until 1440. (Royal MS 16Fii. f73 reproduced by permission of the British Library)

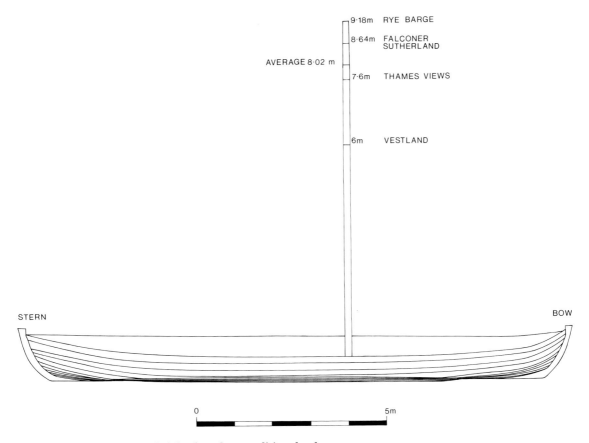

Fig 72 Alternative mast heights based on traditional rules

There are several historical formulae and examples of actual mast structures from which to assess the height of a mast relative to its diameter (Marsden 1994). These fall into two groups, for seagoing sailing ships with fixed masts, and for smaller craft used on inland waterways whose mast could be lowered. Of the latter there are the following (Fig 72):

- a traditional Vestland Norwegian rule that says that the height of a mast from the heel to the halyard hole near the top should equal the girth of the boat at that station (McGrail 1987, 226). The girth of Blackfriars ship 3 at that position was 5.3m, to which should be added a little more to take the mast to its full height, to about 6m.

- W Falconer (1815, 265) 'the length of a mast 'to the rigging-stop or hounds, [should be] three-fourths the whole length' [of the ship]. This means that Blackfriars ship 3, about 14.64m long, should have a mast 10.98m high with a little extra above the rigging-stop, say, about 11.5m high.

- Falconer (*ibid*) also gives the proportion of mast diameter to height as 'one-fourth of an inch to every foot in length'. This proportion is 1:48.

- 'The length of this ship's main-mast being considered, the next thing required is to make her diameter in the biggest place suitable to it, or the stress it will bear.'

(W Sutherland 1711, 109)

Thus for every yard in length of a main-mast for a small ship the mast diameter should be 4/5 or 3/4 of an inch. This too is a proportion of 1:48.

There are two other sources to suggest mast height. The proportion of barge length to mast height above the gunwale, as seen in sketches of barges on the River Thames in views of London by Hollar (1647) and Ogilby and Morgan (1677), are amongst the earliest known detailed and reasonably accurate views of London. The proportions of enlargements of various vessels are in Table 3 which gives an average of mast height above the gunwale to barge length of 47.56%, which, when applied to Blackfriars ship 3 (14.64m long), would give a mast height of 6.96m. To this must be added the depth of the hull amidships (0.88m), giving an overall height of 7.84m.

Table 3   Mast heights

% mast height : barge length	
Hollar	64.5
56.7	
52.0	
Ogilby and Morgan	49.0
36.6	
33.3	
47.9	
47.7	
40.4	

Fig 73 Artist's impression of Blackfriars ship 3 (Karen Guffogg)

Because the hollow in the top of the mast-step block of Blackfriars ship 3 aft of the step shows that the mast was lowered from time to time by being lifted out and slid aft, it would seem that this could best be achieved by two men since there was little space for a third man. The question is, therefore, what mast weight could be lifted by two men? An answer is suggested by a published study of a nineteenth-century Rye barge (Vidler 1935) which had a crew of two and was also used on a river (the Rother, in Sussex). The Rye barge was 16.76m long, 3.73m beam, and had a depth of about 1.52m. Its mast was 9.14m high, with a diameter of 0.177m at the foot, and 0.114m at the top The proportion of maximum diameter to height was 1:51. On this basis the mast height of Blackfriars ship 3 would be 9.18m. The weight of the mast in the Rye barge can be calculated by taking its average diameter of 0.146m and applying this to the formula

Table 4   Estimated mast height of Blackfriars ship 3

Based on Rye barge (f):	9.18m
Based on Falconer (c):	8.64m
Based on Sutherland (d):	8.64m
Based on Thames views (e):	7.84m
Based on Vestland rule (a):	6.00m
Average:	8.06m

$\pi \times r^2 \times h$. This gives $3.14 \times 0.005 \times 9.14 = 0.1435$ cubic metres. Multiplying this by 800kg (the density of one cubic metre of oak) gives 114.8kg. The results of these estimates (Table 4) are reasonably consistent and suggest a mast height of about 8m.

Fig 74   View aft from bow of ship 3, starboard side after removal of floor-timbers. Note sternpost angled over to right

Fig 75   View aft from bow of Ship 3, port side (metric scale)

There must have been rigging to support the mast, taking the form of shrouds from near the mast-head to the sides of the vessel just aft of the mast position; a stay from the mast-head to the stem; and a halyard to raise and lower the yard which carried the sail (Fig 73). Unfortunately all of the relevant parts of the vessel had been damaged at these points so that the means of attachment are not known.

Since the mast lay just forward of the centre of the vessel, and therefore just forward of the centre of lateral resistance (CLR) of the hull, the sail was no doubt square to keep its centre of effort in this position relative to the CLR If instead the vessel had a fore-and-aft sail then the centre of effort would have been aft of the CLR and so would have created steering problems. It is concluded, therefore, that the mast carried a square sail.

Steering

Although the mechanism for steering the barge was not found, there was sufficient evidence to establish how this was probably achieved. Steering on medieval English sailing vessels was normally carried out in one of three ways, by a median rudder mounted on the sternpost, by a side rudder, and by a steering oar. Although it is also possible that oars and poles were used as well at bow and stern to manoeuvre the vessel in the port area, as was the practice on lighters (ie barges without sails), the presence of the mast indicates that the vessel was intended to travel further afield on the Thames and its tributaries, and in that case a fixed method of steering by rudder or steering oar would be needed.

The survival of the sternpost enabled a detailed examination to be made of the fittings for a sternpost rudder. Had one been fitted, there should have been iron ring-bolts (*gudgeons*), fastened to the sternpost, into which were slotted the iron pins (pintles) on the rudder. Although there were iron plates to hold a strip of iron to stop wear to the sternpost, it was clear that there were never any gudgeons, so that the sternpost cannot have carried that form of rudder.

During the medieval period a side (or quarter-) rudder was normally located on the starboard side of a vessel near the stern. This part of the hull of Blackfriars ship 3 was probably not excavated since it lay just outside the north side of the coffer-dam. Occasionally medieval representations of ships do show side rudders on the port side as well, and in that position on Blackfriars ship 3 there was definitely no fitting for such a device. The fact that the barge was built about AD 1400 is significant, for by then side rudders had normally ceased to be used in northern Europe. None of the known side rudder finds from northern Europe, such as those from Bergen, Norway (Christensen 1985, 152–5), can be shown to date from later than the thirteenth century, and side rudders on ships are shown on medieval port seals only up to the beginning of the fourteenth century (eg Dover, dated 1305), after which only median rudders on sternposts are shown (Brindley 1938; Williams 1971, 90). Consequently, it is most unlikely that Blackfriars ship 3, built about a century later, was steered by a side rudder.

The only practical alternative for a vessel of the size of Blackfriars ship 3 was a steering oar or sweep mounted over the stern and perhaps attached to the sternpost. Hollar's view of London in 1647 depicts

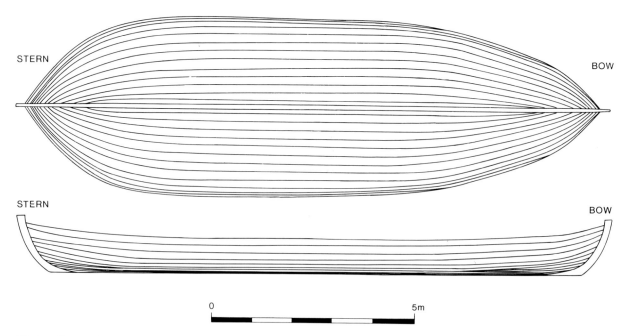

Fig 76 Boatcad view of the planking of ship 3 seen from below (top) and side elevation (bottom)

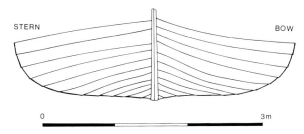

Fig 77 End elevations ('body plan'), forward end (right), and stern end (left) of Blackfriars ship 3

possible steering oars in use on several river craft, and such a use persisted until recent times (Ellmers and Werner 1991, 25).

Conclusions

In conclusion, therefore, it seems that Blackfriars ship 3 was about 14.64m long, with a beam of about 4.3m, a breadth of flat bottom of about 3m, a height amidships of 0.88m, and a planking height at the stern of 1.18m (Figs 71,74 and 75). It was pear-shaped in plan with the widest part of the vessel near the stern. It was clinker-built (Figs 76 and 77) with iron rivets and hair caulking, and, apart from its trenails, was constructed of oak throughout. It was propelled by a square sail on a mast about 8m high, and was probably steered by a steering oar, aided perhaps by poles (Fig 73). Its shape (Figs 78 and 79) and volume (Fig 80)

were ideal for sailing in the shallow water of the Thames and its tributaries whilst carrying tonnes of cargo.

It is now possible to input the results of the recording of these timber remains of Blackfriars ship 3 into the naval architects' computer program Boatcad to obtain an underside view of the hull planking, a side elevation (Fig 76), and a 'body plan' or end elevations (Fig 77). The computer takes the strakes apart and lays them flat to give a strake diagram (Fig 78), and to show the hull shape it gives waterlines (Fig 79), buttock lines (Fig 80) and the distribution of hull volume below the gunwale (Fig 81).

These characteristics appear to match closely what is known of one of the most common of fourteenth and fifteenth-century types of river transporter, the *shout*. There were many other types of vessel then used on the Thames about which little is known: *float, barge, bark, chalkboat, cock or cockboat, cog, crayer, dungboat, eelship, farcost, ferryboat, flune, galley, hakeboat, hookship, hulk, keel, ketch, lighter, mangboat, oysterboat, piker, rushboat, skumer, spindlersboat, tideboat, and whelkboat* (Wright 1988). It is possible that Blackfriars ship 3 was one of these, though it would not have been called a barge since that was a seagoing vessel. Nevertheless, the parallel to the shout is so close, even as regards its apparent use and working environment, as to warrant further consideration of the type. References to shouts were so common in the fourteenth and fifteenth centuries that they may have

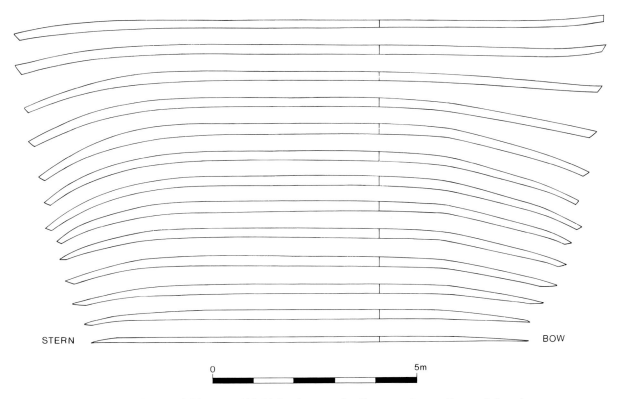

Fig 78 The strakes or planks of ship 3, as if laid flat in a strake diagram, from a Boatcad drawing

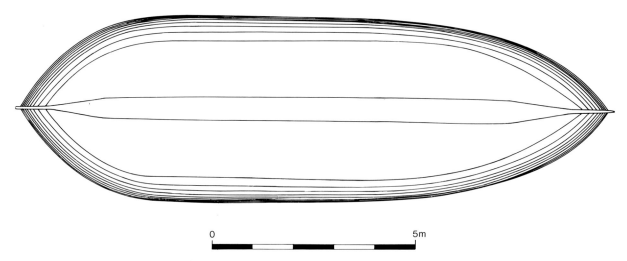

Fig 79 Waterlines, horizontal profiles of the hull, at intervals of 0.084m, to show the hull shape of ship 3 to a height of 0.84m (to the gunwale), from a Boatcad drawing

Fig 80 Buttock lines (vertical profiles of the hull) of ship 3 at intervals of 0.215m from the centreline, from a Boatcad drawing

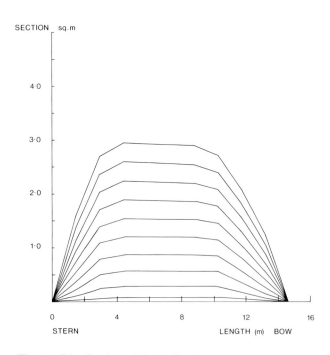

Fig 81 Distribution of the hull volume below the gunwale of ship 3, from a Boatcad drawing

been a basic type on the Thames, but with varying uses as is indicated by a reference in 1394–5 to a dung-boat called a *showt* (Walton 1832, 303) and to a 'masons shout' (Wright 1988, 159–60).

Shouts were clinker-built with iron rivets holding the planks together. They were designed to carry considerable loads in shallow water, as in addition to the Thames they sailed on its tributaries, the Wey as far as Weybridge (Walton 1832, 304), and the Lea as far as Waltham (Wright 1988, 159–60). For this they must have had broad, flat bottoms, as indeed is suggested by the term itself, a variant of the Middle Dutch *schuit*, describing a flat-bottomed river boat (Burwash 1969, 139–40). There are various spellings of the term shout, ranging from 1311 to 1509: *shouta, scutata, shoutis, shoute, showte, shoutes, shoute, scut, escoutes, showtes,* and *shoughtis*, but the most common spellings in the fourteenth century were *shoute* and *showte* (Wright 1988, 159–60). The master of a shout was called a shoutman: 'Johes Wylkyn Schoutman' (1365); 'Thomas Shoutman' (1381); and 'Simon Sergeant Shoutman' (1404) (*ibid*, 199). No indication of the crew size is given.

Shouts were propelled by mast and sail (*Rotuli Parliamentorum* III, 444b), and steered by a 'great oar' (Wright 1988, 159–60). No record has been found, amongst the frequent references in the Bridge House accounts, to them sailing into the Thames estuary or into the River Medway, indicating that their use was restricted to the quiet inland waters.

Nevertheless, it has been suggested that the shouts would occasionally sail at sea (Burwash 1969, 139–40), and that they carried a spritsail. The interpretation of the type of sail is possibly based on the reference to the 'breaking of a cable, rope, spret [ie sprit] or mast of a shout' in a document of 1413–14 (*ibid*). However, in this context the term 'sprit' refers to a pole used for punting a boat (Sandahl 1958, 102–3). Nevertheless, there is a sketch of a *skuta*, which has been identified as a shout, in *The London Journal of Alessandro Magno* of 1562 (Barron *et al* 1983, 137–52). This shows a vessel with a spritsail, a sternpost rudder, and a covered hold, which is very different from the type of craft suggested by the Bridge House records. This vessel was undoubtedly seagoing for it carried its passengers from Margate to London and so was again uncharacteristic of the shouts recorded in medieval London. Furthermore, as the earliest evidence for the existence of the spritsail in northern Europe is an illustration of about 1420, the next dating from 1475, and as it is only during the sixteenth century that it became common (Phillips-Birt 1962, 76), the references in the Bridge House records to shouts as early as the early fourteenth century must relate to vessels with a square sail. Bearing in mind the context of the 1562 *scuta* at Margate it seems more likely that the vessel was a Dutch boat trading with London. This would explain why references to shouts in London appear not to have existed after the beginning of the sixteenth century, as the type may have died out by then.

Sequence of construction

The relationship of timbers and their fastenings in the vessel clarify the stages in its construction. Initially the keel and the stem and sternposts were fastened together on stocks so as to give the shipwright access below to drive in the fastenings. The main tool used was probably an axe to shape the timbers, and cut marks of such tools are often preserved in the plank and scarf laps. In contrast the keel was cut from an oak log that was either sawn or split down the middle near the pith. The garboard strakes, on either side of the keel, were next fastened by rivets to the keel, and to the lower ends of the stem and sternposts. A hole was bored at each rivet position before driving in the nail which was then clenched inboard over a rove. The shipwright must have used a drill bit with a diameter of about 3mm. Each strake was composed of several planks held together endways by overlapping scarfs, whose direction indicates that the lengths of planking were fastened from the stern towards the bow. A layer

of matted hair caulking in warm pine resin (*see Appendix 4*) was placed in each plank lap and scarf to help make them watertight.

Once the bottom planking out to strake 7 had been fastened, the floor-timbers may next have been fashioned and then fastened in position by trenails. Beyond this point came the turn of the bilge, and it was necessary for the bilge and side planking to be attached before the side-frames were fastened. Thereafter, the stringers and mast-block were attached, and finally the rudder, mast, yard, sail, and rigging were lifted into place.

This reconstruction of the stages in building the vessel is based only upon the structural evidence of the craft itself. Fortunately, the contemporary documentary records of the Bridge House, which managed London Bridge in the medieval period, note both the cost of certain materials for building boats for the Thames, and the payments made to shipwrights for building and repairing the vessels. The art of shipbuilding was called 'shipcraft' (Wright 1988, 158), and it was the shipwright's responsibility to locate suitable timber, as is shown by a Bridge House account for 1461–2:

> 'For expenses of John Forster and one horse guided by himself riding to the park of Beckenham to look over timber and wrongs [ie timber for frames] ... 13d ... and to Stephen Leuendale for carriage of one load of wrongs at the park at Beckenham to the said bridge house and 5 loads of wrongs and timber at the said park to Deptford Strand taking for every load, 14d–7s'
>
> (*ibid*, 168).

The time and manpower required to build a shout for the Bridge House is given in the weekly accounts, such as the one commencing on 29 September 1386 (*see Appendix 5*). Under the care of the shipwright William Talworthe, four or five men were employed for about three weeks to build the vessel at daily rates for each of between 2d and 8d. Those extra men included Walter Sakyn and John Stokflete, both shipwrights, and all three named men knew one another well (*see Appendix 7*). Talworth and Stokflete, at least, were near neighbours living in the City of London close to the waterfront just upstream of the Tower of London (*see Appendix 7*). This waterfront region of later medieval London was inhabited by other shipwrights and by mariners, and was clearly the maritime quarter of London. It can be assumed that shipbuilding yards were located there.

The only record of the purchase of materials for this documented shout was for 300 'wrong-nails' (ie trenails to fasten the 'wrong', the frame, to the planks, see Sandahl 1951, 173; Wright 1988, 168), costing 3s, on 13 October 1386. Although the Bridge House appears to have kept a stock of shipbuilding materials and to have bought extra items as needed, it is also possible that this was the full quantity of trenails required for this boat. By comparison, Blackfriars ship 3 used about 530 wrong-nails, so the documented shout may have been smaller.

The Bridge House payments on 10 September 1405–6 record details of materials paid for to repair another shout: 6lb of tow (unworked fibre used in caulking) at 5d, 3 quarts of oil at 7d, 2 pans of earth ('for liquifying bitumen and pitch', see Bridge House Weekly Payments, 1st ser, vol 1, 102), 2 yards of canvas at 7d (the context suggests this was a caulking material), $31^{1}/_{2}$lbs wax at $23^{1}/_{2}$d,

> 'paid to William White for 1 curve of shide [a piece of split wood] bought for a shout, 18d. And to the same for 2 pieces of timber called knees bought for the same, 14d.'
>
> (Wright 1988, 164, 5)

> 'and for blatch bought by William himself and used around the said Shout, 1d' [probably black paint].
>
> (*ibid*, 162)

Materials for other repairs are also given in the Bridge House weekly payments. For example, in 1406–7 there is a mention of rivets, 'for shipnaill and clench for the showte taking for 100–4s 6d' (*ibid*, 168) The payments in 1407 include:

> 'Saturday 20th day of August paid Thomas Clerk of Deptford for timber bought for the shout that is to say for footing (a curved timber, a frame), 1s 1d.'
>
> (*ibid*, 163)

The Bridge House accounts provide a magnificent source of evidence for shipbuilding materials and methods and require further analysis, but in respect of shouts generally two further entries are of value:

> 'ropes cord cables and buckleropes and others for the shouts' 'goathair bought for the shout ... 5 boards called shipboard bought for the shout'
>
> (*ibid*, 159–60)

The reference to goat hair being used as caulking is particularly interesting since this was found in Blackfriars ship 3 (*see Appendix 3*).

Date and place of construction

As Blackfriars wreck 3 was a river craft it could only have been built beside the River Thames or one of its tributaries. This is also indicated by the tree-ring pattern which shows a local growth. The tree-ring pattern contains heartwood dated to 1267–1369 inclusive, with some evidence that the outer rings were close to the sapwood, indicating a boat construction date of about 1380–1415 (*see Appendix 1*).

How the ship was used

The elongated saucer-like shape of the hull and the low gunwale height shows that it was a river barge designed to sail in the shallows of the Thames and its tributaries while carrying a considerable load. The absence of a ceiling of planks on top of the frames suggests that this vessel was not used to carry building stone, some of which would otherwise lie on the planking and could damage the rivets. In fact the contemporary records say that a vessel known as a 'farcost' was normally used to transport Kentish ragstone (*see Chapter 4*). Due to the completeness of Blackfriars wreck 3 it is possible to calculate the maximum weight of that load and also to assess the theoretical stability of the vessel by using the Boatcad program.

Weight of the vessel

In order to undertake a stability and performance assessment the weight of a representative square metre of the hull was calculated, so that the computer could determine the hull's weight and area. The standard structural features were the planks and the frames, of which the former at amidships were broad, narrowing towards the ends. A square metre in an area between the two points was chosen as a mean, where there were parts of six strakes with six laps between. This means that although the planking was 1m long, it was 1m wide plus the width of the laps. The lap widths were about 0.075m each, so that the total width of planking was 1m + (6 × 0.075) = 1.45m. As the planking thickness averaged at 0.035m, the volume of planking in one square metre was 1 × 1.45 × 0.035 = 0.05 cubic metres. As the specific density of oak is about 800kg per cubic metre (McGrail 1987, 20) the volume of the planking, 0.05m, was multiplied by 800 to arrive at its weight of 40kg. To this had to be added the weight of iron rivets fastening the plank laps together. In the average area of planking chosen there were 36 rivets, each weighing about 50gms. The total number of rivets in one square metre of planking weighed 1.8kg.

The weight of the two frames which crossed the planking was added. Each was 1m long, but the average dimensions were 0.115m × 0.119m which allows for the steps (joggling) and limber holes. The average volume of each frame was therefore 1 × 0.115 × 0.119 = 0.0136 cubic metres. The weight of the two frames was 0.0136 × 2 × 800 = 21.76kg. Thus the weight of a representative square metre of hull structure was:

Planks   40.00kg
Rivets   18.00kg
Frames 21.56kg
Total   63.56kg

This figure was read into Boatcad which calculated the total hull area, and from that a total hull weight of 4.052 tonnes. However, there were other features of hull structure to be added to this overall weight.

Keel

This was 10.77m long, and, allowing for the mean width, the rabbets for the garboard strakes, and for the shaped underside, its approximate volume of oak was $10.77 \times 0.385 \times 0.1 = 0.4146$. Its weight was $0.4146 \times 800 = 331.68$ kg. Since about half the keel thickness was included in the total hull area already computed it was necessary to deduct 50%, which gave a weight of 165.84kg.

Mast block

The timber containing the mast-step overlay some frames and the keel. It measured $2.93 \times 0.195 \times 0.365 = 0.2$ cubic metres (allowing for the step socket and the rebates for frames). This is converted to the weight: 0.2×800 which equaled 160kg.

Stringers

This timber was originally about 13m long, and was triangular in shape with its two right-angled sides each being 0.12m wide. Its volume was therefore $13 \times 0.12 \times 0.12 = 0.1872$, $\div 2 = 0.0936$ cubic metres. Its weight was therefore $0.0936 \times 800 = 74.88$kg. Since there were two stringers their total weight was twice this figure which equaled 149.76kg.

Sternpost and stempost

Only the sternpost had survived almost in its entirety, and although its approximate volume was constantly changing shape and dimension, a mean average seems to be about 2.2m long $\times$ 0.18 thick $\times$ 0.2m wide $= 0.0792$ cubic metres. The weight of this would be $0.0792 \times 800 = 63.36$kg. Since enough of the stempost survived to show that there is good reason to believe that it was roughly of similar dimension the total of the two is $63.36 \times 2 = 126.72$kg.

Mast

In order to arrive at the weight of the mast as reconstructed with a lower diameter of 0.18m and a height of 8.06m it is necessary to find its average diameter. Its top diameter may reasonably be based on the fact that the top of the mast of the Rye barge was 64% of its diameter at the foot. On that basis the top of the Blackfriars mast would be 0.115m in diameter, and its average diameter would be 0.147m (radius 0.0735m). Thus the weight of the Blackfriars mast would be $\pi \times r^2 \times h = 3.14 \times 0.0054 \times 8.06 = 0.136$ cubic metres. Multiplied by 800 (the average density of one cubic metre of oak) = 108.8kg.

Judging from seventeenth-century pictures of barges on the Thames, and allowing for the fact that Blackfriars ship 3 had to pass under bridges (eg London and Kingston), it seems likely that the yard from which the sail was hung did not exceed the beam of the vessel, 4.3m. Its diameter was perhaps about 0.115m, as at the top of the mast. From this it is possible to calculate an approximate weight for the yard based upon the formula: $\pi \times r^2 \times h = 3.14 \times 0.003 \times 4.3 = 0.04$ cubic metres: multiplied by 800 = 32kg.

The sail would probably be about 3.5m wide and about 4m high, with a weight of about 80kg. The weight of the rigging to support the mast, already described, is estimated at about 80kg. This gives a total additional weight for the mast, yard, sail, and rigging of 300.8kg.

Weight of crew and fittings

An anchor and rope (50kg), a crew of two men (160kg), and various other equipment such as a gangplank, wheelbarrow for loading goods, as well as personal supplies of food and water (150kg) would give a total weight of 360kg.

Conclusion

The estimated total weight of the vessel is:

Hull	4052.00 kg
Stempost/sternpost	126.72 kg
Mast block	160.00 kg
Keel	165.84 kg
Stringers	149.76 kg
Mast	300.80 kg
Crew and fittings	360.00 kg
Total	5315.12 kg

Theoretical stability and performance

A measure of the stability of a ship is its ability to right itself when heeled (Hind 1982; Taylor 1984; Kemp and Young 1987; McGrail 1987, 12–22). This righting lever is proportional to the metacentric height (or GMt), which is the distance between the centre of gravity (CoG) and the transverse metacentre (Mt) (Fig 82). For a ship to be stable the righting moment must be positive, that is the Mt must always be above the CoG (Fig 83). However, a large metacentric height can make an uncomfortably stiff vessel that pulls itself

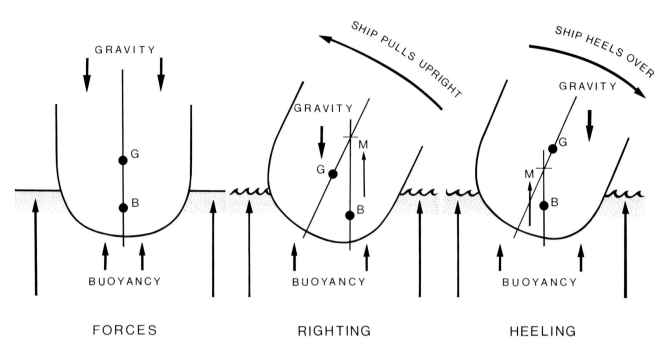

Fig 82 The forces exerted on a floating ship

upright too quickly, but a small one makes the vessel tender with a possibly dangerous weak righting moment (McGrail 1987, 15). It is difficult to judge what was an ideal metacentric height in an ancient ship, but nowadays in sailing ships a large GMt separation is needed to counteract the heeling force on a sail, whilst in large modern powered ships it is considered desirable that it should not exceed about 3–4% of a ship's beam (Kemp and Young 1971, 65). However, the broad flat bottom of Blackfriars ship 3 gave considerable stability, and it is important to take into consideration that its environment on the River Thames was very different from that of a seagoing sailing ship. Much more study is needed of the theoretical stability of ancient ships of various types from several environments before it is possible to generalise. Ideally such vessels should be tested with full-size working reconstructions.

The method used here to examine the theoretical stability and performance of Blackfriars ship 3 was to input its shape into Boatcad, with these specifications:

length:	14.64m
beam:	4.30m
height:	1.36m at ends
hull density:	63.56kg/m²

The computer program then calculated the hydrostatics both in tabular and graphic form for interpretation.

Waterlines and righting moment

Since the calculations mostly relate to the displacement of the vessel, and displacement determines waterline (Fig 84), it is necessary to establish what working waterlines the vessel used. There are no clues from the remains of the wreck itself, though had there been more time and facilities a careful examination of the hull planking outboard for evidence of water erosion might have established the normal working draught. However, by using the computer it is possible to examine the vessel in three states, lightship (which is the vessel without any of its crew and fittings) fitted (which includes the crew and their equipment) and while carrying the maximum load of cargo.

Lightship

In its lightship state, without any cargo, crew, or supplies, Boatcad calculates that Blackfriars ship 3 would have a freshwater waterline of 0.23m, a metacentre above the keel (KMt) at 6.37m, a centre of gravity (CoG) at 0.52m, giving a metacentric height of 5.85m. This shows that it was a very stiff vessel in an unladen state.

Fitted

The weight of the crew and their equipment is estimated to be 0.36 tonnes, giving a total displacement to the vessel of 5.321 tonnes. Boatcad calculates that this will give a waterline of 0.235m, a CoG of 0.52m, and a KMt of 6.25m. This gives a metacentric height of 5.73m, which, again, implies a very stiff vessel.

Maximum load

A medieval Icelandic law concerning clinker-built boats states that the minimum freeboard of a cargo ship should be two-fifths the depth of the hull near

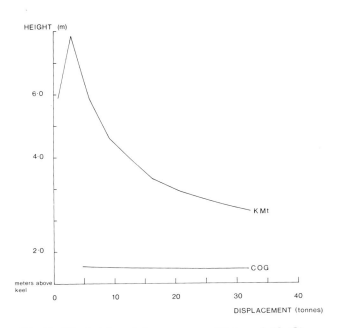

Fig 83   The heights of the transverse KMt and (CoG) above the keel of ship 3, from a Boatcad drawing

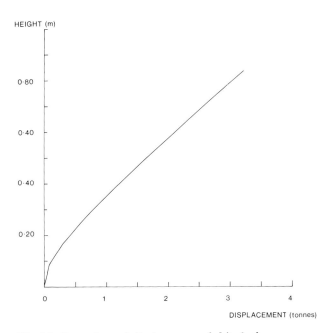

Fig 84   Draught and displacement of ship 3, from a Boatcad drawing

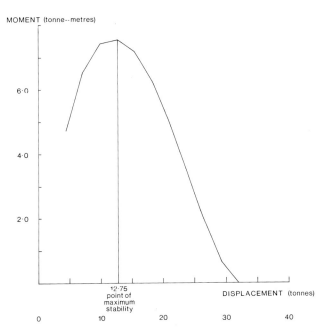

Fig 85   Heeled righting moments of ship 3, from unloaded to maximum displacement, from a Boatcad drawing

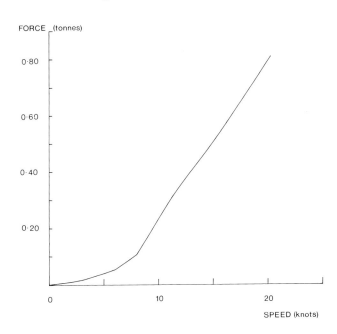

Fig 86   Resistance against hull at a waterline of 0.23m, based on 'one wave speed' from a Boatcad drawing

amidships (McGrail 1987, 13), which would give a waterline of 0.53m and a freeboard of 0.35m. At this waterline Boatcad calculates a CoG of 0.49m, a KMt of 3.18m, and therefore a metacentric height of 2.69m. The displacement would be 17.70 tonnes, of which the cargo load would account for 12.385 tonnes evenly distributed about the vessel. However, such a low freeboard could place the vessel in danger of being swamped, particularly when sailing close to structures, like London Bridge, that created wave eddies, and a lower waterline may have been preferred.

A safer freeboard is indicated by the heeled righting moments of Blackfriars ship 3, calculated by Boatcad, which show that the point of strongest righting ability, and therefore the point of greatest stability, would be at a displacement of about 12.75 tonnes (Fig 85). If the loading, and therefore the waterline, were to be increased beyond that point, the ability of the vessel to pull itself upright from a heeled position becomes weaker. At that displacement the waterline would be about 0.40m with a freeboard of 0.48m. At that waterline Boatcad calculates that the centre of gravity

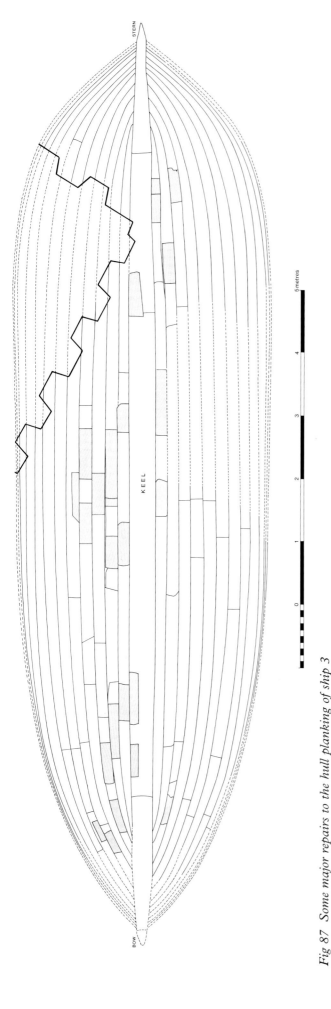

Fig 87 Some major repairs to the hull planking of ship 3

lay at 0.5m above the bottom of the keel, and the transverse metacentre was at 4.08m. Thus with a metacentric height of 3.58m the vessel had considerable stability.

If the weight of the ship in its fitted state (5.322 tonnes) is deducted from the total weight at the 12.75 tonnes displacement, the difference represents the load of cargo that could be carried by the vessel, 7.43 tonnes. Since the hold or cargo area is not defined in the wreck it is assumed that the load carried was evenly distributed about the vessel. Because the vessel had a broad flat bottom in which to lay out its cargo it is difficult to reconstruct how any cargoes were stowed, and therefore to find their CoG and stowage factors. A cargo of oak timbers weighing about 7.5 tonnes, for example, could consist of about 100 logs, each weighing 0.75kg (a weight which a strong man could carry), and each 3m long and 0.20m in diameter. They could be laid out in two piles, one before and one behind the mast, each of fifty logs, and their centres of gravity can be calculated so as to establish the CoG of the logs and the vessel. But as there was enough space for them to be laid out in other ways such a theoretical calculation is pointless in this particular vessel. The message of this hydrostatic study is that the vessel could carry these substantial loads, and that it was extremely stable.

Speed

The theoretical maximum speed of the vessel, which is related to the hull's waterline, length, and to the stage at which the vessel would be travelling fast enough for its stern to drop into the trough caused by the bow wave, is calculated by Boatcad at 9.1 knots (Fig 86). This is unrealistically high for this vessel since it was a river craft and its hull shape was clearly designed for carrying goods in very shallow water, and not for speed. In any case such a propulsion power was probably not available.

Evidence of repairs

There was considerable evidence of repairs, particularly in the form of patches on the planking both inboard and outboard (*see above*). Where these were investigated they seem to have related to the refastening of rivets or to the trenails which attached the frames, as if these fastenings had worked loose and were leaking, presumably by frequently running aground. This also seemed to apply to the patches on the starboard side of the keel (Fig 87), probably indicating that lengths of planking were replaced, and multiple trenail holes in some frames must reflect the refastening of frames. Finally, the worn hollow in the mast-step timber suggests the frequency with which the mast was lowered, presumably mostly for passing under low bridges.

Fig 88 Artist's impression of the fourteenth-century East Watergate (Peter Warner, 1976)

Documentary records

Whether or not Blackfriars ship 3 was a shout, its use and features were evidently so similar that the documentary records referring to shouts during the fourteenth and fifteenth centuries are a valuable general guide to the use of this vessel. The Bridge House accounts are a prime source:

'for a Shout of hay that comes two pence' (1316–17), ...'for carriage of 1 shout full of piles from Wallham [Waltham] for the Bridge House by water' (1384–5), ...'the boat called the masons shout laden with the pot called the cement pan'(1472–3)

(Wright 1988, 159–60)

'paid for cleaning one ditch called a dock for shining the shout for carrying bricktiles to Deptford, 2s. 1d'(1419–20)

(*ibid*, 70)

Other sources confirm the general picture of the use of shouts:

'and that all ships shouts and boats of whatever kind that bring corn to Billingsgate as well as elsewhere on the Thames ...'

(*Liber Albus* 1419, fo 198)

'and from two boats forfeited anew in this year [1393–4], of which one dung-boat, called a showte ...'

(Walton 1832, 303)

in 1393–4,

'carriage of timber from Wyldwood shoutemen, for the carriage of 74 loads of timber from the wood of Wildwood, carried from Weybridge to the Manor of the Savoye, by the river Thames, carriage at 12d a load, and 17s. 6d. for drawing the said 74 loads of timber from the showte'

(*ibid*, 304)

Of particular interest is the dispute in 1343 which shows that shouts used the public berthing place known as East Watergate (Chew and Kellaway 1973, 453), much of which was excavated in 1972–3 and can be fairly accurately reconstructed (Fig 88).

When not in use the Bridge House berthed their boats in a dock probably at Deptford, which seems to have been an excavated inlet from the river, judging from the entry for 1419–20 referring to the cargo of bricktiles quoted above. The creation of this or another dock is referred to in 1417–18:

'And paid to 6 men guiding for 2 days for the manufacture of the dock for the shout at Deptford'

(Wright 1988, 69–70)

This protected them in winter:

'for placing boats and shouts belonging to the bridge in a certain place there called a dock for the safe custody of the said boats in time of ice in this year [1468–9]'

(*ibid*, 70)

The voyage routes were up and down the Thames and its tributaries, and the vessels must frequently have passed beneath bridges and run aground. This accords with what is known about Blackfriars ship 3, whose mast was so often lowered that a hollow was worn in the mast-block, the rivets and trenails had in places worked loose and required replacing, and the planks needed patching. There were hazards, as in 1413–14 when Parliament was petitioned concerning the reduction in the number of shouts on the river, because, if the breaking of a cable, rope, sprit (a pole used for punting, see Sandahl 1958, 102), or mast, any man, woman, or child was killed, the shout was forfeited as *deodand*. This was the term for an inanimate object which had caused the loss of life, which was forfeited and its value given to charity by the King's almoner. The result was that victuals and other merchandise reaching London by water had become more expensive than elsewhere in England (*Rotuli Parliamentorum* III, 444b). A particular problem causing loss were the locks on the river,which somewhat resembled modern weirs, for sometimes the cables broke that winched the boat up the weirs. Once at London there could be further problems of access to the quays, as in 1343 when the local inhabitants of Castle Baynard Ward complained to the Mayor of London that the prior of St Mary had built a quay that encroached into the public quay, East Watergate:

'to the nuisance of ships (*navium*), shouts (*shoutarum*) and boats (*batellorum*) putting in there (*applicancium*)'

(Chew and Kellaway 1973, 453)

1

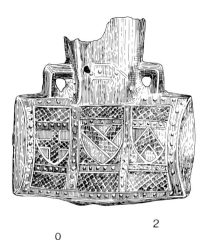

2

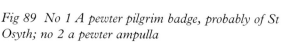

0   5cms

Fig 89 No 1 A pewter pilgrim badge, probably of St Osyth; no 2 a pewter ampulla

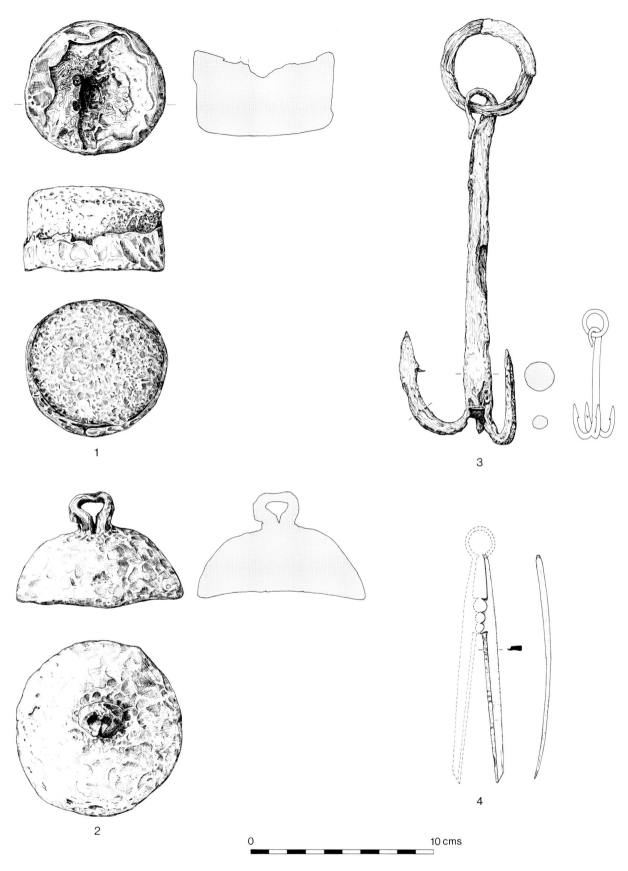

Fig 90 Nos 1 and 2 lead weights; no 3 a wrought-iron grapnel originally with four hooks; no 4 part of a pair of bronze shears

Loss of the ship

On sinking, Blackfriars wreck 3 lay roughly east-west, with its stern at the east end near the shore, and the bow in deeper water facing west and the oncoming river current. There was no evidence for a cargo in the wreck; instead there were layers of clean sand and gravel containing rubbish in the form of broken pottery, bones, etc, of the latter part of the fifteenth century. On the bottom of the wreck were found two pewter badges (Fig 89), nos 1 and 2, one a figure and the other an ampulla, identified by Brian Spencer as probably of St Sythe (ie St Osythe). Also a small wrought-iron grapnel was found at the bow, on the starboard side above strakes 4-6 (Fig 90, no 3), the bronze arm of a pair of shears with its iron blade missing was found in the stern (Fig 90, no 4), and a domed lead weight was found in the bottom of the wreck (Fig 90, no 2). Just outside the starboard side of the wreck near the bow another lead weight was found weighing 1.5kg, which seems to have been suspended originally by an iron loop, since corroded, set into the lead (Fig 90, no 1). These could have been lost by members of the crew, or dropped with other objects into the sunken vessel.

No damage to the hull was found that would indicate the cause of the loss of Blackfriars ship 3, though it is always possible that there was damage to the recently destroyed parts. It is clear, however, that the low freeboard could have caused the sinking, particularly if the vessel was swamped in a collision. The presence nearby of the wreck of Blackfriars ship 4 carrying a cargo of Kentish ragstone suggests a collision. The two ships lay only a few metres away from each other, and the coincidence that they were at about the same level and of a similar date suggests that they may have sunk together in the same incident.

The wreck of Blackfriars 3 lay only about 6.6m south of the contemporary waterfront, with the top of the sternpost, the highest part of the wreck, at 1.69m below OD, which was about 1.6m below the foreshore in front of the fifteenth-century stone waterfront (Milne and Milne 1982, 61–2). It would seem from this that the wreck was permanently submerged and followed the deepening slope of the contemporary river bed, with the lowest part of the ship lying at about 4m below OD (the top of the scarf between the stem and keel was at 3.78m below OD, and the top of the scarf between the sternpost and keel was at 3.2m below OD).

For the wreck to remain largely intact it must have been quickly buried by sand and gravel. There had been some distortion to the hull and the side-frames on the starboard side were all lost, presumably because they were at a higher level than those on the port side, and had been exposed to the river erosion longer. One loose side-frame was found caught in the wreck. A quantity of pottery and building materials lay in the gravel alluvium in the wreck, all of which seems to have been washed into the vessel fairly soon after the sinking since the alluvium protected the hull from much erosion.

The fishing net

A scatter of lead weights from a fishing net was found in the bottom of the wreck, which had presumably become caught soon after the vessel had sunk, though it is always possible that the vessel itself was engaged in fishing. As no fish-well or other evidence of fishing was found in the wreck it seems more likely that the net had become snagged in the wreck. A total of 1109 weights were recovered, each made from a roll of lead between 14mm and 45mm long (Fig 91), around a cord of unidentified fibre. This was not the total number in the wreck as not all were collected, and there could have

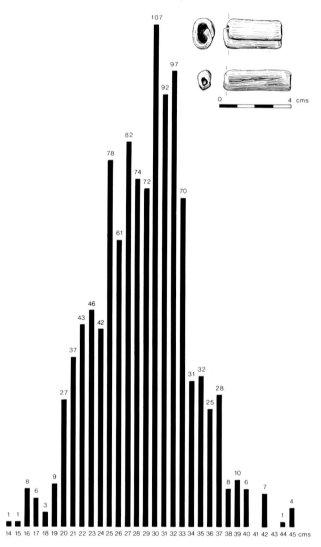

Fig 91 A graph of the frequency of lengths of cylindrical lead net weights found in ship 3

been as many as 300 more, missed in the rush to uncover the vessel. At least enough were found to gain some idea about the size and possible mesh of the net, assuming that the leads all came from one net.

The weights were probably from a seine net, one of the oldest types used in rivers (Aston 1988, 156–9), and would have consisted of a long train of netting with the weights on the bottom and floats at the top. It would be cast into the river in a semi-circle, and hauled in either to the shore or into a boat; in this connection it may be significant that the wreck lay only about 6m from the shore.Various types of fishing net are mentioned in fourteenth and fifteenth-century records for London, but it is not known what they were like:

berd, berdpot, blee, bleenet, castingnet, codnet, drayney, dredge, forstate, hebbingnet, hose, hooknet, peternet, pursenet, shotnet, shovenet, smeltnet, stalker, trink, and *trinkersnet.* Their mesh was called *mask, mash, maskel,* and *mesh*
(Wright 1988, 92-121)

Some of these terms are found in a fourteenth-century fishing ordinance of the time of Edward III (1327–77) which relates to London and established some net types and mesh sizes. This refers to 'the great nets which take smelts', and:

'another manner of large net, that is called codnet, so called from the cod or pouch in which a stone was placed to sink it.'

Moreover,

'there is another manner of large net, towards the west of London Bridge, that shall go on all the year, [the meshes of which are] two inches [51mm] wide, and not more narrow...'

'There is another manner of net, which people call peteresnet [the meshes of which are] two inches wide, and not more narrow; and it shall go on all the year, except in the season when they take smelts...'

'There is another manner of net, that they call treinekes, of the width [in the meshes] of one inch and a half [38mm], and not more narrow...'

'There is a kind of garee; which things are not at all advantageous, as they are too narrow [in the mesh], to the undoing of the waters. There are other manners of nets that are forbidden, that is to say, chotnet, chofnet, and kidel'
(*Liber Custumarcum,* in *Liber Albus* 1861, 331–2)

The meshes of such nets were measured 'from one knot across to the second knot'(*ibid*, 333)
Each weight was measured and most were found to be around 30–33mm long (Fig 91). It is not known if they were attached to the lowest line of the mesh, or to an even lower line hanging from the net, as suggested by Aston (1988), but in the former case they would indicate a mesh of at least 1.25in (32mm). At this size the net would have a minimum length of 1109 × 1.25in = 115ft 6in (35.2m). However, if an allowance is made for the knots, and bearing in mind the general documentary preference of net mesh to 2in (51mm), the minimum net length could have been 1109 by 0.051m = 56.56m long (ie 185ft 6in). Whichever was the case, the net itself was clearly very large and heavy, and would have required several people to handle it.

Dating the wreck

A small amount of pottery was recovered from a shelly deposit beneath the boat. Within the boat itself was aslightly larger group of pottery (a minimum of twenty vessels) together with fragments of brick and roof tile.

The pottery
by Lyn Blackmore

Five sherds of pottery were found beneath the boat: one of possible Kingston ware (residual), three of Coarse Border ware 1350–1500), and the rim of a pitcher in Late London ware (1400–1500).

The pottery from inside the boat comprises fifty-four sherds deriving from twelve locally-produced vessels (Late London ware, Late London slipware, Cheam redware and Tudor Brown, some quite reduced) and from eight imported vessels (Rhenish stoneware, Dutch earthenware, and part of an amphora), the dating of which is summarised below.

Production of Siegburg stoneware started *c* 1300 –1350, but both vessels from the boat, a squat *trichterhalsbecher* and a bowl, date to 1450–1500 (Beckmann 1974, Types 132 and 163; Hurst *et al* 1986, 177 pl 30, 178, no 257). Production of Langerwehe stoneware started *c* 1350, but while one sherd is from a fourteenth-century Type 1 rouletted jug, the other two vessels, a globular costrel and a large fragment of standing costrel, are types dated to 1350–1450 (Hurst *et al* 1986, 190, fig 92, nos 294, 295), and are probably of fifteenth-century date. The two Dutch redware pipkins are dated by the form of the rim and applied tripod feet to *c* 1400–25 and 1400–50 (Hurst *et al* 1986, 134, fig 60, nos 188, 191, and 194). The amphora is of interest in that the very fine fabric is unlike that of the Spanish examples found in sixteenth-century and later contexts in London, and in fact is macroscopically very similar to the Roman type Pelichet 47, produced in Southern France *c* AD40–250, although these lack the surface slip and band of rilled decoration present on the Blackfriars example. As such an early find would be quite out of place in the context of this otherwise homogenous late medieval group, it must be concluded that this amphora is probably of fifteenth-century date, although the source remains to be determined.

The redwares comprise one base sherd from a fourteenth-century London-ware baluster jug, but otherwise range in date from *c* 1400–1550 to 1600. Late London slipware (one base sherd) is currently dated to 1400–1500. The dating of Cheam red ware (one jug and a large globular cistern/pitcher) is problematical, but is thought to be to after *c* 1440, and possibly after 1480 (Orton 1979, 357–8; 1982, 82). Tudor Brown (one cistern, one possible cistern, and one sherd from a ?cooking pot), formerly dated to after 1550, has been shown to occur in contexts dating from *c* 1480 in Southwark (Stephenson pers comm), but is unlikely to be much earlier than this. An overfired jug with reduced surfaces and sherds from three other vessels may be of either Cheam Red or Tudor Brown ware.

The building material
by Ian Betts

The finds comprise a single fragment of roofing slate, peg and ridge roofing tile, and a piece of yellow brick. The earliest example of slate as a roofing material in London is dated to *c* 1320–50, but it is not common until after the Great Fire of 1666. The roofing tiles include pieces typical of the later medieval period, with fine moulding sand. This type was introduced by at least 1480–1520, and possibly as early as 1450, but is very unlikely to predate 1450. The yellow brick is of a type probably introduced around the mid fifteenth century.

Conclusion

Taken together, the pottery and building materials suggest a date of 1450-1500, and possibly 1480–1500, for the fill of the boat. Therefore it can be assumed that the vessel sank towards the end of the fifteenth century.

4 Blackfriars ship 4, probably fifteenth century, City of London, 1970

Summary

The wreck of a clinker-built vessel, probably of the fifteenth century, was found with a cargo of Kentish ragstone lying close to Blackfriars wreck 3.

Discovery

This wreck was found on 1 December 1970, lying roughly north-south a few metres east of Blackfriars ship 3. A mechanical grab had dug through the vessel in the night while excavations continued on ship 3, and in the morning a section across the vessel was visible in the side of the hole. Unfortunately there was no time to excavate and little time to clean and record this new find, and its position in the side of the deep hole within the coffer-dam was very dangerous since the waterlogged sides of the hole were collapsing. A sketched cross-section was drawn, some measurements were taken, and the section was photographed (Fig 92). From these the accompanying section was drawn (Fig 93).

Description of the ship

The keel of the vessel was 0.415m wide and about 0.10m thick, and the garboard strakes were riveted into rabbets in the sides of the keel. Six strakes, probably of oak, were noted on each side of the keel, and the garboard strake was found to be only about 10mm thick. The garboard strake was 0.23m wide, and the other bottom strakes were 0.24–0.30m wide, with laps between of about 30–40mm. It was not absolutely clear if these were the maximum strake widths at the widest part of the vessel, but as the section crossed the cargo of building stone, and as the short length of exposed strake edges seemed to be parallel to the keel, it was evidently in the main body of the vessel and probably at about its widest point. The section suggests a vessel about 3.2–3.5m wide.

One frame was noted, which seemed to be of oak. It was 0.12m thick over the keel, but had been slightly inset. Over the planking it was 0.13m thick, but tapered to 0.07m near its end. The method of attaching the frames to the strakes was not established but was presumably by trenails since iron fastenings were not seen. The underside of the frame did not seem to be particularly notched for the overlapping strakes, though two limber holes were found cut into the underside to allow the flow of bilge water

How the ship was used

Overlying the frame in the bottom of the vessel was a spread of irregular lumps of Kentish ragstone, some of which were quite large (up to 0.5m across). This is presumed to be the cargo. No ceiling planking to protect the hull was found. The stone was no doubt quarried in the Maidstone region and had been brought down the River Medway and up the Thames to London where it was presumably intended for building purposes.

The Bridge House weekly payments for 1381–1405 (*Appendix 6*) include a record of many ship voyages that brought ragstone from the Medway to London, from which it is possible to place the wrecked vessel in its context. Since the normal type of vessel that carried ragstone to London was called a *farcost* during the fourteenth and fifteenth centuries (Wright 1988, 151; Salzman 1967, 350), it is possible that Blackfriars ship 4 was such a vessel, though the 10mm thickness of the garboard strake was probably too thin for a vessel undertaking such a long voyage with a substantial load.

The Bridge House accounts are a useful guide to the sizes of farcosts and their loads, for they include payments for 162 voyages to London with ragstone cargoes at prices per boatload ranging from 11s to 26s 8d. These can be converted into weights, for the records show that a cargo costing 11s was 16 tuntight, that cargoes costing 15s and 16s were 18 tuntight, that cargoes costing 18s and 20s were 24 tuntight, and that cargoes costing 24s were 26 tuntight. It is difficult to be precise about how a tuntight converts to a modern weight (Murray 1923, vol X, pt 1, 23, under *Tight*), though between the fourteenth and seventeenth centuries *tuntight* was a measure of capacity in a ship, as well as a measure of weight for stones, gravel, salt, etc carried in them. Salzman (1967, 122) says that the term was based upon the weight of a tun of wine (2000 lb), its half being called a 'pipe'. Thus, for work at St Pauls in 1382 Henry Yevele supplied '30 tunnetyth and 1 pipe of northern stone' at 9s the ton. Although a modern ton weighs 2240 lbs, for the purpose of this study it is assumed that a tuntight weighed approximately one tonne.

On this basis it is possible to use the cargo costs as a rough indicator not only of the volume of the ragstone cargoes (1 cubic metre of loose ragstone weighs 1.3 tonnes, see Marsden 1994), but also of the sizes of vessel used. The relative frequency of voyages at different prices shows that the boatloads seem to fall into two groups: 14–15 tonnes and 18–20 tonnes. This

Fig 92 The only photograph of ship 4, showing the keel-plank (centre), the clinker planking, and a frame. Part of the ragstone cargo has fallen into the foreground (metric scale)

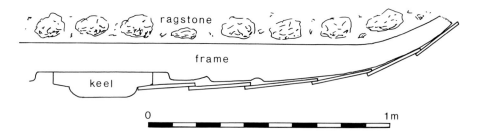

Fig 93 A sketched cross-section of ship 4

is a substantial difference that probably reflects two basic sizes of ship. The variations in price under the same quantity are possibly due to the stone having been brought from different sources near the River Medway, depending upon their relative distance from London. For example payments for the stone were made to Stephen Charles of Hoo (16s, 10 October 1388, and 22 August 1405), Simon Sherman of Gillingham (13s 4d, 10 October 1388), John Scoven of Stroud (18s, 14 March 1405) and John Attemylle of Maidstone (15s, 23 May 1405). As far as size is concerned these vessels had a ragstone cargo weight carrying capacity that was two to three times that of Blackfriars ship 3 (*see Chapter 3*), which suggests that the vessels were much more substantial than ship 4. On balance, it seems likely that Blackfriars ship 4 was a local river craft, perhaps a lighter used for unloading a farcost moored in the stream.

Loss of the ship

There was no direct evidence to show why this vessel had been sunk, but its proximity to Blackfriars ship 3 and its apparently similar age suggests that the two vessels might have been in a collision, particularly as this was a frequent cause of shipping loss on the river.

Dating evidence

There was no opportunity of recovering any dating evidence from this wreck, though, as it lay at about the same level in the undisturbed river bed as ship 3, which is dated to the fifteenth century (*see above*), it is likely to be of similar date. This conclusion is reinforced by the fact that the workmen found large quantities of fifteenth-century pottery at about this level very close to wreck 4.

5 Ship and boat fragments of the twelfth to early fifteenth centuries

Summary

The fragments of ship and boat timbers found on the sites mentioned below appear to date from the twelfth to the fifteenth centuries. The dating is sometimes provisional pending the completion of full site reports and consideration of the dating evidence. Meanwhile, brief details of the contexts in which the fragments were found derive from the site archives preserved at the Museum of London and further dating evidence was obtained from a tree-ring study of individual ship and boat timbers. As a result, the value of the medieval collection lies in what it shows about methods of medieval ship and boat building as practised by a number of shipwrights. Although the fragmentary state of the planking has nothing significant to say about the shape of the hulls from which they came, it is important to compare these pieces with the more complete vessels from the Custom House and Blackfriars ship 3 sites. Since there would be considerable repetition if the fragments were to be individually described, each has been illustrated, and two fragments from Abbots Lane have been described in some detail. The significant features of each piece from every site have been tabulated to enable comparisons to be made (*see Appendix 1, Tables 6 and 7*). Summaries of the finds from each site are given below, and at the end of this chapter are some conclusions. The descriptions given below are a summary of the records preserved at the Museum of London, which can be referred to for further information

Hays Wharf to Abbots Lane, Southwark, 1987 (site code ABB 87)

Large piece of ship planking

A large slab of ship planking was found reused in the medieval revetment of a channel (context: revet [029]). Several phases of the revetment existed from which boat timbers were recovered, including samples from the large slab for dating or detailed study. A few of these fragments have been tree-ring dated to the latter half of the fourteenth century, and it seems likely that this is the date of the large slab of clinker planking. The slab was drawn in elevation while *in situ* by tracing it on polythene sheeting, and this was photographically reduced to 1:5 and redrawn for publication (Fig 94). As it was not seen by the writer, the description and interpretation given below is based wholly upon the site drawing.

Up to four strakes (Fig 94, A–D) appear to have been articulated, held together by rivets, presumably of iron. The general absence of rivets along the upper edge of strake D suggests that the plank edge had been broken away, presumably in antiquity, and that strakes E and F were not part of the articulated boat structure. Strakes H and I may well have been a broken extension of strakes A and B, but although this cannot be confirmed it should be noted that the scarf at the eastern end of A could have continued as the scarf at the western end of H. If it is accepted that H is part of A, then the apparently articulated plank fragment G shows that A cannot have been a garboard strake lying next to the keel. Although it is possible that J was found articulated with I, it seems that K, L, and M were separate pieces of planking since they overlapped in an opposite direction to the rest of the planking. At the western end fragments N, O, and P were clearly loose.

On this basis it is now possible to examine the planking as part of a boat. For this purpose strakes A–D are the most valuable. Based upon the usual clinker rules that roves were placed inside a boat, that upper strakes overlapped the lower outboard, and that scarf joints faced the stern on the outboard side, it is clear that this planking was from the starboard side of a boat, and that the bow was at the western end and the stern at the east.

Strake A was about 0.2m wide, but as it had rivets only along its upper edge it is clear that the lower edge had been broken off, presumably as the row of rivets presented a line of weakness when the boat was broken up. Rivets along the upper edge were spaced between about 0.13m and 0.18m, though the wide space of 0.35m in the middle of the plank could represent a rivet that was not recorded. The strake fragment was 3.85m long and contained two scarfs whose rivets suggest that they had overlaps of about 0.35m. It seems that at each end of the lap scarf there was a single rivet. Two holes, probably for trenails to fasten the planks to frames, were recorded 0.8m apart. The smaller hole was recorded as being about 0.04m in diameter.

Strake B survived to 4.8m in length, and, judging from its rivet positions, was probably about 0.23m wide. The rivets at the east end were spaced at 0.14–0.18m intervals, but in the rest of the strake were at about 0.23–0.24m intervals. Rivets in the breadth of the strake indicate that there were scarf joints or repair patches in at least four places, though it is difficult to establish

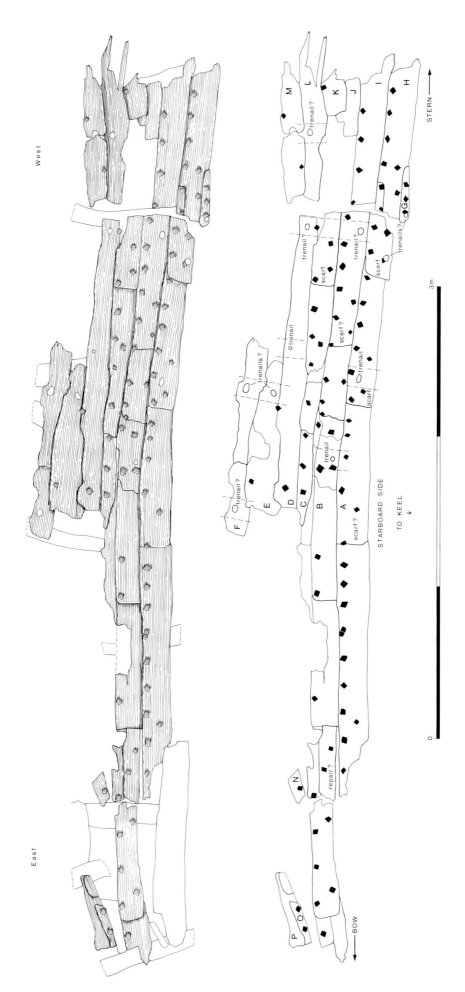

Fig 94 Abbots Lane, 1987: context 029, elevation recorded on site of a large piece of boat planking reused in a waterfront (top); an interpretation (bottom)

which was which. Towards the western end one group of fastenings seemed to be for a repair. Two round holes for trenail fastenings to frames were recorded at the eastern end, each hole being about 30mm in diameter. These holes were 0.151m apart centres, indicating the frame spacing.

Strake C was 2.07m long and appeared to have two scarf joints, the right-hand-end one, judging from the rivets at each end, probably being about 0.35m long. The strake was about 0.23m wide, and the rivets were spaced between 0.17m and 0.26m apart. A possible scarf may have existed near the western end of the strake, but associated rivets were not seen.

Strake D was 1.92m long, and had only one rivet in position along its upper edge, indicating that the strake edge had been split away along the rivet line. It would seem to have been originally about 0.23m wide. Two trenail holes were recorded with centres about 0.8m apart.

Strake E was only about 1m long, and was probably about 0.2m wide originally. It had one trenail hole.

Strake F may have been attached to strake E, but only one rivet that may have held them had survived. The importance of this strake is that it apparently had two trenail holes whose centres were 0.8m apart at their centres. Since the east end trenail hole was in line with the trenail hole in strake E it is likely that strakes E and F were originally joined.

Other fragments of planking were recorded which appear to have the same constructional characteristics, and therefore were presumably from the same boat. They do not add much to the overall evidence from which the construction and form of the vessel can be reconstructed, for crucial information about the timbers, particularly relating to their thickness and the angle and width of the laps, was not recorded. To obtain such information the timbers would have to have been recovered from the site and cleaned for detailed study. If the trenail holes all represent former frame positions then there is considerable uncertainty about the original frame spacing, particularly as no trenail holes were recorded at the centre and western end of the planking. The trenail holes mostly do not line up, making it difficult to reconstruct the frame positions. Nevertheless, the site record shows that this clinker-built boat was possibly about 8m long, with frames spaced 0.8m apart. The gentle curve of strakes A and B in plan suggests that they formed part of the bottom of a vessel.

Planking from context 199

Several separate pieces of oak planking from this context, believed to be from the slab of planking, are worthy of description. They were of radially-cut oak and were free from knots.

The first (Fig 95, no 9) was 0.875m long and about 0.12m wide, but as both edges were broken it is clear that the plank was originally wider. One edge had been broken along the rivet line, and had traces of a lap with a caulking of hair. This incomplete lap was 30mm wide, but judging from a complete lap on the second fragment (described below) it seems likely that the whole lap was originally 60mm wide. The plank had a maximum thickness of 26mm, but at its unscarfed end this thinned down to 18mm. At the other end the plank thinned on its outboard face to the feather end of a scarf with a caulking of hair. The scarf was 0.225m long. The inboard face at this end was flat, but had been shaved down slightly to receive a repair patch at least 0.46m long, held by an iron nail at one end. The patch was held by an iron rivet further along showing that its thickness was 14mm. An oak trenail 23mm in diameter passed through the centre of the plank and the patch, confirming that the plank face with the rove was inboard, as did the deep erosion on the outboard face of narrow channels which were possibly caused by *Teredo*. There was no evidence of a surface dressing of tar either inboard or outboard. The scarf indicates that this fragment is probably from the starboard side of the boat.

Planking from context 205/86

An oak plank fragment (Fig 95, no 10), quarter cut and reasonably straight-grained with no knots, was 0.495m long and about 0.17m wide. It had an oak patch inboard, and had heavy erosion on its outboard surface, which was presumably the reason for the repair.

The plank was 15mm thick at its single surviving edge, and up to 25mm thick in the middle of the plank. However, its faces were deeply eroded, particularly beside the lap where the plank was only 5mm thick. There is no indication of the original width of the plank, but the surviving piece shows that it was more than 0.17m. The lap was up to 44mm wide, and the adjoining plank, although missing, had the two surviving iron rivets 0.232m apart between centres in the adjacent planks, which show that it was 23–25mm thick. There is no trace of any caulking on the lap face.

On the inboard face of the plank was an oak patch, fastened by iron rivets both at the lap and in the centre of the plank. This patch had increased the thickness of the eroded plank. It was 0.764m long, and 18mm thick in the middle, thinning down to 5mm at the ends. One end was broken. Between the plank and the patch was some caulking of black felt-like hair about 2–3mm thick. This seemed to have been laid in thin flat layers.

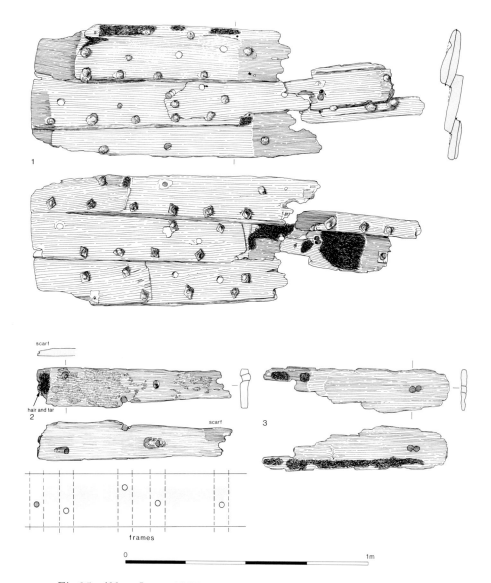

Fig 95 Abbots Lane, 1987: no 1 contexts 184/63, 186/65, 191/70; no 2 context 185/64; no 3 context 199/78

The nails in the iron rivets have square shanks about 8mm square, and their roughly circular heads show marks of hammering. The roves lay inboard and were diamond-shaped and cut from iron bars 3–4mm and 6.5mm thick. There were V-shaped cuts at opposite ends of the rove, showing that they were cut from an iron bar by a chisel. The roves were also slightly raised in the middle as a result of the central hole being punched through over a larger hole in the blacksmith's anvil. The point of each nail had been beaten out to a diameter of about 18–20mm over the rove to hold it in place.

Two-thirds of the thickness of the outboard surface of the plank had been worn away beside the lap, and further deep erosion had occurred around the nail heads in the middle of the plank. A rivet nail showed that the plank was originally 25mm thick, but had been eroded down to only 10mm in a hollow 55mm across around the nail. This shows that considerable erosion had occurred after the repair patch had been added. The excessive wear on the outside of the planking suggests that this fragment may be from the bottom of the vessel.

This fragment is particularly interesting for showing the extremely worn condition to which a boat could be reduced, even after repair, probably before being finally abandoned, though it is possible that some wear occurred during its use as a revetment. To fasten the patch required the removal of a frame and some existing rivets.

Other boat planking

There were seventeen significant pieces of boat planking from this site, in addition to those described above. Four pieces have given the following tree-ring dates in the heartwood: context 205/86, AD 1296–1352, context 187/66, AD1266–1333; context 185/64, AD1196–1344; and context 195/74, AD1296–1368. These suggest that the collection as a whole dates from the late fourteenth century. (Figs 96–100)

All samples of planking were of oak and all were radially-cut, and although the construction was similar there were some characteristics which suggest the work of several shipwrights. In many cases the lap and scarf caulking was of matted hair, but in two fragments (contexts 236/154 and 199/78) the hair caulking had been carefully laid across the plank laps. In most cases the planks were up to 21–30mm thick, but in three

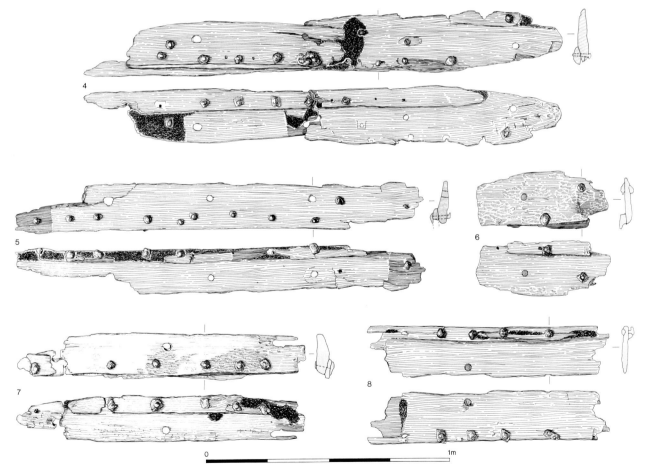

Fig 96 Abbots Lane, 1987: no 4 context 155/152; no 5 contexts 235/153, 236/154; no 6 context 195; no 7 contexts 238/156, 358/157; no 8 context 201/81

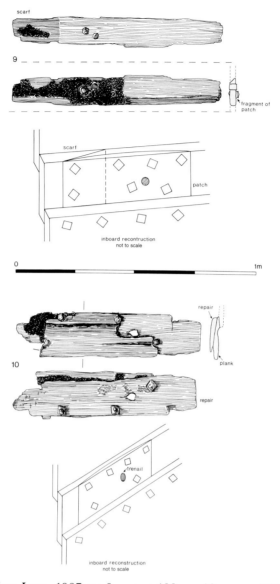

Fig 97 Abbots Lane, 1987: no 9 context 199; no 10 context 205/86

instances (contexts 237/8/155/157, 236/154, and 154/5/150/2) the planks were 41–45mm thick as if these were from a larger vessel. Although some of the tree-ring dating shows the use of local oak (contexts 205/86 and 187/66), other planks were of Baltic oak (contexts 185/64 and 195/74). Three planks had evidence of use, one having a slightly burnt surface (context 237/8/155/7), and three others had what seemed to be eroded *Teredo* borings (contexts 199, 189/68 and 201). As it is not clear what timbers were from the large slab of planking, it seems that the caulking and the plank thicknesses suggest that there could be a minimum of three vessels, though the Baltic timbers in addition to the English, and the *Teredo* could mean there are two or three more.

The repairs are particularly interesting, for in one the plank lap had to be patched and re-riveted (context 205/86), and in another a scarf was patched (context 199). In three examples of re-riveting the old rivets had been removed and the holes plugged with pieces of square oak, and new rivets had been inserted in alternative positions (contexts 154/5/150/2, 195, and 188/67). In another a trenail was expanded by having an iron nail driven into it (context 185/64), and in another re-trenailing of a frame was represented by two adjacent holes 23mm and 26mm in diameter (context 199/78). Damage to the planking was represented by splits along lap rivet lines (contexts 195/74 and 199/78), and in one piece (context 205/86) the plank had been deeply water-eroded, a rivet showing that the plank was originally 15mm thick at the lap, but had been eroded down to only 5mm thick. Whether or not this happened during the use of the vessel or during its reuse in the revetment is not clear. However, all these pieces show a great concern for repairing old leaking boats. Some repairs required skilled re-riveting and were probably carried out by shipwrights, but other repairs lacked skill, such as the iron nail driven into the end of a trenail, and may have been carried out by the boat owners.

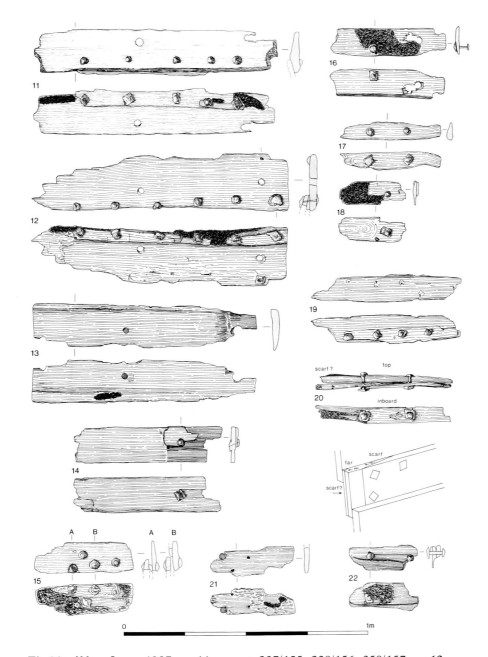

Fig 98 Abbots Lane, 1987: no 11 contexts 237/155, 238/156, 358/157; no 12 context 178.56/54; no 13 context 195/44; no 14 context 201; no 15 context 175/53; no 16 context 216/99; nos 17 and 18 context 209/91; no 19 no context; no 20 context 199; no 21 context 188/67; no 22 context 206/87

5-15 Bankside, Southwark, 1987

(site code 5BS 87)

Excavation revealed a revetment dated to the fourteenth century 10m south of the modern river bank, containing some boat timbers. Two associated fragments of oak planking from the same vessel (context 3163/84) were recovered (Fig 101), one of which is tree-ring dated in the heartwood to 1028–1137. Although this suggests a building date for the boat in the late twelfth century, the provisional date of the revetment suggests that a thirteenth-century date is more appropriate.

The two fragments include part of a clinker plank of radially-cut oak, which originally had frames attached by trenails. The plank had split at the trenails and was repaired inboard with an oak patch fastened by small bent iron nails. There was a matted caulking of hair (cattle and wool) beneath the patch.

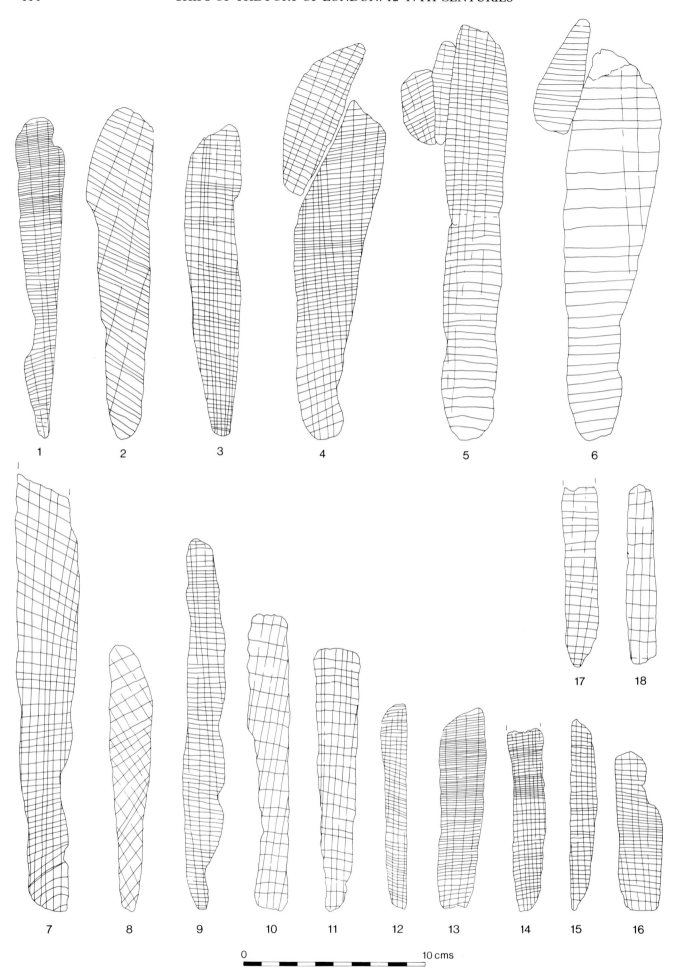

Fig 99 Abbots Lane, 1987: Tree-ring sections of planks: no 1 context 205/86; no 2 context 236/154; no 3 context 195/74; no 4 context 153/150; no 5 context 178/56; no 6 context 155/152; no 7 context 186/65; no 8 context 190/69 upper plank; no 9 context 193/72; no 10 context 189/68; no 11 context 201; no 12 context 187/66; no 13 context 199; no 14 context 188/67; no 15 context 216/99 patch; no 16 context 206/87

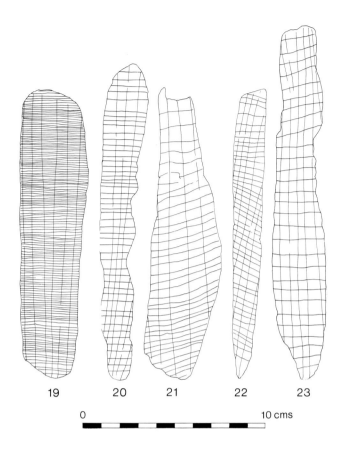

Fig 100 Abbots Lane, 1987: Tree-ring sections of planks: no 19 context 185/64; no 20 context 199/78; no 21 context 238/156; no 22 context 205/86; no 23 context 201/81

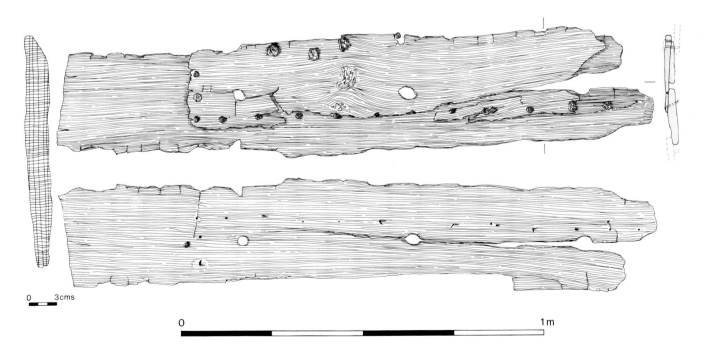

Fig 101 5–15 Bankside, 1987: context 3163/84, plank B

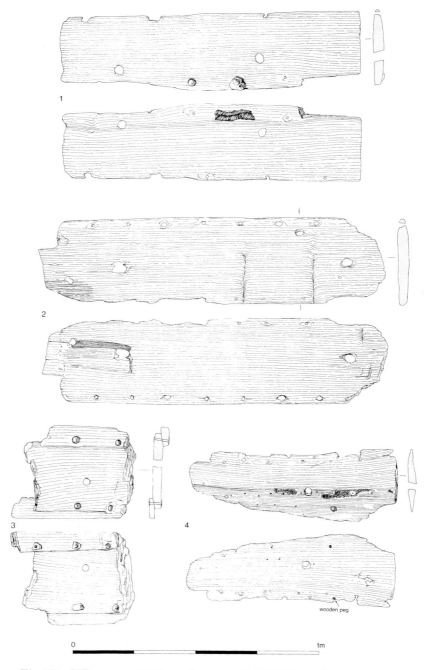

Fig 102 Billingsgate, 1982: no 1 context 6281/3578; no 2 context 3534/5047; no 3 context 3058/4924; no 4 context 2606

Billingsgate, City of London, 1982 (site code BIG 82)

Excavations uncovered ship timbers (Figs 102 to 105) reused in waterfronts of the twelfth and thirteenth centuries (Steedman *et al* 1992, 51, 61, 68). Two were probably from context 2724, and others from contexts 4924/3058, 5047/3534, 3058/9-4923/4, 4925/3056, 6281/3578, and 6373/3582. Three were tree-ring dated in the heartwood, contexts 6794/3579 to AD 1027–1115, context 2606 to AD 1034-1183 and contexts 4445/3065, a' to 1081–1181 and b' 1075–1179. Most of the vessels were probably built during the early thirteenth century.

The planks, all clinker-built of radially-cut oak, had been fastened together with iron rivets. Some planks had traces of hair caulking, probably mostly matted (contexts 4924/3058, 3058/9/4923/4, and 4925/3056), but in one (6281/3578) the caulking was of twisted strands. Most of the plank lap faces were flat, but in two there were traces of caulking grooves (contexts ?2724, 4445/3065). A trenail in one plank had

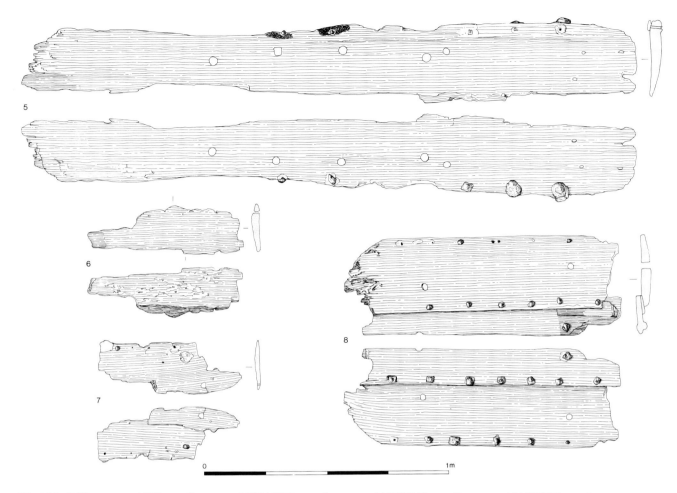

Fig 103 Billingsgate, 1982: no 5 context 3582/6373; no 6 context 4445/3065; no 7 context 4445/3065; no 8 context 3059/49.23

survived and was of poplar/willow (context 4924/3058). There were traces of repairs, and in one (context 2724) a patch with a caulking of hair laid in strings covered a split (Fig 106). In another (context 2606) a line of rivets had replaced an earlier line which had been removed and the holes plugged with small square oak pegs.

The different methods of laying the lap caulking (matted and in strings), the presence of the caulking groove in a few planks, but not in others, and the existence of two sizes of trenails (23–6mm and 30–35mm) suggest that at least three vessels may be represented.

Hays Wharf to Symonds Wharf, Southwark, 1988 (site code SYM 88)

Fragments of substantial ship's oak planking (Figs 107 and 8) were recovered from a single revetment (revetment 123), possibly fronting onto the River Thames. The tree-ring dating of the reused ship timbers, all of which were of Baltic oak (*see Appendix*

1), shows that the ship or ships were probably built about 1350. The timbers had the following date ranges in the heartwood: context 141/168, AD 1177–1332; context 168, AD 1222–1325 and 1230–1327; context 175/164, AD 1133–1243, 1134–1231, 1238–1330, 1251–1328, 1173–1231, and 1237–1333; and context 196/120, AD 1193–1307.

The timbers fell into three groups, perhaps representing three distinct vessels. The first were planks with a thickness of 55–8mm, and with laps 40–60mm wide (context 141/168, 168 and 175/164). The rivet nails were thick (mostly 8–10mm square) (Fig 109), and the caulking in two pieces was of hair in strings (contexts 141/168, 168) (Fig 110). This group seemed to belong to a single vessel, and as the latest tree-ring dates fall into a narrow band (AD 1332, 1325, 1327, 1330, 1328, and 1333) it seems likely that this was close to the sapwood, and that the construction of the vessel dated to the mid fourteenth century.

The second group was represented by one fragment (context 194/136) which was much thinner, even though it too had hair caulking. It was presumably from a smaller, slighter vessel.

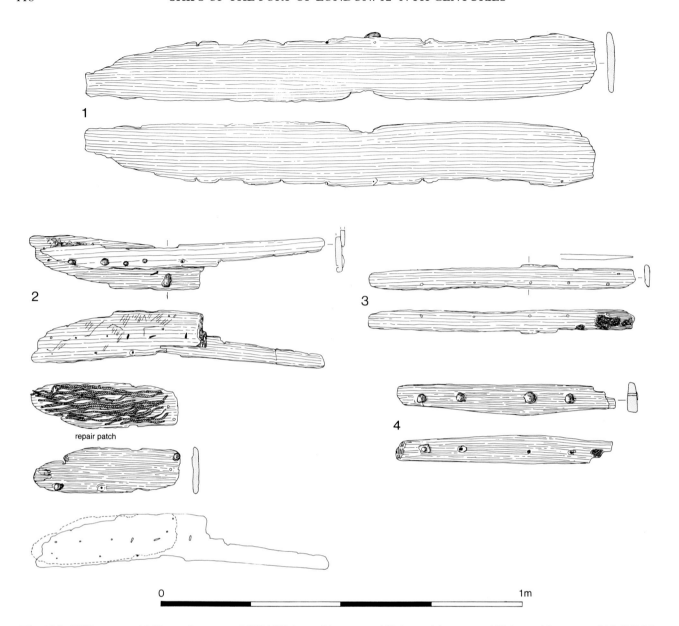

repair patch

0   1m

Fig 104 Billingsgate, 1982: no 9 context 3579/6794; no 10 context 1124; no 11 context 1121; no 12 context 3056/4925

However the third group was also represented by a single piece (context 196/120) which, although from a substantial ship like those above and of Baltic oak, differed in that the caulking was of moss (Figs 111 and 112). The moss could represent a repair, and that piece could be derived from the group 1 vessel described above.

Hays Wharf to Gun and Shot Wharf, Southwark, 1988

(site code G&S 88)

Articulated fragments of a narrow section of ship planking (Figs 113 and 114) were recovered from a medieval timber revetment on the west side of an inlet

from the River Thames. The planking was from a single context (contexts 158/159/160/449/450 /451/452/453), and was of radially-cut Baltic oak which had the following tree-ring dates in the heartwood: 1174–1358, 1084–1159, 1136–1335, 1089–1172, 1146–1370, 1073–1146, 1077–1133, and 1055–1159. The end dates suggest a vessel built perhaps about AD 1400.

The ship from which this sample was cut was probably the largest of the London medieval vessels and must have been seagoing. The four large oak planks were clinker-built and had been joined together by iron rivets. One plank was scarfed, and two others contained trenails which originally fastened the planks to a frame. There were no tool marks. The full width of only two of the planks had survived.

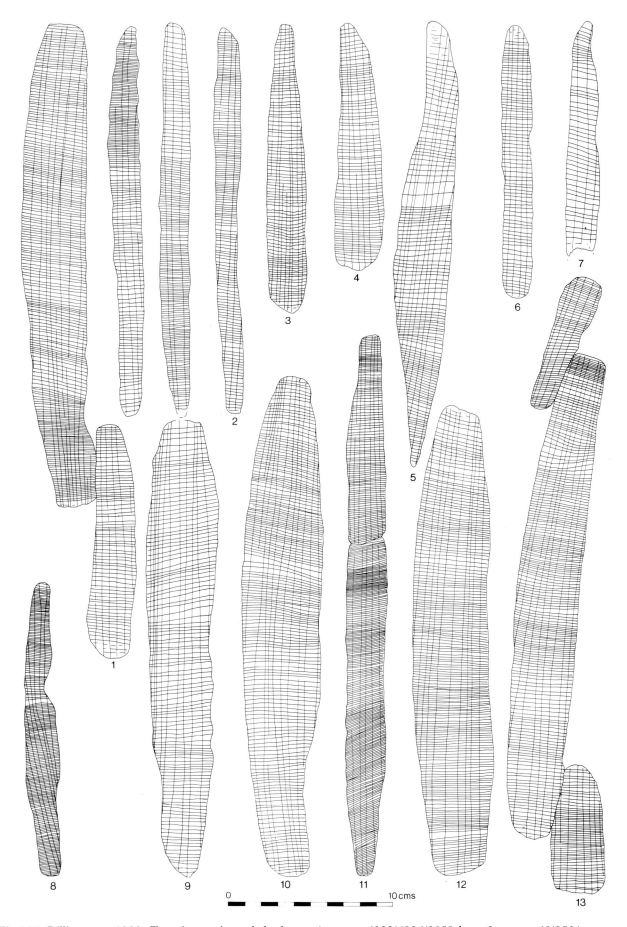

*Fig 105 Billingsgate, 1982: Tree-ring sections of planks: no 1 context 4923/4924/3058A; no 2 context 68/3581;
nos 3 and 4 context 4445/3065; no 5 context 2606; no 6 context 6794/3579; no 7 context 4445/3065; no 8 context
6698/3563; no 9 context 5047/3534; no 10 context 6281/3578; no 11 context 6697/3583; no 12 context 6373/3582; no
13 context 4924/3058B*

Fig 106 Caulking of hair in strings under a patch repair to a plank, twelfth century Billingsgate 1982 (context 2724)

These were 0.35m and 0.36m wide, 54mm, and 60mm thick in the middle, and 31mm and 40mm thick at the edges. One plank was scarfed, but only 0.28m of the length of the scarf had survived. Judging from the angle of the overlap it seems that the scarf was originally about 0.4m long. Two iron rivets existed in the centre of the plank to hold the scarf together, and in the middle was a caulking of moss, which smells like tar. A sample of the moss was identified as *Weissia* spp, a genus of about 150 species which occurs worldwide and therefore is no indicator of the place at which the ship was built (kindly identified by Dr J Hather, Institute of Archaeology, London).

Three complete clinker laps survived, 94mm, 73mm, and 77mm wide, and at least two held a hair caulking up to 5mm thick. The planks at the laps were held by iron rivets, two of which were 0.163m apart, centre to centre. Each rivet had a domed nail head about 47mm in diameter and 5–9mm in height. Only one nail shank could be seen, and this was 8mm square. The roves were well-cut iron plates, 35–40mm square and about 3mm thick, and slightly domed in the centre.

In the middle of each pair of two adjacent planks was an oak trenail 37mm in diameter, which once held the planks to a frame. The trenails presumably had been driven into the planks from outboard, and in the centre of each was a square oak plug, evidently driven there so as to expand the trenail.

In the planks were also holes left by five metal nails, four of which passed completely through the planks. As most of these lay in the area of the former frame it seems likely that they had served as an additional method of attaching the planks to the frame, but that when the ship was broken up the nails were removed. Two of the nails passed through the clinker laps, one through a plank, one through the planking scarf, and the fifth passed through only one plank of a clinker lap, suggesting that the planking at the lap had been partly replaced. The shaft of each nail was about 10mm square, and the impression of the missing nail head shows that it was about 40mm in diameter. Impressions of the nail heads lay on the outboard face of the planks, and as there was no impression of roves on the inboard face this tends to confirm the interpretation that they held the planks to the frames.

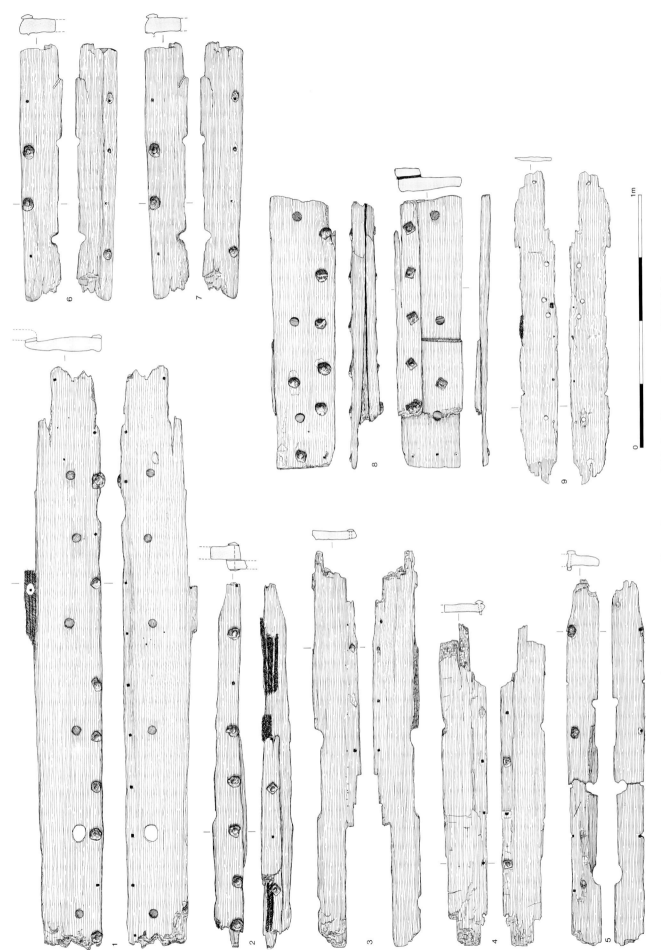

Fig 107 Symonds Wharf, 1988: no 1 context 141/168; no 2 context 168; no 3 context 164, frag B; no 4 context 175/164A; no 5 context 175/164; no 6 context 168; no 7 context 168; no 8 context 196/120; no 9 context 194/136

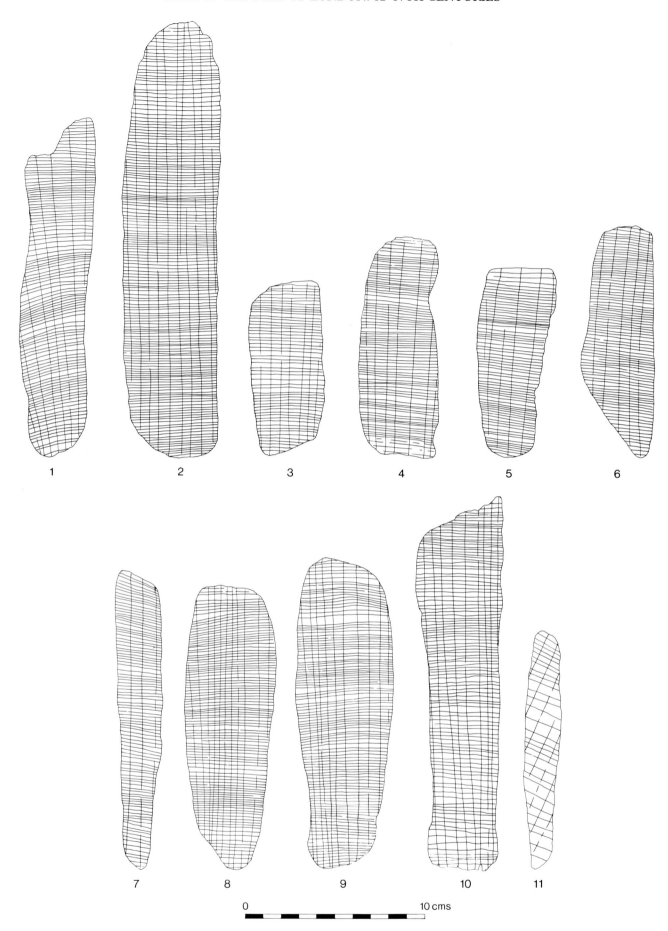

Fig 108 Symonds Wharf, 1988: Tree-ring sections of planks: no 1 context 175/164; no 2 context 147/168/141; no 3 context 168/175; no 4 context 164/175; no 5 context 164/175; no 6 context 164/175; nos 7–9 context 168; no 10 context 196/120; no 11 context 194/136

Fig 109 *The shank of a rivet driven through oak planking showing only slight deformation of the wood grain, indicating that a hole had been drilled first, fourteenth century (SYM 88 88, context 175/6) (metric scale)*

Fig 110 *Two lengths of twisted hair caulking in a plank lap, fourteenth century (SYM 88, context 168) (metric scale)*

Fig 111 Inboard view of a scarf with rivets at the outboard end (left) and one rivet near the inboard end (right), fourteenth century (SYM 88, contexts 196/120). A trenail passes through the scarf (metric scale)

Fig 112 Iron roves and a trenail, fourteenth century (SYM 88, context 196/120) (metric scale)

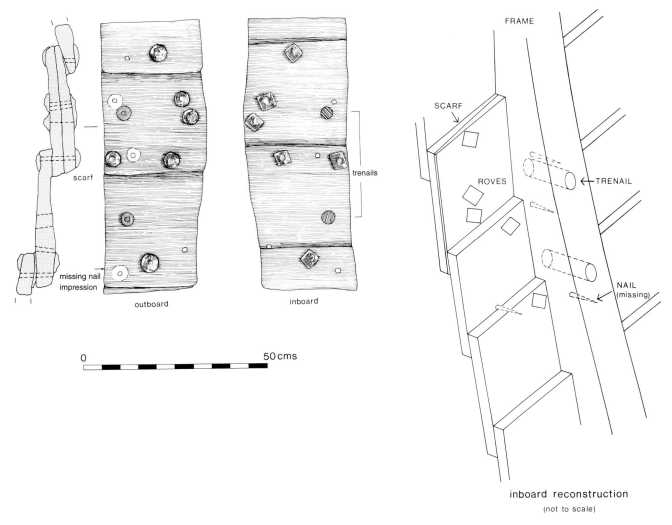

Fig 113 Gun and Shot Wharf, 1988: Ship planks, from contexts 449/450/160/452/457/159/451, and inboard reconstruction

No surface dressing of tar or trace of water erosion or wood borers were found to suggest that this timber was from the underwater part of a ship. However, the angle of the clinker laps suggests that these pieces of planking perhaps derived from a flat part of the hull, probably the side. Assuming that the usual rules of clinker planking applies then the scarf indicates that these planks were from the starboard side of the vessel.

Trig Lane, City of London, 1974
(site code TL 74)

Fragments of boat planking (Figs 115–17) were recovered from this site (contexts 1384/5/ 1136/4, 1382, 1383/1136/1, 1381, and 1353/1136/1), and two further fragments without numbers are probably from this site (NL 10, NL 11). They were from a timber waterfront revetment built during the fourteenth century (Milne and Milne 1982, 26–7), so

it is likely that the vessel or vessels represented by the timbers dates from the late thirteenth or fourteenth centuries.

They had no great variations in constructional features and could all have been derived from one vessel. They were of oak radially-cut, with a lap caulking of hair and tar. The felt-like hair caulking in one fragment (NL 11) might suggest another vessel or a repair. Although there was evidence of repair patches (contexts 1384/5/1136/4, and 1353/1136/1), it was clear that one of these had probably been attached over a scarf and at a trenail which had presumably become leaky.

Bridewell, City of London, 1978
(site code BRI 78)

Associated fragments of planking from the same boat (Figs 118–20) were found in deposits beneath the Tudor royal palace of Bridewell built in 1515–23

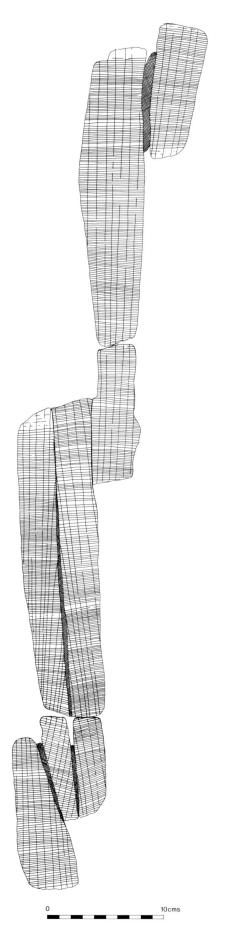

Fig 114 Gun and Shot Wharf, 1988: Tree-ring sections of ship planks, from context 449/450/160/452/457/159/451

(Gadd and Dyson 1981, 20), under which were found dumps of the fourteenth and early fifteenth centuries. The fragments therefore probably date from the fourteenth century.

The clinker planks were of radially-cut oak, held by iron rivets, with a matted hair caulking in the laps. Substantial repairs in the form of oak patches lay both inboard and outboard, and covered a split in the planking at the trenails. The inboard patch extended to the rivet line and was fastened by nails and rivets.

Baynards Castle, City of London, 1972 (site code BC 72)

Part of an oak frame (Fig 121) was found in a medieval dump of rubbish filling the fourteenth-century East Watergate (Marsden forthcoming). It was 1.75m long, about 0.15m wide, and up to 0.115m thick. The underside was notched or joggled for nine strakes (missing), each of which was originally 0.275–0.3m wide and about 0.03m thick. The planks had evidently been held together by rivets whose rove positions were marked on the frame by rectangular recesses cut in its underside. There was also an intermediate recess in the width of a former plank, which must mark the position of a plank scarf or repair. The planks had been held by trenails that were wedged at the upper face of the frame and across the grain of the frame so as not to split the timber. Two adjacent trenails indicate a re-fastening of the frame.

At the former plank overlap positions were limber holes for the flow of bilge water, showing that this frame was from the bottom of the vessel. At one end there were no joggling, trenails, or limber holes, and this should indicate the former position of the keel. Since the joggling was at a right angle to the frame this timber was evidently from about the widest part of the bottom of the boat. This frame, then, must be from the flat bottom of a vessel which was more than twice the length of the fragment, that is more than 3.5m. Therefore, allowing for the sides, the vessel itself can hardly have been less than 4.5m wide.

Two rectangular notches had been cut into the top of the timber, as if they were tenons for posts, one post being probably vertical and the other raking, as if the frame had been reused as the base of a revetment support. When found, the bottom of the vertical post was still in position. Each tenon was held by a trenail driven in from the side of the frame. The ends of the frame were squared off as if they had been sawn away for reuse.

By the time the frame was discarded in the dock it was already old, for it had already been used in the repaired boat, and then had been reused probably in a revetment. Its date is probably late thirteenth to early fourteenth century.

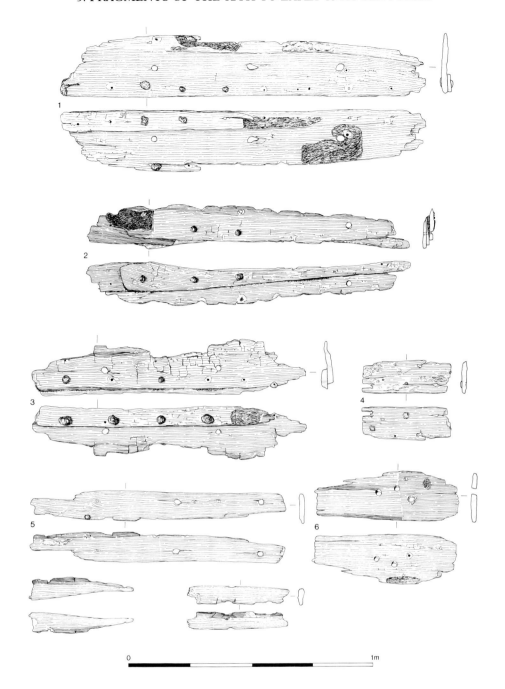

Fig 115 Trig Lane, 1974: no 1 context 1353/1136/1; no 2 no context, NL 11; no 3 context 1136/1; no 4 context 1384/5; no 5 context 1381, three pieces; no 6 context 1384/5

Anchor fluke, River Thames off Custom House Wharf, City of London, 1987

A wrought-iron anchor fluke (Museum of London acc no 87.107/4) was found at low tide in 1987 in the bed of the Thames, a short distance off the western end of Custom House Wharf (Fig 122). It lay at a depth of approximately 3m, and about 0.3m above it were two groats of Henry VI. One coin was the Annulet issue (1422–27), and the other was the Rosette-Mascle issue (1427–30). The finder, Terry Letch, noted that in this general area of the foreshore the eighteenth-century layer is approximately 1.5–1.8m below the surface. Since it is clear from riverbed excavations at Blackfriars and on waterfront sites (eg Trig Lane, Custom House) that the natural alluvial deposits of the riverbed are stratified, it is likely that the two groats of Henry VI are a true indication of the date of the anchor, and that it was probably lost in the fourteenth or fifteenth centuries.

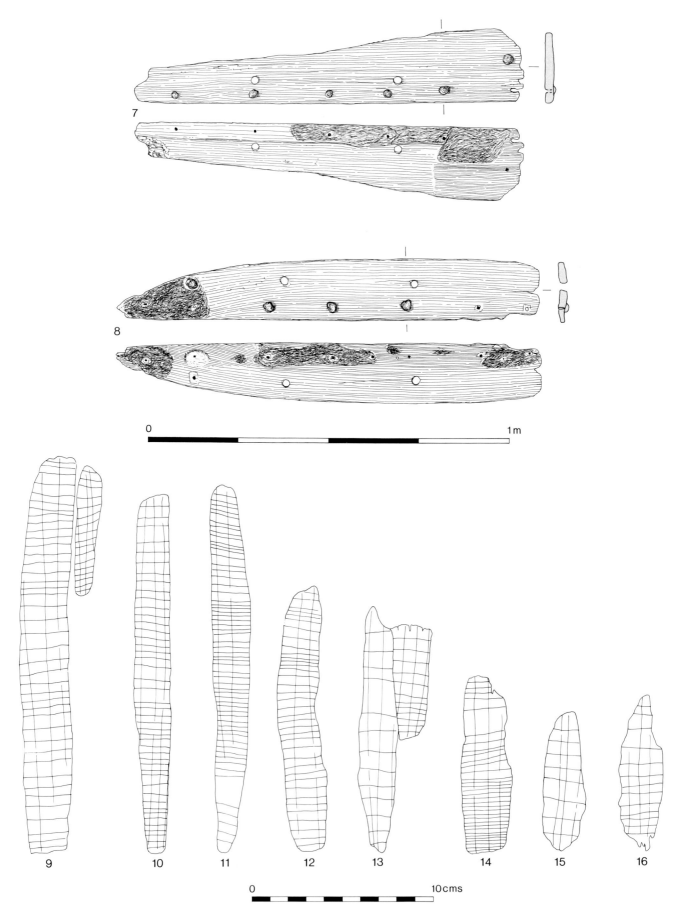

Fig 116 Trig Lane, 1974: no 7 no context, NL 10: no 8 context 1384: Tree-ring sections of planks: no 9 contexts 1383 and 1136/1; no 10 no context, NL 10; no 11 contexts 1384/5, 1136/4; no 12 context 1382; no 13 no context; no 14 contexts 1383 and 1136/1; nos 15 and 16 no contexts

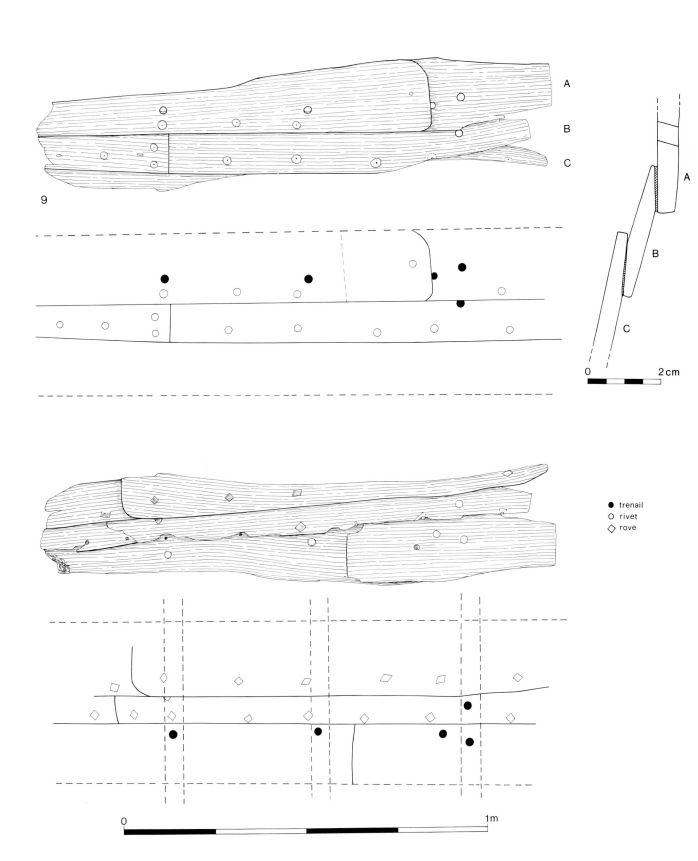

Fig 117 Trig Lane, 1974: no 9 context 1381, outboard, top inboard, with frame positions indicated at bottom

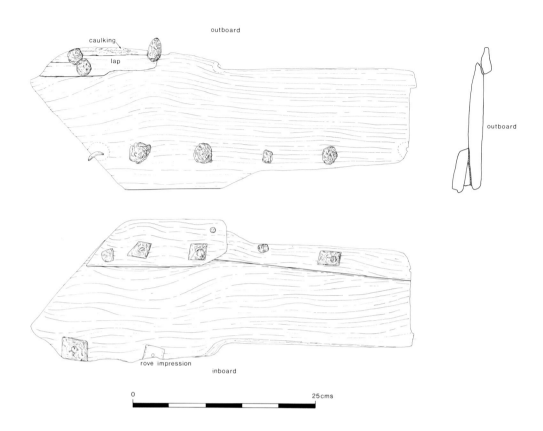

Fig 118 Bridewell, 1978: planking

The fluke (Fig 123) is roughly triangular in shape, 0.388m along the arm, 0.271m wide, and about 13mm thick. It bears clear traces of hammering, with circular hollows 20mm in diameter suggesting the shape of the hammer head. The fluke was hammered onto the pointed end of the anchor's arm, which, under the fluke, is rectangular in section, and the join is clear. The arm is broken, and just in front of the fluke it is round in section with a maximum diameter of 62mm, suggesting that the rest of the arm was also round.

Dated medieval anchors from northern Europe are rare, as they are difficult to date by their form. However, the rough wrought form of this fluke is unlike the usual post-medieval anchors. Medieval illustrations from northern Europe show ships with similar large flukes (Fig 124) (Villain-Gandossi 1979, 214–6), but the general form continued into the nineteenth century (Peterson 1973, 172–9). Probable medieval anchors of this type have been found at Kalmar, Sweden (Akerlund 1951, pl 27d). One of these had a fluke measuring 0.22 × 0.22m, with an arm 50mm thick (Fig 125). As this is only a little smaller than the known parts of the London anchor, the overall size of the Kalmar anchor is therefore a useful indicator of the original size of the London specimen. The Kalmar anchor had a shank 2.7m long, a wooden stock 2.7m long, and the distance between the ends of the arms was 1.33m. On this basis it is likely that the London anchor was about 3m long.

Considerable stress must have broken this anchor's arm, and it seems most likely that the find spot indicates the position of a large later medieval mooring site, and that the fluke had been broken when a ship tried to raise the anchor on setting sail.

Conclusions

The significant details of each fragment are given in Table 6 and many pieces are illustrated. However, it is important to consider the group as a whole as examples of medieval shipbuilding from the twelfth to the fifteenth centuries, taking account also of the parts of the more complete vessels; the Custom House boat from the late twelfth century and the Blackfriars ship 3 dating from about 1400.

Among the fragments are a few pieces of Baltic oak which were used in building the more substantial

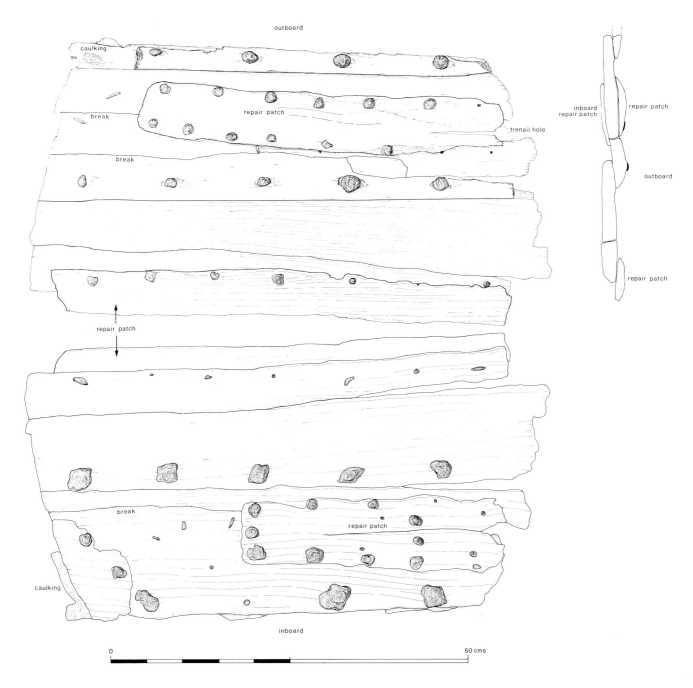

Fig 119 Bridewell, 1978: planking

vessels, and these were presumably seagoing. They date from the fourteenth century, a time when such timber is recorded as being imported into England for local use, so that it is uncertain whether the ship planks were from English-built vessels or from foreign ships. A comparison with the construction of foreign medieval ship finds may suggest an answer in due course.

The rest of the fragments were mostly of less substantial timbers, and the tree-ring studies of samples do show a local growth. These are most likely fragments of river vessels rather than seagoing ships, though the possible *Teredo* borings suggest that some at least did venture into the estuary for long periods and were perhaps from fishing boats.

The timbers are all of oak and seem to have been radially-cut from the logs. Few tool marks were found, even in the laps between planks, often because the fragments had become eroded while being reused in revetments. The woodworking tools represented seem to have been the axe and the auger or drill. A record was made of the diameters of 63 trenail holes from all of these medieval fragments, including a random sample from the Custom House boat and Blackfriars ship 3. These show that the drill bit sizes ranged from 17mm to 37mm in diameter, but that there was a peak in drilled holes at 23–26mm, at 30mm, and at 35mm diameters. These presumably reflect the most commonly-used drill sizes.

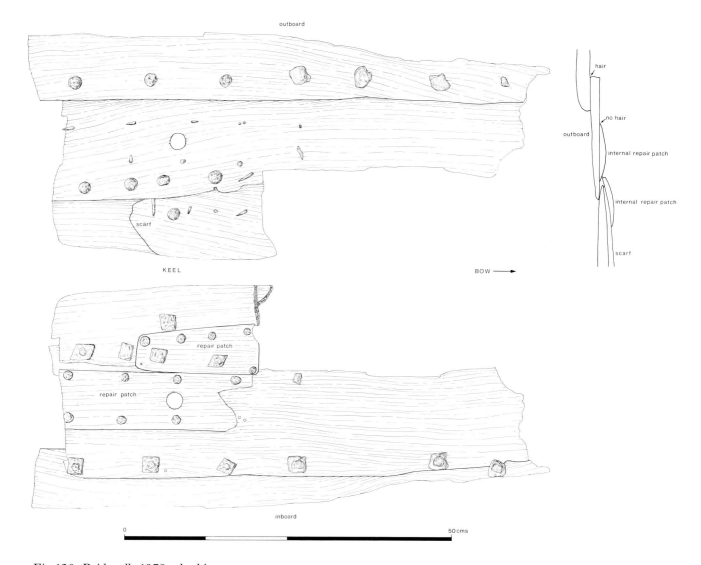

Fig 120 Bridewell, 1978: planking

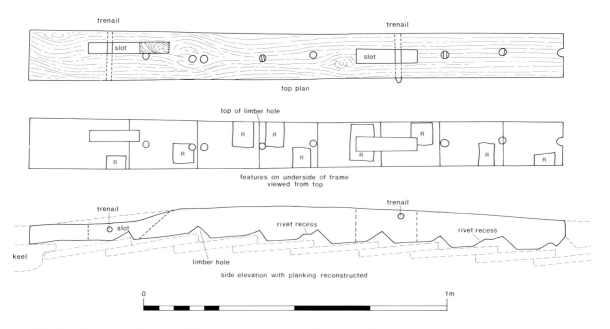

Fig 121 Baynards Castle, 1972: frame from fourteenth century dock

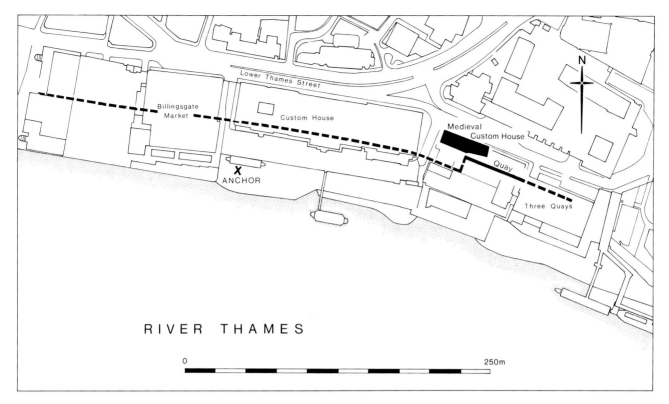

Fig 122 Location of a medieval anchor fluke from Custom House Wharf

The timbers were examined to establish whether or not particular proportions of timber shape and spacing of fastenings were favoured by shipwrights. The results show that there was considerable variation even in the same vessel, so there were no exact rules. However, the following were the averages: plank thickness:maximum plank width was 1:6.66 (based on 22 examples); maximum plank thickness:lap width was 1:1.7 (based on 51 examples); lap width:plank width was 1:4.38 (based on 22 examples); plank thickness:maximum rivet spacing was 1:5.15 (based on 49 examples); and maximum plank thickness:scarf length was 1:7.93 (based on 35 examples). The significance of these proportions may only become apparent when compared with ship finds elsewhere, but already a brief comparison of plank thickness:scarf length amongst the Bergen finds (Christensen 1985, 92–113) has shown a significant difference. This may reflect different traditions of the shipwrights who constructed the London vessels and those responsible for the Bergen vessels about what constituted a safe and watertight construction.

An estimate has been made to suggest how many different vessels the fragments represent. This has proved particularly difficult for it can only be based on differences in the timber sizes and in construction details. The scantling of timbers varied in different parts of the same ship, and repairs would introduce alternative methods of joinery and caulking, so that the conclusion cannot be other than speculative. Nevertheless, this matter should not be evaded, and it

seems most likely to the author that at least 15 medieval vessels were represented by actual hull structure, including the Custom House vessels and Blackfriars ship 3.

The repairs to the planks were all intended to make the vessels watertight, for they show that the most common damage took the form of splitting along the plank grain at riveted laps and at trenails, and it is clear that the stresses caused by the movement of timbers in the hull were considerable. Such movement was evidently the cause of felting in some of the hair caulking (*see Appendix 3*). Patches nailed or riveted onto the existing planks might stop a leak, but in the Custom House and Blackfriars ship 3 vessels it was necessary go further and replace whole lengths of planking. Another common problem was leakage at rivet and trenail positions, resulting in the need to refasten or even to use thicker trenails in a redrilled hole in the plank. Another feature, frequently noted, was a deeper erosion to the outboard face of the planking beside the laps. This was apparently due to eddies in the flow of water caused by the laps themselves, and also had the effect of eroding the caulking out of the laps. Similar plank erosion also occurred sometimes around nail heads on the outboard face of planks, resulting in an oval hollow.

When a ship or boat became too old and unsafe for further use it was broken up, and parts were often reused, as were the fragments described here which were mostly from waterfront revetments.

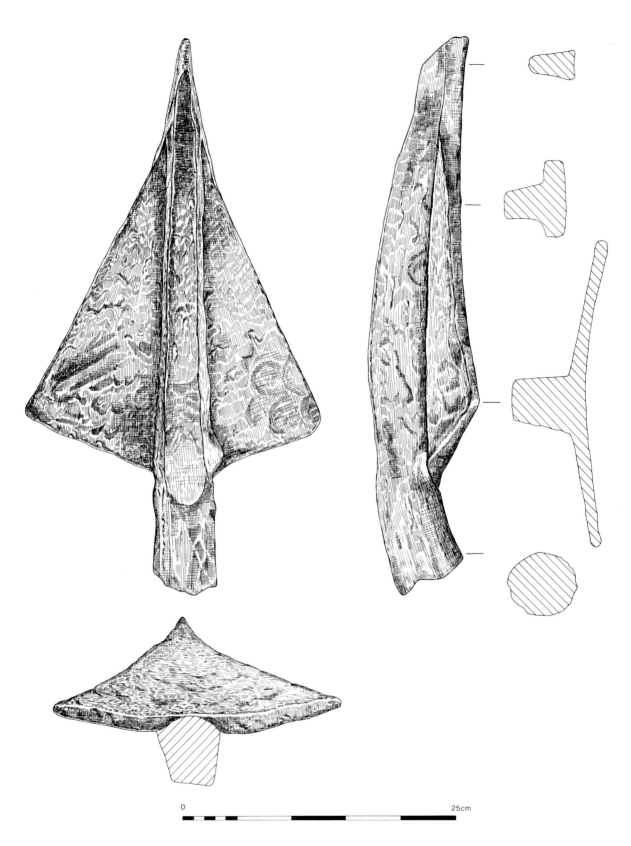

Fig 123 Medieval anchor fluke from Custom House Wharf

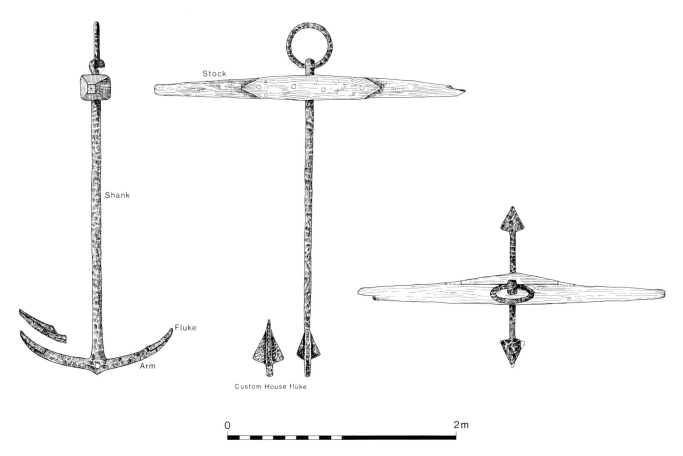

Fig 124 Medieval anchor fluke from Custom House Wharf, compared with a complete anchor from Kalmar, Sweden

Fig 125 The stowage of a medieval anchor (from Villain-Gandossi 1979)

6 Sixteenth-century reverse clinker boat, Morgans Lane, Southwark, 1987

Summary

Seven articulated planks were recovered from a late sixteenth-century waterfront, on a site excavated in 1987 by Alan Thompson (Figs 126 and 7). They were from the stern of a boat that had been built in 'reverse clinker', where the top of each lower plank overlapped outboard the bottom of the plank above. The vessel probably had a specialised use.

Site context and date

The fragments were found reused on the outer revetment of a moated house in Morgans Lane, Southwark. The revetment dated from the late sixteenth or early seventeenth centuries, which should be the approximate date of the reuse of the boat timbers (site context Tr G, NE cut, 722/89-727/67). Straight cuts across the planking indicate that it had been sawn from the remainder of the vessel's planking, and broken away from the sternpost. Four planks were sampled for tree-ring dating, and two (722 and 725) gave end dates in heartwood of 1555 and 1567. These indicate a felling date after 1577, but since both planks had felling dates close to each other, and bearing in mind the date of the context on site, they indicate a similar date also for the building of the boat. The fragments have been preserved at the Museum of London.

The planks are of oak, with an oak trenail, iron rivets, a caulking of hair and tar, and with outer surfaces coated with tar.

Bow or stern?

Six of the strakes (Figs 129–30, strakes A–F) end in a rough curving line of plank ends which suggests the form of the missing stem or sternpost, and in spite of

Fig 126 Part of a sixteenth-century reverse clinker boat found reused in a revetment at Morgan's Lane, Southwark. Note the curved end of the outboard face of the boat planking beside the left hand post (metric scale)

Fig 127 Inboard face of the reverse clinker planks at the end of the boat (metric scale)

the unusual reverse clinker construction, this and other features demonstrate that the planks are from a boat.

Although the end of the boat was pointed, which might suggest that it was the bow, it was then common for vessels to be pointed at both ends. Fortunately there are two scarf joints, one in strake G and the other in strake B, which were feathered outboard towards the surviving end of the boat, indicating that it was probably the stern. On this basis all the planking would be from the starboard side.

Log conversion

Each plank was of radially-cut oak (Fig 131), and reasonably free from knots. There was a definite twist in the planks as they curved towards the stern, but as the planks were damaged it was only possible to record this accurately in strake C. Without cutting sections through this plank it is not possible to establish how the twist was created, though a study of the grain suggests that the twist may have been caused by being bent into the required shape during the construction rather than by having been cut to that shape. No tool marks were noted.

Description

Each fragment was drawn, individually, from inside and outside, and in an assembled state, and a diagrammatic reconstruction of the end of the vessel was made (Fig 135).

Strakes

The six strakes were between 145–87mm wide, and 20–30mm in thickness. They tended to thin towards the sternpost, but only on the external face, and each had a bevel on the lower outboard edge where they overlapped each other (Figs 132 and 133), the laps being 37–50mm wide, and held by iron rivets.

The iron rivet nails had shanks 5mm square, and flat heads about 15mm in diameter on the outside of the boat. On the inboard side of the vessel the nails held diamond-shaped roves about 18mm × 28–20 × 22mm. Unfortunately the rivets had corroded, and it was difficult to establish their original appearance. One rove seemed to have been held by a bent nail, and two others by nails that might have had burred ends. A careful examination could not disclose any evidence that holes had been drilled through the overlapping

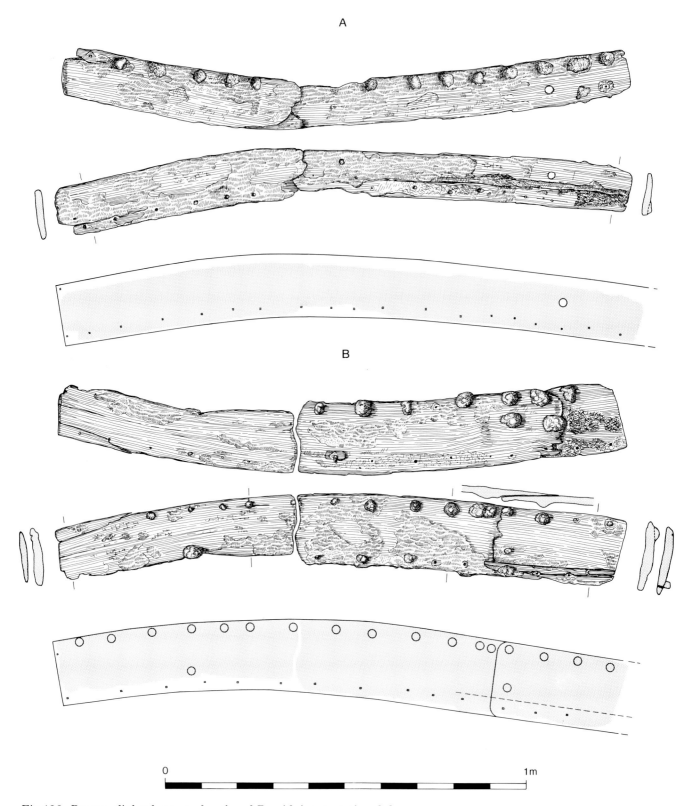

Fig 128 Reverse clinker boat: strakes A and B, with interpretations below

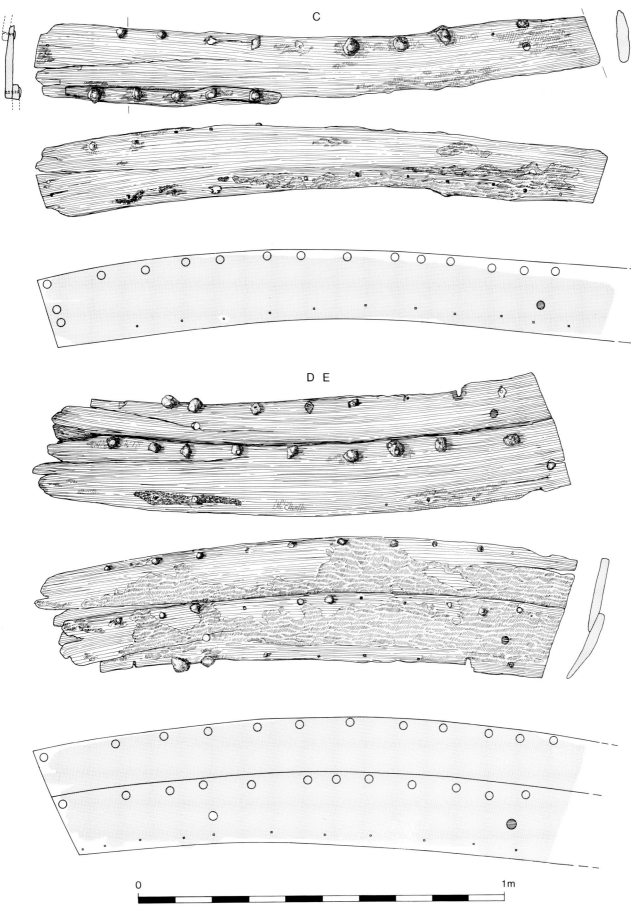

Fig 129 Reverse clinker boat: strakes C, D, and E, with interpretations below

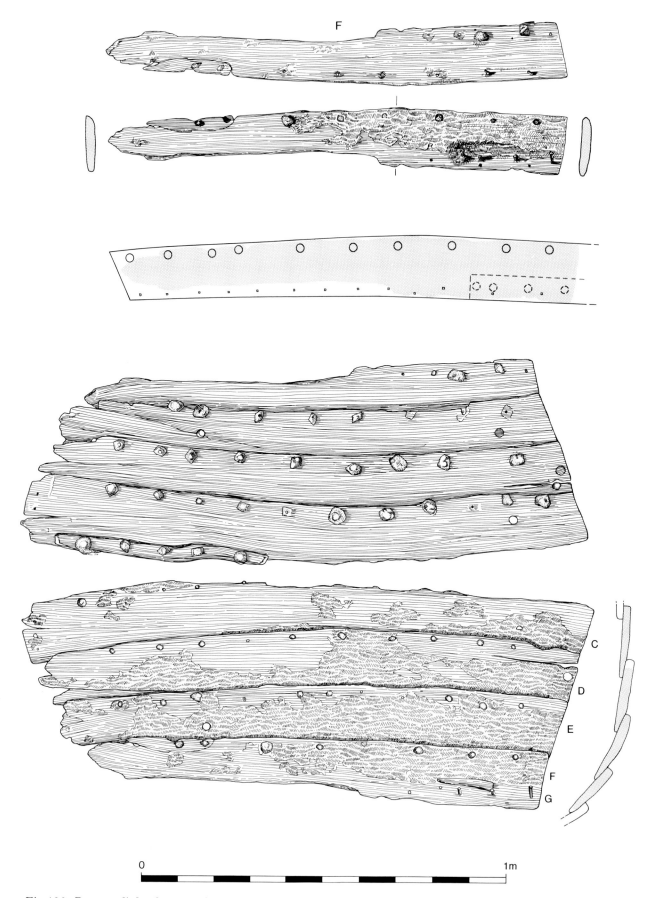

Fig 130 Reverse clinker boat: strake F and strakes C–F assembled, inboard (top) and outboard (bottom)

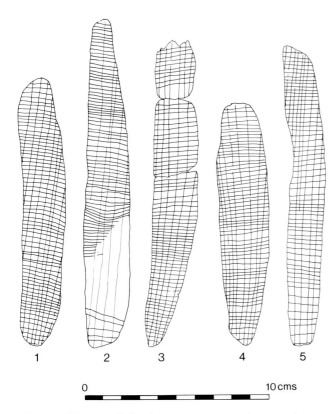

Fig 131 Reverse clinker boat: tree-ring sections: no 1 plank F; no 2 plank E; no 3 plank D; no 4 plank C; no 5 plank B

planks before the rivet nails were driven in place, particularly as in some cases the nails had distorted the timber. This is curious because a line of nails driven through near the edge of a plank could have split it, and it is more likely that the holes had been drilled. The rivets were spaced at 70–175mm centres, but on average were 100–140mm apart, except at the stern end where the sternpost presumably made it difficult to attach the fastenings.

Within the laps between the strakes was a caulking of hair and tar pressed flat by the adjacent planks. The hair was patchy, as if parts had been eroded out during the life of the boat and had not been replaced.

Of the two scarf joints, that in plank B was complete, 185mm long, with each plank feathered off to a sharp edge. The interior of the scarf had been caulked with hair, and each end was held by a rivet. The additional rivets holding the strake laps above and below the scarf made it a tight construction. Of the other scarf, in plank G, only an impression in a small piece of the planking remained in the tar coating the outside of the boat, so that the size of the scarf cannot be determined.

The external surfaces of the planks had been coated with a layer of tar up to 4mm thick in places, but elsewhere it was absent, as if it had been eroded away (Fig 134). Around the scarf in plank F the tar

was 10mm thick. On the outboard surfaces of planks A and C were traces of scorching.

Sternpost

Although the sternpost was not found, the ends of the planks provided useful information about that missing timber. The planks had been thinned to about 10mm thick externally towards the end where they originally joined the sternpost. The end was slightly bevelled inboard, though this was not always clear as the plank ends had been damaged, particularly where they had overlapped each other. Only on the end of plank C were found any of the holes left by nails which joined the plank to the sternpost. These reflect the shape of two nails, one with a shank 5mm square, but the other was round with a diameter of 8mm, and could have held a larger nail. The absence of nail holes in the width of the other plank ends, where they had survived, suggests that the planks had probably been fastened to the sternpost at the overlaps, as occurred in

Fig 132 Outboard face of the reverse clinker boat (metric scale)

Fig 133 Section through the reverse clinker boat planks (metric scale)

Fig 134 Detail of tar dressing on the outboard face of the reverse clinker boat planks (metric scale)

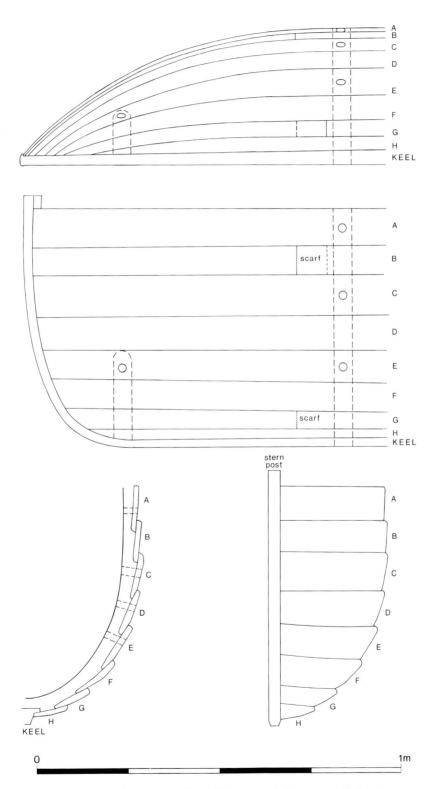

Fig 135 Suggested reconstruction of the stern of the reverse clinker boat

Blackfriars ship 3 (*see Chapter 3*), and that this accounts for the plank breakages at the laps.

The plank ends were presumably fastened into a rabbet in the side of the sternpost. A stain ending in a line at the end of plank C may reflect thewidth of the rabbet and show that it was 57mm deep. Furthermore the bevel at the end of the plank may reflect, very roughly, the angle of the sternpost at the end of the rabbet.

Frames

The trenail holes in the planks indicate the position of two frames in the boat. These are important, for the frames probably lay at right angles to the line of the keel, and thus allow the position of the planking to be reconstructed relative to the keel, indicating the width of the vessel at those frames. The trenails had been positioned in the mid-points of the planks, though there was unfortunately no impression of the frame on the planking surfaces.

The trenail holes in the planks show that the frames were 0.815m apart centre to centre. One trenail hole in the lower plank nearest the sternpost was 20mm in diameter, and another in a higher plank, was 19mm in diameter. The lower trenail hole penetrated the plank at an oblique angle.

The frame furthest away from the sternpost had been held by two trenails in the middle of alternate planks. The head of the lower trenail, still in position in the frame, was 25mm in diameter and not wedged, and the higher trenail hole was 20mm in diameter. No indication of the width of the frame was preserved on the inner face of the frame. The greater diameter of one trenail hole suggests that it was a replacement.

Reconstruction

There are several important clues to make possible a tentative reconstruction of part of this boat. Most important are two scarf joints, both facing the same direction, which show that the boat fragment is probably from the starboard side at the stern; and the vertical downward curve of the hull is preserved in the angle of the lap joints of the clinker planks furthest away from the sternpost (Fig 135).

The twist in plank C is also important for, just as the face of the feathered end of the plank was presumably vertical where it was fastened to the sternpost, so, forward of this position, the plank soon became inclined at an angle of about 52° from the horizontal, thereby producing the angle of this part of the side.

A side elevation of each plank shows that it curved down towards the stern, but when allowance is made for the horizontal and vertical curvature of the side of the boat it becomes clear that the edges of the strakes ran horizontally towards the sternpost.

Since the trenail holes reflect the frame positions, and the frames probably lay at a right angle to the line of the keel and sternpost, it would seem that the width of the boat just forward of the second frame from the stern was about 2.8m.

Sequence of construction

As the boat has a reverse clinker construction, the lower planks overlapping the upper, the sequence of building is unusual. Roves on the planking under the frame positions show that the two frames must have been fastened in position after the planking had been completed. The horizontal run of the strakes to the stern, the need to fasten each lower strake above the upper, and to fix upper strakes to the sternpost before the lower strakes had been fastened together, all suggest that the boat had been built upside down, starting at the sheerstrake or gunwale and ending at the keel. Establishing exactly how this was undertaken in this particular case would depend upon the survival of more boat structure, especially the stem and sternposts and the keel.

Reverse clinker boatbuilding is still carried out occasionally, and various claims have been made in its favour. For example, it is supposed to be easier to fit the planks as they lie flatter on the boat's sections, and there are thought to be benefits for faster sailing but these are unlikely to have influenced the sixteenth-century boatbuilder. The most practical gain, which might well have concerned the sixteenth-century owner, is that the interior of the boat would have been easier to clean out (Leather 1987, 102–3).

Use of the boat

Since the only apparent benefit of building a boat in reverse clinker is to enable it to be more easily cleaned out, this perhaps provides a clue to its use. Possibly it carried dung or some such cargo that had to be shovelled out. Certainly, the vessel seems to have had a fairly short life, perhaps as little as twenty-five years, but during that time it had received considerable wear, the thick tar coating of the outer planking having been applied to help waterproof a leaking vessel. In spite of such efforts, the hair caulking was absent in some places, and would have caused leaks, and the outer face of the planking had been burnt in one area.

7 Blackfriars ship 2, seventeenth century, City of London, 1969

Summary

Blackfriars ship 2 was a clinker-built river vessel, perhaps a lighter with no mast and sail. When it sank *c* 1670 it was carrying a cargo of bricks, and in its bottom were traces of a previous cargo of coal.

Discovery

Blackfriars ship 2 was found on 5 June 1969 during the mechanical excavation of a large coffer-dam sunk in the bed of the River Thames in the Blackfriars area, just west of the foot of Paul's Stairs. It lay roughly east-west, aligned with the tidal current, about 2m below the modern river bed and with the bottom of its surviving eastern end at about 2.56m below OD, and the surviving western end (in reality about the middle of the vessel) at about 2.87m below OD (Fig 136).

The vessel was discovered when a mechanical grab dug away its western end within the coffer-dam, and the site contractor alerted the Guildhall Museum to the find. In the absence of the author Roger Inman, a volunteer site supervisor with the City of London Excavation Group, was asked to excavate and record the wreck quickly with the help of volunteers, and Ralph Merrifield from the Guildhall Museum undertook the photography. The excavators uncovered the cargo of bricks and the visible inner planking and frames of the vessel which they recorded (Fig 137), but as no nautical specialist was present the excavation team was unable to compile a detailed record of the construction. As a consequence scarf joints in the planks were not recorded and it is not now known which end was the bow. The excavators were able to record carefully the dating evidence of objects within the wreck.

Later the author examined the wreck which had by then been broken up and its timbers scattered, though a small portion of the hull remained along part of the edge of the coffer-dam (Fig 137). The scattered timbers were collected and taken from the site for study and recording. The result was the publication of a short report (Marsden 1971), but with no attempt at interpretation. In the light of more recent boat discoveries from London, it is now possible to understand better how this vessel was built, and, as much more information has recently been recovered from the surviving timbers, it is also possible to suggest what it looked like. Little of this vessel has been preserved, but most of the frames described and two small pieces of planking are at the Shipwreck Heritage Centre, Hastings.

Dating evidence

The dating evidence, described in detail elsewhere (Marsden 1971, 96–7), comprised several clay pipes of the period 1650–70 which were found on the bottom boards, together with part of the stem of a wine glass. Immediately beneath the vessel were twenty-five pipe bowls, all of the period 1650–70, a broken wine glass

Fig 136 General view of ship 2, west to the right, seventeenth century (scale of feet)

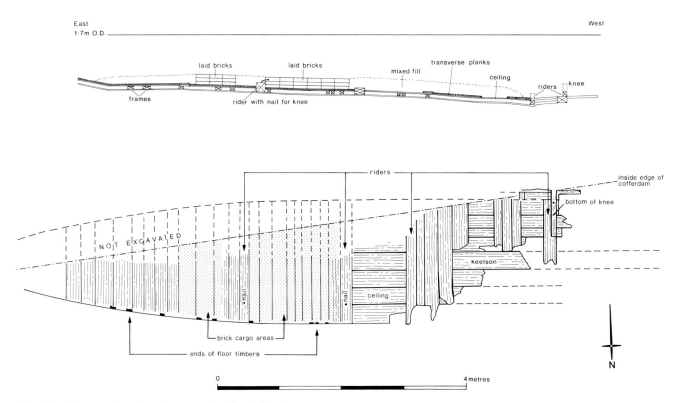

Fig 137 Plan and section along north side of ship 2

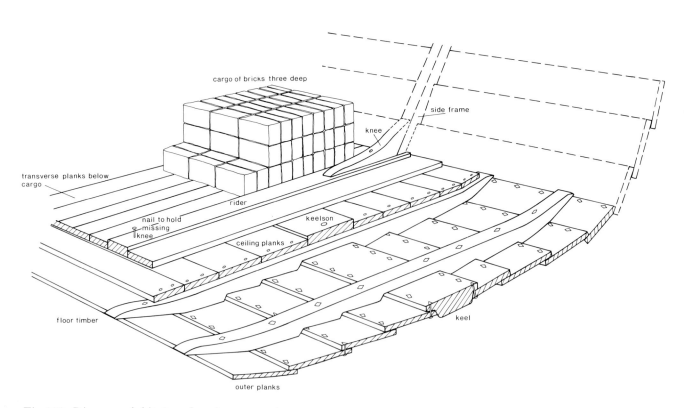

Fig 138 Diagram of ship 2 to show its construction

stem, parts of a Bellarmine jug, and several fragments of other pottery including buff ware with the pale greenish-yellow glaze typical of the seventeenth century. These objects seem to have been rubbish dumped into the river rather than items used on the vessel. They indicate that the vessel sank in the third quarter of the seventeenth century, and as the period when building bricks were needed in very large quantities occurred soon after the Great Fire of 1666, this is the most likely historical context for the barge and its cargo.

Ship construction
(Fig 138)

Materials

The keel was of elm, the frames and outer skin planks were of oak, a sample of an inner plank was of pine, and the planks and frames were fastened together with iron nails and rivets. The species of timber were kindly identified by Dr M Stant of the Royal Botanic Gardens, Kew. Animal hair had been used as caulking.

Keel

The keel (Fig 139) was tangentially cut, and was plank-like, about 0.2m wide and 0.05m thick, with a rabbet 0.02m deep on each side for the garboard strakes (Figs 140 and 141). The frames included a rebate over the keel and thus fixed the relationship of the keel to the hull bottom.

Frames

There were two forms of frame: the floor-timbers in the bottom (Fig 142), and side-frames reinforcing the sides. Of these only parts of the floor-timbers were saved for study. They were between 0.04m and 0.07m wide and roughly 0.05m deep, and were stepped (joggled) on their undersides to take the clinker planking. Some retained a little sapwood, showing that limited care had been taken in the choice of the timber. The spacing of the frames was not clear for they were covered by a ceiling of planks. However, the upper surface of a fragment of the keel bore the impression of two frames 0.494m apart, although in a drawing of the vessel in situ the spacing of frames at their ends was given as 0.076m, 0.152m (twice), 0.355m, 0.457m, and 0.533m. The cause of the apparent irregularity in this spacing is not clear and the photographs, which show the ends of those frames, do not suggest that they had been displaced.

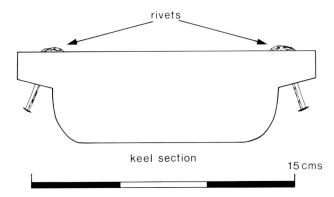

Fig 139   Section of elm keel from ship 2

Fig 140   Upper face of the keel of ship 2 showing rivets and the impression of a frame, left

Fig 141   Underside of the keel of ship 2 with traces of the garboard strake riveted to the rabbet

Ten of the recovered floor-timber fragments were drawn mostly in side elevation, and one was drawn in plan (Fig 142). The shaping of their outboard faces shows that there were three strakes on each side, beyond which was the turn of the bilge. The frames are particularly valuable because they reflect the changing shape of the bottom of the hull. In some cases they show the rebate for the keel, and from that it is possible to calculate the middle line of the keel almost exactly. It is clear from this that the lap between strakes 3 and 4 at the turn of the bilge was at the following distances from the centre line: 1.02m, 1.00m, 0.99m, 0.97m,

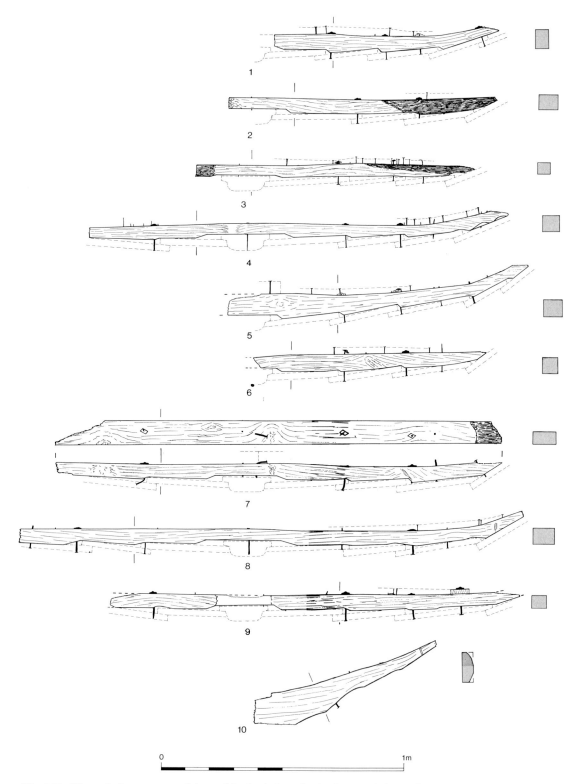

Fig 142 Floor-timbers recovered from ship 2; their order in the wreck is not known

0.92m, 0.90m, 0.89m, 0.88m, and 0.80m. Where the longest frames reflect a flat bottom in the central part of the vessel, the two shorter frames, 0.92m and 0.80m long, show a more rounded bottom towards one or both ends of the vessel.

The relative position in the vessel of some of the detached frames is suggested by the points at which they had been severed by the southern wall of the coffer-dam which cut across the wreck diagonally. The eastern end of the vessel lay just outside the south side of the coffer-dam, and the western end lay wholly within the coffer-dam but had been destroyed by the mechanical excavator before the wreck was found. Thus the ends of the frames which are almost complete mostly derive from the northern side of the vessel.

In the centre of the vessel the floor-timbers were approximately horizontal and reflect a hull bottom about 2m wide. At the eastern end, however, the bottom appears to have narrowed to nearer 1m, and to have become slightly more rounded. A photograph of the broken western end of the wreck shows that there too the hull bottom was beginning to become a little more rounded, so that it seems that the widest part of the vessel was just west of the brick cargo.

Outer planking

The outer skin of planks was clinker-built and held by iron rivets. Each plank was about 25–30mm thick and had been radially cut. In a small fragment one strake had overlapped the next by 30–40mm and contained a caulking of felt-like hair, the lap being held by iron rivets spaced at intervals of about 0.07m. At the east end of the north side of the vessel the bottom planking, 25mm thick, had been sheathed, probably in oak about 5mm thick. This was fastened by many small iron nails with square shanks, spoon-shaped pointed ends and with waisted flat heads (Fig 143). The iron rivets were unusual, the point of each nail having been pulled through the hole in each rove and simply bent over, leaving about 20mm of the pointed end hanging down. In this case the nail shank was about 4mm square.

There were scarf joints in the planks, though none was recorded *in situ*. One was found in a loose plank fragment that was over 0.105m long and seemed to be a simple lap scarf, held by at least one rivet near the outboard end, and by several small tacks along the outboard (presumably) edge. The roves were about 14–20mm square or slightly diamond-shaped and 1.5mm thick, and were distinctive for being high-domed. The roves were cut from an iron bar by a chisel whose shape was preserved on two edges of the rove, and in one case two roves were found still partly joined together.

The strakes were held to the frames by iron nails driven from outboard and bent over diamond-shaped iron roves on top of the frames inboard. Each nail shank was rectangular in section, about 6mm × 4mm. with an almost flat head and a chisel-shaped point. The nails presumably took this rectangular shape to enable them to be driven into the wood with their narrow sides across the grain so as to minimise the risk of splitting frames. However, they were not always used in this way. In one frame four of the rivet nails were used properly, but in two others they were not. The general lack of distortion in the wood surrounding the nail shanks suggests that a small hole had been drilled through each frame before the nail was driven into place, but this is far from clear.

Although the planking was no longer attached to the frame fragments, the surviving nail heads and notches in the undersides of the frames show almost exactly where the planks had lain. The nail shanks were either about 25mm or 50mm long below the frame, indicating that some rivet nails allowed for the thickness of one strake, and in other cases allowed for two overlapping planks. Where the nail had been driven through two thicknesses of planking it was sometimes possible to see an impression of the central joint on the faces of the nail. Cut into the outboard or lower face of the floor-timbers were small hollows for the roves of the rivets that held the overlapping planks

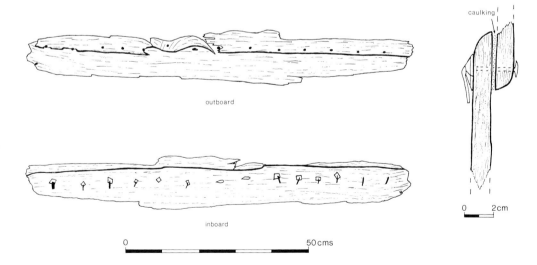

Fig 143   Fragment of clinker planking from ship 2 with bent nails through the roves

Table 5   Strake widths in cm

frame	strake 1	strake 2	strake 3	strake 4
1	24	24	26	–
4	26	26	26	?21
5	26	27	30	19
6	26	27	–	–
7	26	28	31	–
8	26	30	30	–

together. By using the step sizes, the rivet nail positions, and the rove hollows on the frame an accurate reconstruction of the missing plank widths can be shown (Table 5).

At the eastern end of the remains the author found a small portion of planking still *in situ* which appeared to be curving into the eastern end. It was here that the width of the planking narrowed to 0.15m, 0.177m, and 0.216m. The rivets were spaced at intervals of about 70mm with the roves inboard and with the turned nail points bent towards the keel. The lap between the clinker strakes was 30mm wide. A frame lay on top of the planks at an oblique angle to them and was therefore evidently running in towards the stem or stern. At that point the outboard face of the planking was covered with a thin skin of wooden sheathing fastened by many short iron nails.

Ceiling

Above the floor-timbers was a ceiling of planks, 30–40mm thick and approximately 0.25m wide, held to the top of the frames by iron nails (Fig 144). These nails had rectangular shanks about 6 × 3mm, slightly domed faceted heads and chisel-shaped points, and they were driven down into the frames at various angles, with their long sides both along and across the grain of the wood. On the flat top of the frames there were generally only a few such nails, but at the turn of the bilge there were many, no doubt to ensure that the ceiling planks remained in place. One frame, only 0.07m wide at that point, contained ten nails holding the ceiling.

Keelson

There was a keelson along the centreline of the vessel above the floor-timbers (Fig 145). It was about 0.28m wide and was fastened through each frame and into the keel by an iron nail driven from inboard. The

Fig 144 Fore and aft ceiling planks (below scale), keelson (under point of scale), and transverse riders, from ship 2. View to east (scale of feet)

Fig 145 The keelson of ship 2 (under scale) below transverse planks (scale of feet)

Fig 146 Transverse riders overlying the ceiling planks of ship 2. The nails (left) once fastened a side knee. View to south-west (scale of feet)

Fig 147 Knee fastened to a rider on the south side of ship 2 (scale of feet)

Fig 148 Knee overlying a rider, view to east, ship 2

thickness of the keelson was not recorded, but, judging from the height of a nail that apparently held it in position, was 45mm thick.

Transverse riders

Five transverse timbers, each about 0.16m square, were found on the bottom of the vessel, apparently overlying the ceiling (Fig 146). It is not absolutely

clear how they were fastened to the bottom. Their purpose was evidently to hold at each end the lower part of the knee which supported the now missing side-frames of the vessel. One knee remained (Figs 147 and 148), at the surviving western end of the wreck, and this was held to the rider by a long iron nail with its head inboard. Other knees had been broken off, but long nail fastenings remained and are visible in the photographs to show their location (Fig 146). One photograph suggests that the knees held the lower ends of side-frames on the outboard side of the knees, though no side-frames had survived.

Transverse planks

The longitudinal ceiling planking was covered by transverse planks about 20mm thick and 0.09–0.25m wide (Fig 145), lying immediately beneath the cargo of bricks, possibly to protect the hull, including the ceiling. The planks were probably loose and only a temporary protection, unlike the ceiling which was nailed to the top of the frames. The transverse planks also lay between the transverse riders.

Damage and repairs

No certain evidence of damage or repair was noted in the fragments recovered. It might be said, however, that the presence of many iron nails in the top of the frames at the turn of the bilge was probably due to the need to make extra sure that the ceiling planking there was held in place.

Reconstruction of the vessel

The aim of a reconstruction is not only to establish what the vessel looked like and its size, but also to show how it had been used. In this case the central part of the hull had a cargo of red bricks lying in groups between the knees that supported the sides, so it would seem that the vessel was a barge of some kind. Its flat bottom, plank-like keel and the small scantling of its frames all show that it was probably a river craft that would not have sailed at sea. There are important limitations, however, since not only was the vessel's bottom incomplete when excavated, but also its sides were lost and the archaeological record was only partial. It would have been particularly valuable if the scarf joints in the planks had been recorded as evidence of the bow end.

The greatest width of the flat hull bottom was, judging from the longest frame fragments, about 2m. The lower part of the curve of the turn of the bilge is preserved in the ends of the floor-timbers, indicating a beam of roughly 3–4m. Naturally, the original height of the sides amidships cannot be calculated.

Although the bow end is not known there was some suggestion that the eastern end was sharp. The survival of some lower planking at that end was examined by the author, and was found to be sloping at an angle of about 20 degrees, as if the bottom was forming a V-shape as it approached that end. Some of the frame fragments show that towards the eastern end the vessel's bottom was becoming narrower and more

rounded. It is just possible that the vessel had an inclined flat 'swim head' end like a modern punt, but in that case the bottom would be expected to have been flatter and broader.

As the wreck appeared to include the widest, and therefore probably the midships, part of the vessel, it is significant that no evidence of the method of propulsion was found, for if it had been a sailing craft the mast was likely to have been stepped near amidships or towards the bow. The alternative possibility is that the vessel was a lighter without a mast and sail, and that it worked with the tides and was guided by oars and poles. Further excavation in the river bed at the eastern end could be extremely helpful, not only in searching for a possible mast-step but also in seeking the plank scarf joints that would show which was the bow end.

In conclusion, then, it seems that the vessel was a river barge of some form, about 3–4m in the beam, and with a probable length, judging from the discovered remains, of between 12m and 16m.

Sequence of construction

The method of construction can in part be reconstructed from the fragments of timber, though these relate only to the ship's bottom. It is clear that the keel must have been laid first and that the lower outer planking was attached to it by iron rivets clinkerwise. The form of the rivets that held the overlapping planks is unusual for although they comprised a nail and diamond-shaped rove or washer, the nail point had been bent over the rove. This is in contrast to the (probably) normal method of riveting at that time, which is described by Moxon in his account of smithing (1703, 26–7) and which was used on all the earlier boat remains from London. Moxon says that 'rivetting is to batter the edges of a shank over a plate, or other iron'. The nails used to 'rivet' the overlapping planks in Blackfriars ship 2 were 55–60mm long, and those used to hold the planks to the frames were about 0.13m long. In both cases the points of the nails overhung the rove by about 15mm. The distinctive features of these nails were the rectangular shank and the fact that the end was not pointed but formed a chisel-like edge. This must have been a type of nail used in carpentry to help avoid splitting timber. That there were various types of nails used in wooden shipbuilding a century and a half later than this wreck is shown by Falconer, who describes, for example,

> 'Four-penny nails, are one inch and a half long, have sharp points ...', but 'Six-penny nails, are one inch and a half long, they have flat points ...'
> (Falconer, 1815, 291)

A layer of felt-like hair caulking was placed between the overlapping planks before the rivets were fastened.

After the clinker outer planking was fastened together the floor-timbers were attached by iron nails driven from outboard and turned through roves on top of the frames. It is clear that the frames had been secured in position after the shell of planks had been fastened together, for there were small hollows cut in the undersides of the frames to accommodate the inboard ends of plank rivets.

It is not absolutely clear if the riders or the ceiling planks were next fastened into position. However, drawings made on site indicate that the ceiling planks did not pass under the riders, in which case the riders and the knees which they supported to hold the side-frames, and the side-frames themselves, were probably next erected inside the shell of clinker planking. After the longitudinal ceiling planks of the hold were attached by iron nails driven from inboard, the transverse planking was next placed in the hold, though this may have been merely a temporary feature to protect the hold from damage.

Use of the ship

Cargo

The vessel was carrying a cargo of red bricks, each of which measured about 0.216 × 0.114 × 0.07m (8.5 × 4.5 × 2.75ins) (Figs 149 and 150). They lay on their edges along the long axis of the vessel in two areas of the hull on top of the transverse planking (Fig 151). A third area of transverse planking at about the middle of

the vessel did not include bricks, as if some had already been unloaded. The easternmost group was three bricks deep (Fig 152), three fore-and-aft, and there were at least eleven rows across the vessel, seven of which lay north of the central longitudinal axis of the vessel. This means that there were probably at least fourteen rows of bricks, giving a minimum total of about 126 bricks.

The western group was three bricks deep, six fore-and-aft, and there were about ten rows north of the centreline of the vessel. This would give a total of about twenty rows across, and a total of 360 bricks in that group. Thus there were about 485 bricks still lying in the hold, though between these two groups there were many loose bricks, so that it would be fair to say that the vessel was carrying a cargo of well over 500 bricks. A possible earlier cargo is suggested by the presence of small pieces of coal at the east end in the bottom of the vessel. These were mixed with brick fragments.

Contemporary river vessels

Many of the common types of river vessel in the port are pictured in the seventeenth-century views of London by Visscher (c 1616), Hollar (1647), and Ogilby and Morgan (1677). Of these the Visscher view is poorly drawn and has little value in this context. However, a detailed comparison of the archaeological and pictorial evidence for Baynards Castle shows that the most reliable view is that of Hollar, though the types of vessels that he depicts are no different from those shown by Ogilby and Morgan.

Fig 149 Cargo of bricks from ship 2, view to south-west

Fig 150 Cargo of bricks from ship 2, view to south

Fig 151 Two areas of stacked brick cargo from ship 2, separated by a rider, partly removed (scale of feet)

Fig 152 Section of ship 2 through the stacking of the western group of bricks, view to south (scale of feet)

The river vessels shown by Hollar (Fig 153) comprise swim-head barges, here shown each with a mast and square sail on a mast stepped well forward, and with a long rudder on a sternpost, and lighters which were pointed at both ends, with no mast and sail, but with a steering oar at the stern and two sweeps at the bow. They had a short deck at bow and stern and a crew of three. The third type were wherries, small rowing boats for carrying passengers.

The vessels shown in Ogilby and Morgan (Fig 154) were *wherries*, *swim-headed barges* with a mast and square sail mounted well forward, and at the stern a long median rudder, *hoys* with a mast stepped well forward for a fore-and-aft sail, and *lighters*, short and rounded with no mast and sail, but steered by two men with sweeps at the bow. These vessels were between a half and one-third of the length of a swim-head barge. David Sturdy has identified the most common vessel types as western barges, lighters, hoys, and wherries (Sturdy 1977).

It is unlikely that Blackfriars ship 2 was a swim-headed barge since it seemed to have had at least one pointed end. Although the missing keelson could have included a mast-step or towing post, the vessel does seem to fit the known characteristics of lighters, which used the tides, were guided by oars and a steering oar

and were primarily used to lighten cargo ships moored in the stream, hence their name. Having no method of sustained propulsion it is unlikely that they travelled far to collect their cargoes. The cargo of bricks and the probable previous cargo of coal are consistent with what is known about lighters, for there were sources of bricks close to the River Thames. Blackfriars ship 2 was wrecked soon after the Great Fire of London in 1666, and it seems relevant that after an Act of Parliament had been passed in 1667 for the rebuilding of London, lifting building restrictions to encourage rebuilding (Bell 1938, 38–41), many brickworks were established to supply the City, though their locations are not always known since many were short-lived. Brickworks were certainly situated at that time at St Giles in the Fields, Islington, Moorfields, Spitalfields, Whitechapel, Shoreditch, Hoxton, and Clerkenwell, though these were all some distance from the river (Reddaway 1951; pers comm Ian Betts).

However, the suggested earlier cargo of coal is also a useful clue to the type of vessel, for it was almost certainly sea-coal from the Newcastle area that had been shipped down the east coast of England in colliers. On arrival at London it was normally discharged into lighters, though in the Plague year, 1665, this transfer had to take place downstream

Fig 153 River craft on the Thames, from Hollar's view of London, 1647: A swim-head barges; B lighters; C moored lighters; D wherries

Fig 154 River craft on the Thames, from Ogilby and Morgan's view of London, 1677: A swim-head barges; B hoys; C lighters; D wherries

between Deptford and Blackwall, so as to avoid contact with the people of London (Broodbank 1921, I, 65). There is no possibility that Blackfriars ship 2 itself could have carried the cargo of coal by sea.

Loss of the ship

Although the cause of the loss of the vessel is unknown, it is clear that it sank aligned with the river current and that the alluvium soon buried the wreck.

Her bottom lay at about 2.9m below OD, but although nowadays mean high water is at 3.47m above OD it was rather lower than that in the seventeenth century, so that at high tide the wreck lay fairly deeply submerged. Immediately below the wreck there was a layer of grey silt 13mm thick, below which was a layer of sand almost 80mm thick. That in turn overlay a thicker layer of grey silt. These deposits indicate that the river was probably muddy and locally not too fast-flowing when the vessel sank.

8 Ship and boat fragments of the sixteenth to seventeenth centuries

Summary

These fragments of ship and boat timbers are from deposits provisionally dated to the sixteenth and seventeenth centuries, pending a full site study. Summaries of the likely contexts are given below from information in the Museum of London site archives.

37-46 Bankside, Southwark, 1987

(site code 37BS 87)

Excavations on this site exposed three parallel timber revetments, probably fronting the River Thames, and parts of boats that had been reused in them (Figs 155–58). Almost all the boat timbers were recovered from revetment 21, and seven of these were tree-ring

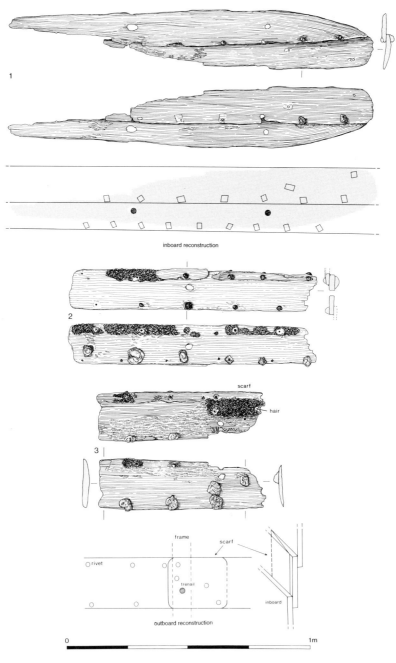

Fig 155   37–46 Bankside, 1987: no 1 context 199/200; no 2 context 183; no 3 context 184

160

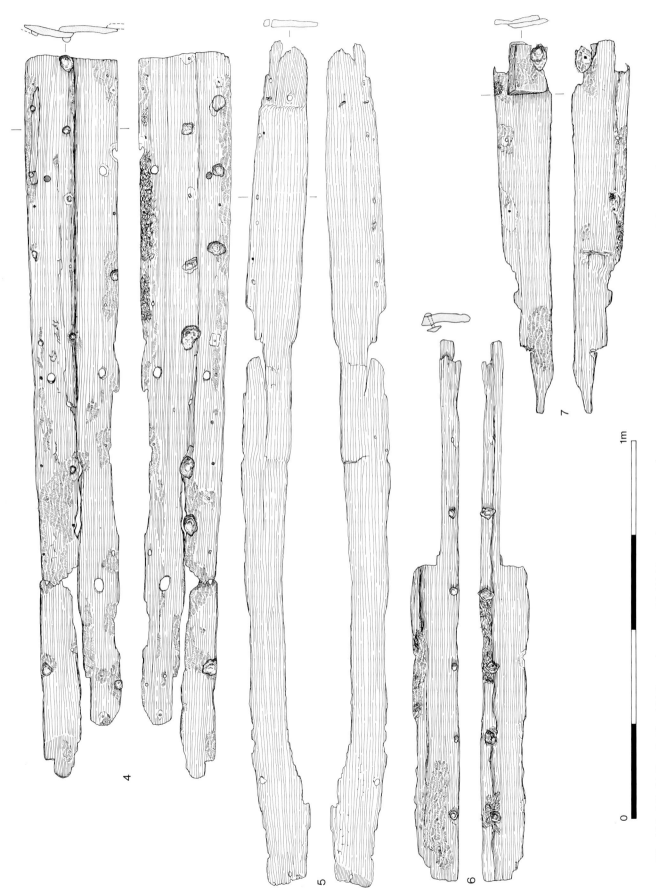

4

5

6

7

1m

0

Fig 156   37–46 Bankside, 1987: no 4 context 296/157; no 5 context 193, revet 21; no 6 context 196; no 7 context 185, revet 21

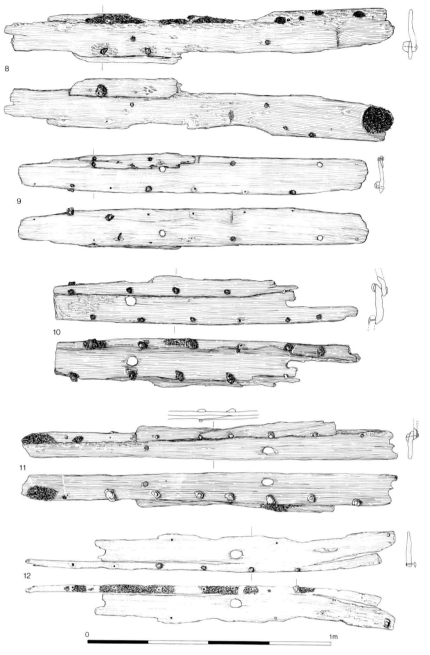

Fig 157 37–46 Bankside, 1987: no 8 context 188/197; no 9 context 205/268,
revet 21; no 10 context 267/261, revet 21; no 11 context 267/266; no 12
context 202, revet 21

dated in heartwood to between 1416 and 1476, so that
the likely building date of the latest boat (contexts 188-
197) was about 1500. Allowing some years for the use
of the vessel, it seems that the revetment was being
repaired during the sixteenth century.

Of the fragments of clinker planking that were
recovered all were of oak and most radially cut, though
four planks (contexts 205/268, 188-197, 200-199,
181) may have been tangentially cut (Fig 158). The
maximum plank thicknesses ranged from 15mm to
36mm, and the laps, all of which were held by iron
rivets, were mostly about 40mm wide. There was little

distinctive about the wood construction, though the
caulking methods did show some variety. The lap
caulking was generally of matted hair impregnated in
tar, but in one case (contexts 267-266) it was mixed
with thick tar. In three planks (contexts 202, 298-299,
183) the hair had been carefully laid across the laps
(Fig 159). Hair was also used in the planking scarf
joints. Two trenails that once held the frames and
planks together were of oak.

Two planks (contexts 200-199, 184) had possible
Teredo channels (*Fig 17*), each about 3mm wide,
and in another plank (contexts 267-266) the lap

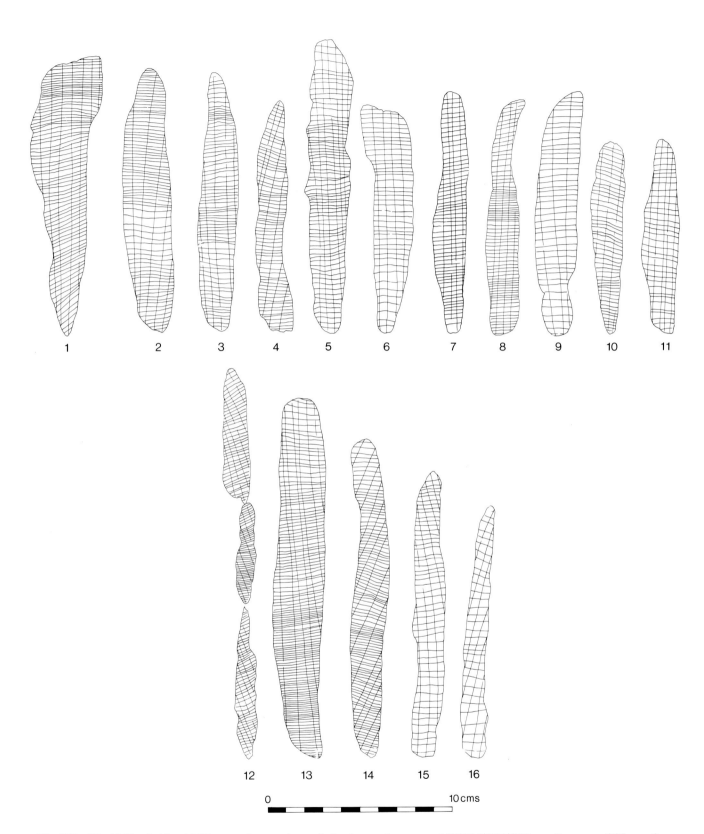

Fig 158 37–46 Bankside, 1987, tree-ring sections of planks: no 1 context 165/194/254/297; no 2 context 200; no 3 context 202; no 4 context 199 fastened to 200; no 5 context 183, in revet 21; no 6 context 195/196; no 7 context 187, A; no 8 context 266, revet 212; no 9 context 187, revet 21; no 10 context 182, revet 21; no 11 context 187, revet 21; no 12 context 181, revet 21; no 13 context 184, revet 21; no 14 context 188/197; no 15 context 185, revet 21, no 16 context 205/268

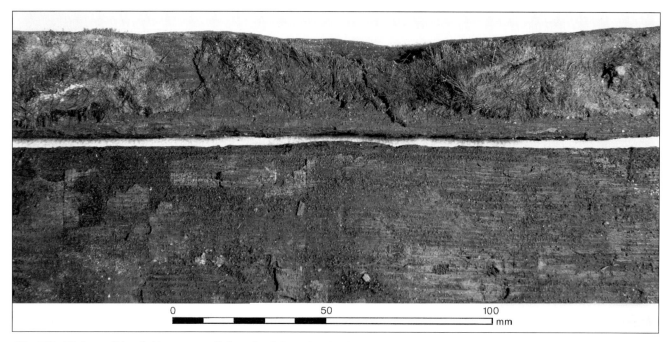

Fig 159 Hair caulking laid across a clinker plank lap, ?early sixteenth century (37 BS 87), context 202

had been water-eroded to only 5mm wide in places, though this may have happened after the planking was reused.

Repairs were apparent, and in one (contexts 187-296) a former row of square rivet holes had been filled with small oak pegs (Fig 160), and new iron rivets had been fastened in the intermediate positions. An

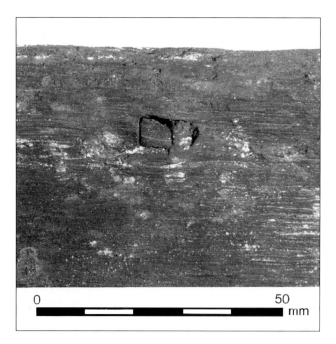

Fig 160 Oak peg filling a former rivet hole, ?early sixteenth century (37 BS 87, context 187)

individual oak peg filling a rivet hole was also noted in another plank (context 183). A patch 13mm thick, held by small iron nails, had been inserted into the face of a further plank (context 205/268), but it is not clear what damage it was repairing. One unusual repair was a trenail hole which had been bunged with a piece of cork (contexts 187-296).

This collection was very similar as a group, though the different caulking methods could suggest that at least two vessels were represented.

Site context no 184 in revetment 21
(Fig 155, no 3)

An oak plank fragment 0.69m long, from a clinker-built boat, was 0.19m wide and up to 24mm thick. It was radially cut, and on one lap face there were the cut marks of an axe or adze lying at an oblique angle to the edge. Two laps survived, 30mm and 40mm wide. There was a caulking of hair about 1.5mm thick, possibly mixed with tar. Iron rivets were spaced between 182–88mm apart, and the rivet nails had shanks about 4mm square. The rivets were too corroded to show the size and form of the roves.

There was a single lap scarf 0.23m long at one end, with the plank feathering off. A central iron nail at one end had a shank 4mm square, and its circular head had a diameter of 10mm, judging from the clear impression left in the wood surface. Within the scarf was a caulking of hair about 1.5mm thick. An irregular

Fig 161 (opposite) Gun and Shot Wharf, 1988: no 1 context 120/39, outboard (top), inboard (middle), without patch (bottom); no 2 context 119/38; no 3 context 139/37; no 4 context 119/38; no 5 context 118/40; no 6 context 117/41; no 7 context 149/274; no 8 context 158/449, 451; no 9 context 138/36; no 10 context 139/37

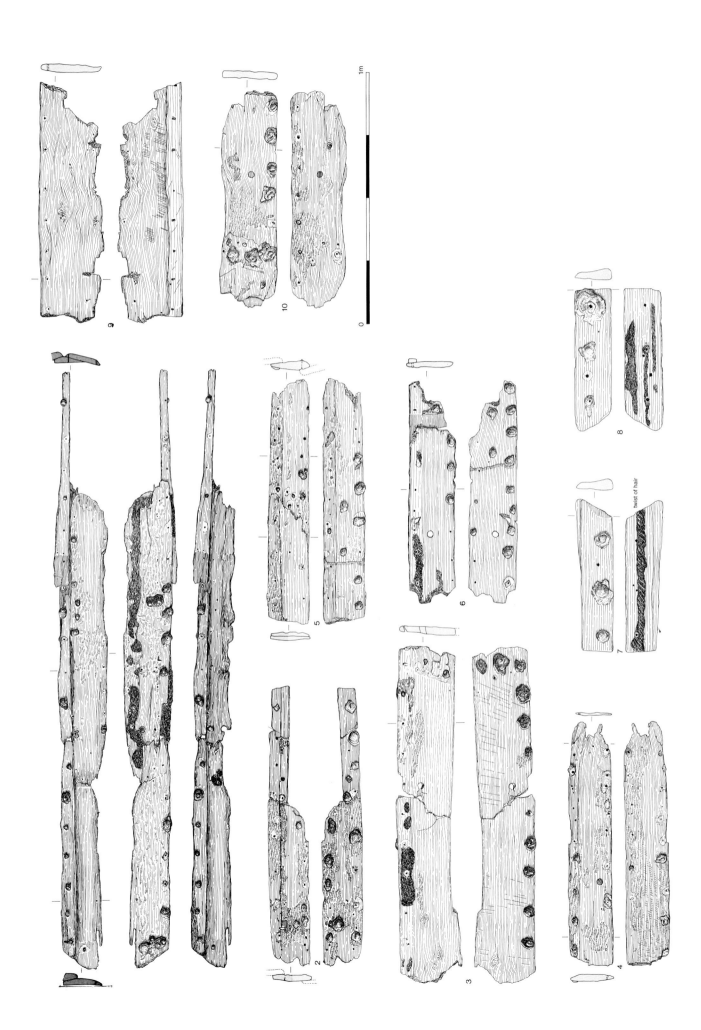

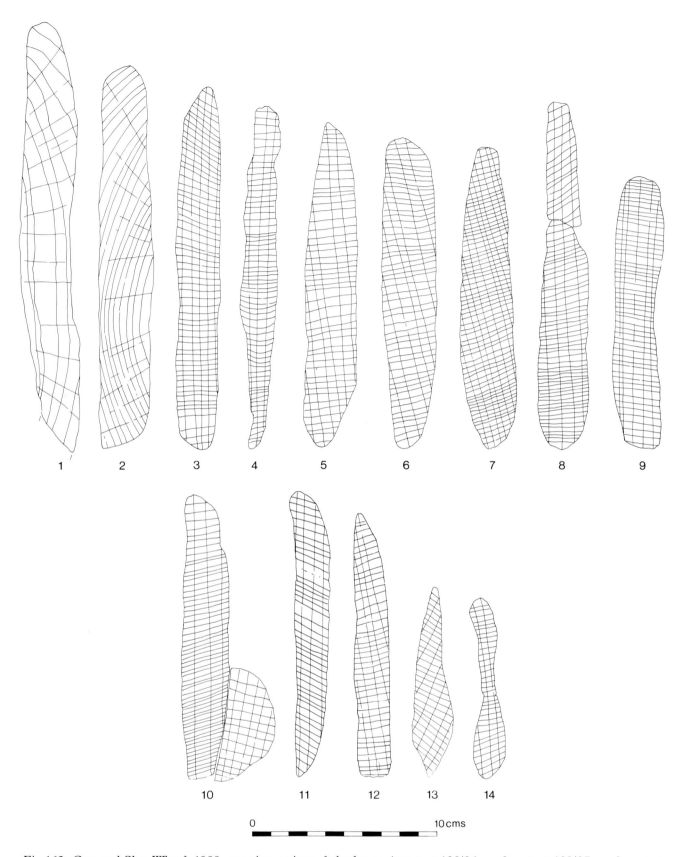

Fig 162 Gun and Shot Wharf, 1988, tree-ring sections of planks: no 1 context 138/36; no 2 context 139/37; no 3 context 117/41; no 4 context 116/30; no 5 context 119/30; no 6 context 118/40; no 7 context 118/40; no 8 context 116/30; no 9 context 119/38; no 10 context 120/39; no 11 context 120/39 B; no 12 context 120/39 D; no 13 context 120/39 C; no 14 context 119/38

Fig 163 Clinker boat planking reused in a sixteenth-century moat revetment (MOR 87), (metric scale)

eroded hole with a minimum diameter of 19mm suggests the location of a trenail fastening to a frame. It passed through the scarf joint.

The inboard surface of the plank had a patchy brownish deposit, up to 2–3mm thick near the lap, which was the remains of tar (*Appendix 4*). The outboard surface had a light grey-bright yellow surface coating which seemed most likely to be a phosphate deposit and not an original surface dressing.

The eroded outer surface contained many hollows up to 3mm wide, all of which followed the wood grain and resembled the eroded borings of *Teredo*. If correctly identified these indicate that the boat had been in the sea for some time. The angles of the laps suggest that this plank came from a slightly curving part of the hull, and the possible *Teredo* borings indicate that it lay below the waterline. The scarf suggests that it was from the starboard side.

Hays Wharf to Gun and Shot Wharf, Southwark, 1988 (site code G&S 88)

Fragments of clinker boat planking (Figs 161 and 162) were recovered from the revetment of a moat around a late medieval and sixteenth-century house. Six pieces (contexts 116-30, 117-41, 118-40, 119-38a/b, and

Fig 164 ?Repair on clinker planking (MOR 87)

120-39) were from the same vessel, and were of radially-cut oak. The latest tree-ring dates for the pieces are 1514, 1549, 1550, 1553, and 1568 in the heartwood, showing that this vessel should be of late sixteenth-century date. The lap caulking was of matted hair, and the laps were fastened by iron rivets. Oak trenails had fastened the frames to the planking.

The boat had been repaired, small nails having been driven in along the outboard end of scarf joints (contexts 116-30, 117-41, 118-40, 120-39). The laps had been re-riveted (contexts 118-40, 119-38), and in

MOR 87

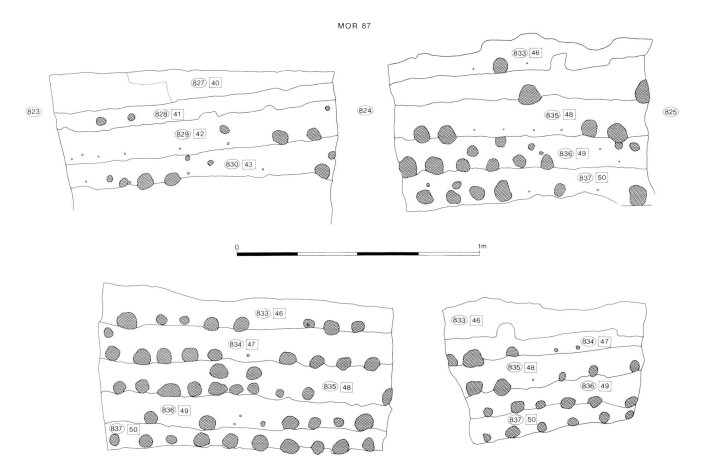

Fig 165 Morgans Lane, 1987, site drawings of fragments of reused boat planking, with their site context numbers

one there were two rows of rivets. A split plank had been repaired by a wooden patch with tar and hair beneath.

The remaining pieces of boat planking, also from the moat revetment, were from another vessel or vessels. Three were of elm that had been tangentially cut (contexts 138-36, 139-37a/b). These planks were much wider than the oak planks above, even though the thickness of all was similar. The only traces of repair were small nails driven into the outboard end of a plank scarf. The remaining fragment (contexts 149-274) was of oak radially cut, and this had a string-like caulking of hair in the plank lap. Also, the lap had been repaired with an extra iron rivet.

Hays Wharf to Morgans Lane, Southwark, 1987 (site code MOR 87)

Excavations exposed the sixteenth-century timber revetment (Figs 163 and 164) of a moat that had encircled a house, and in it were many reused parts of boats (Fig 165), some of which were saved for study (Fig 166).

Two pieces of planking gave the following tree-ring dates: 1387–1480 (contexts 735-123), and 1467–1525 (contexts 829-42). These indicate that the construction of the vessels occurred during the first half of the sixteenth century. Some plank fragments were of radially-cut oak (contexts 735-123, 837-50), others were of tangentially-cut oak (context 623/4-32/34), and in one (contexts 837-50) the plank had an oak repair tangentially cut. In another the plank was of tangentially-cut elm (contexts 659-35). The clinker planking was held by iron rivets, with a caulking of hair in the laps. A trenail of oak was identified.

Repairs were in evidence: in one plank (contexts 030/1-23/4) the lap required extra nail fastenings, and another (contexts 625-13) was re-riveted. One plank included a wooden patch with hair caulking fastened over a trenail and lap rivets, and tacks held the inboard edge. These were evidently intended to make the vessel waterproof, but another plank seems to have had its out-board face re-faced with a large patch (contexts 837-50)

Hays Wharf to Morgans Lane, Southwark, 1988 (site code MOR 88)

Excavations revealed further parts of the moat found on this site in 1987. There were many phases of revetment, but parts of broken-up boats were found reused in revetment 004 (Figs 167 and 168), which has been provisionally dated to *c* 1480–1550.

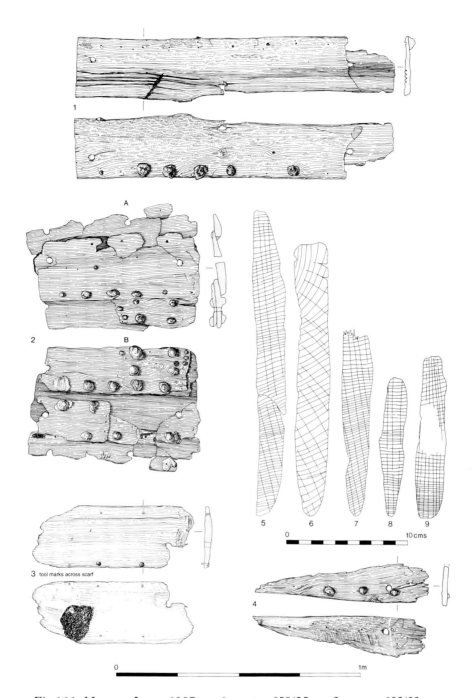

Fig 166 Morgans Lane, 1987: no 1 context 659/35; no 2 context 632/32–634/34; no 3 context 735/123, G NE cut; no 4 context 025/83. Tree-ring sections of planks; no 5 context 735/123; no 6 context 625/13; no 7 context 735/123; no 8 context 829/42, plank 2; no 9 context 829/42

Of the fragments recovered from this phase (contexts 025, 028, 029, 030, 031, 034, 040), none could be tree-ring dated because all but one (contexts 029-22) were of elm, mostly tangentially cut. The exception was a piece of oak that was tangentially cut by a saw which had left distinctive marks (Figs 169 and 170). The caulking in the laps and scarf joints was of hair, which, where undisturbed, was always matted.

Evidence of repairs included extra nails to strengthen a lap (contexts 030-031), and small nails to hold the inboard and/or outboard ends of plank scarfs (contexts 025-83, 028-21, 033-26, 034-27). In one instance (Fig 171) a scarf had many extra fastenings (contexts 034-27). Clearly, the scarfs had been leaking. These timbers could all have been from one boat.

Other boat timbers were found in the dumped infill of the moat, which is dated *c* 1550–1600. There were five pieces which were of radially-cut oak (contexts 101-84, 103-86, 107-90), one of oak that was either

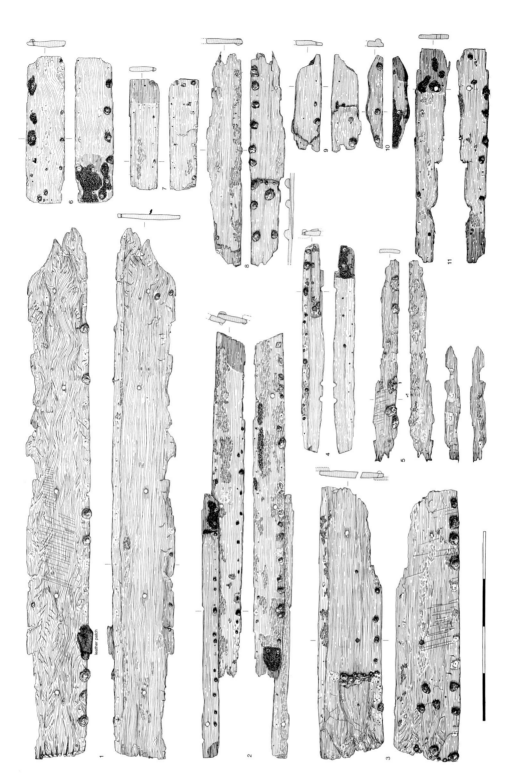

Fig 167 Morgans Lane, 1988: no 1 context 033/26, the piece of leather is not related to the boat; no 2 context 104/105; no 3 context 034/27; no 4 context 107/90; no 5 context 029/22, two pieces; no 6 context 102/85; no 7 context 103/86; no 8 context 031/24; no 9 context 028/21; no 10 context 040/033; no 11 context 101/84

radially or tangentially cut (contexts 101/104-6), and one of elm that was tangentially cut (contexts 102-85). These may be from two vessels, one oak and the other elm. One oak plank (contexts 101-84) was tree-ring dated in the heartwood to 1471–1551, and 1480–1568 with some sapwood rings, suggesting a shipbuilding date of about 1580.

Repairs resulted from leaking laps, which had been re-riveted (contexts 104/6, 101-84, 103-86). A scarf also was re-fastened (contexts 101-84), and the outboard edges of others fastened with small nails (contexts 102-85, 103-86). Trenails also seem to have been leaking for the heads of two outboard were strengthened by a wooden patch (contexts 107-90).

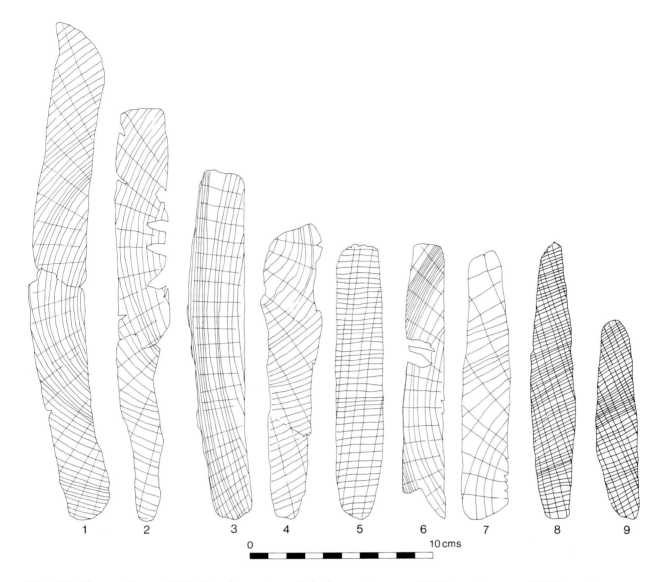

Fig 168 Morgans Lane, 1988: Tree-ring sections of planks: no 1 context 033/26; no 2 context 659/35; no 3 context 102/85; no 4 context 030/23; no 5 context 103/86; no 6 context 025/83; no 7 context 028/21; no 8 context 84/101, 89/106; no 9 context 84/101, 89/106

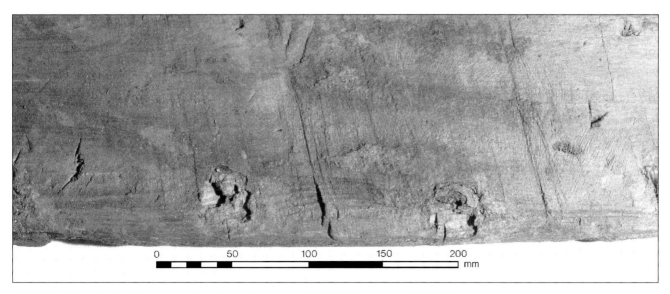

Fig 169 Elm plank with saw marks, sixteenth century (MOR 88, context 034-27)

Fig 170 Plank, split through drying, with saw marks, sixteenth century (MOR 88, context 029-22) (metric scale)

Fig 171 Heavily reinforced outboard end of a scarf, sixteenth century (MOR 88, 034-27) (metric scale)

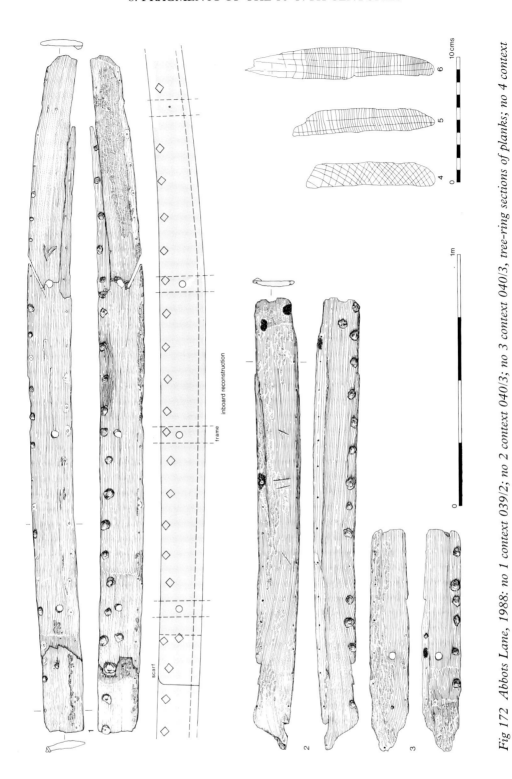

Fig 172 Abbots Lane, 1988: no 1 context 039/2; no 2 context 040/3; no 3 context 040/3, tree-ring sections of planks; no 4 context context 038/1; no 5 context 040/3; no 6 context 030/2

Hays Wharf to Abbots Lane, Southwark, 1988 (site code ABB 88)

Fragments of a boat (Figs 172 and 173) were recovered (context 038-1/039-2/040-3) during a two-day watching brief, but their site context is not known.

One was tree-ring dated in the heartwood to 1501–71, suggesting a boatbuilding date of at least 1600. Both were of oak, one radially cut and the other tangentially. There was no evidence of repairs, though one (context 039-2) had slight traces of burning outboard. Another (context 040-3) had drilled holes at the edge but these had not been used for rivets (Fig 174).

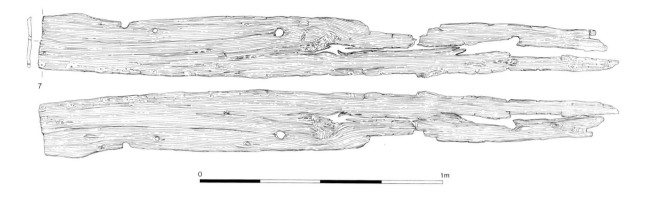

Fig 173 Abbots Lane, 1988: no 7 context 038

Fig 174 Circular rivet hole near edge of plank, one of several about 4mm in diameter which seem to have been drilled but not used, ?seventeenth century (ABB 88, context 040-3) (metric scale)

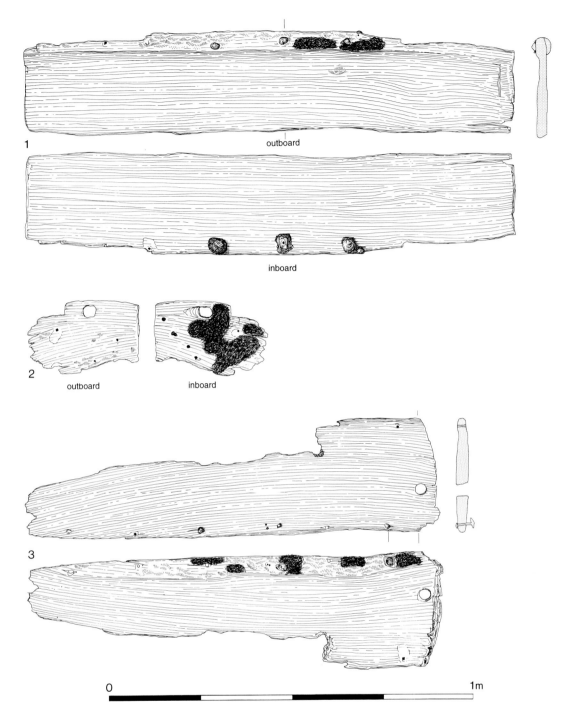

Fig 175 Butter Factory South, 1988: no 1 context 158; no 2 no context; no 3 context 158

Hays Wharf to Butter Factory South, Southwark, 1988 (site code BFS 88)

A fragment of boat planking from part of a pond and a north to south watercourse, provisionally dated to the fifteenth to eighteenth centuries (Figs 175 and 176), with a tree-ring date in the heartwood of 1442–1531, suggesting a building date around the middle of the sixteenth century. The planking was of oak radially cut. There was no evidence of repair.

Cherry Garden Street, 1987

(site code CG 87)

Three boat timbers (Fig 179) were recovered from an unknown context. One was tree-ring dated to 1488–1554 suggesting a building date in the latter half of the sixteenth century. The planks were of oak. Two (contexts 2-6/32-7, 3-8) were radially cut while another (context 84-46) was tangentially cut, and had been sharpened as if for reuse as a post.

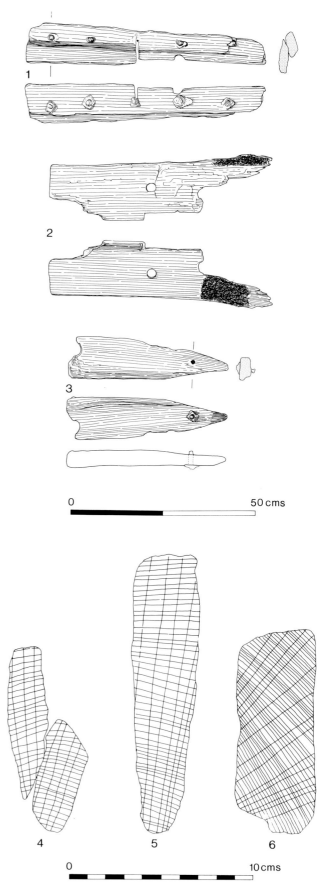

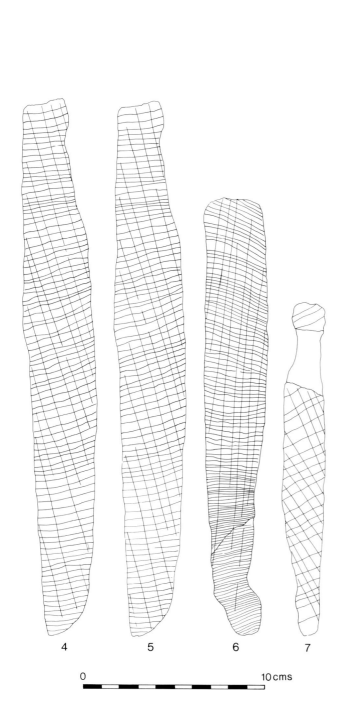

Fig 176 Butter Factory South, 1988, tree-ring sections of planks: no 4 contexts 118/49, 153/50, 154/51, 158, no 5 context 158; no 6 contexts 118/49, 153/50, 154/51, 158, no 7 context 158

Fig 177 Cherry Garden, 1987: no 1 context 3/8; no 2 contexts 2/7, 6/32; no 3 context 84/46, tree-ring sections of planks; no 4 context 3/8; no 5 contexts 2/6, 32/7; no 6 context 84/46

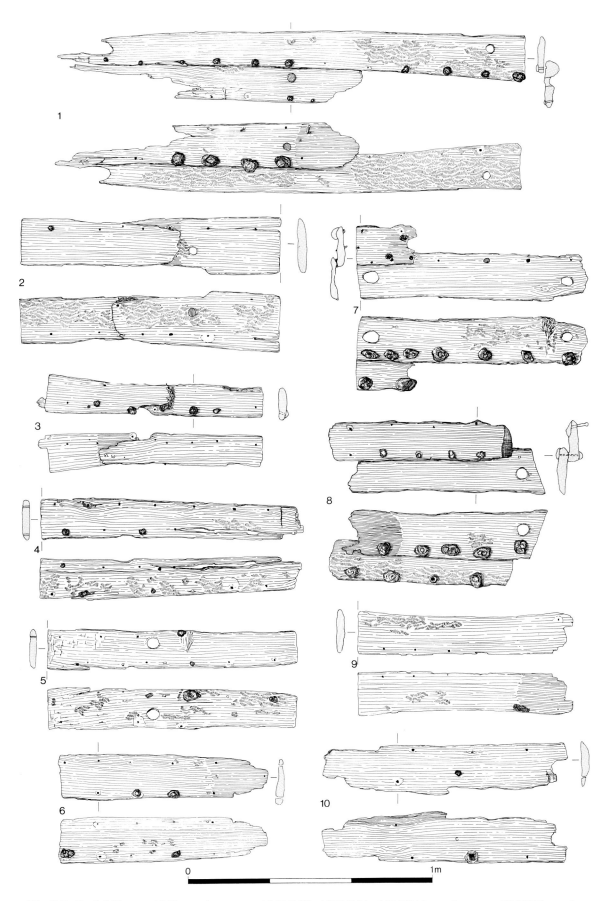

Fig 178 Bethel Estate, 1988: no 1 contexts 1000/217, 1001/231, 1002/218; no 2 context 795/230; no 3 contexts 796, 797; nos 4 and 5 context 794/229; no 6 context 793/228; no 7 contexts 711–713, 719, 720; no 8 context 53/488; no 9 context 1000/271, with 1000–1002; no 10 context 312/741

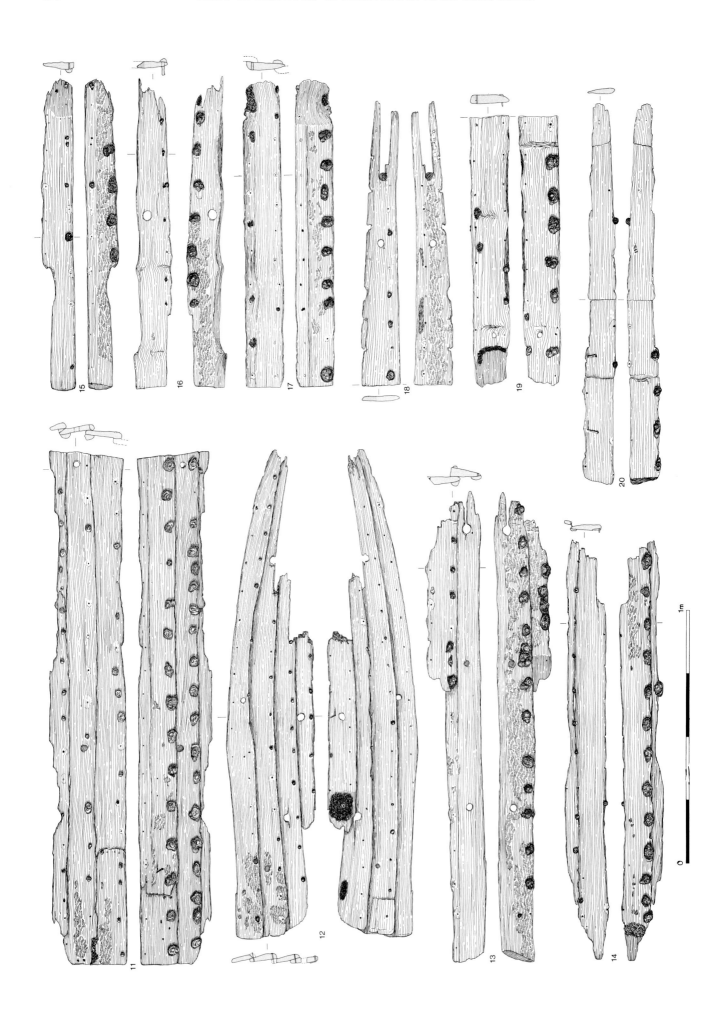

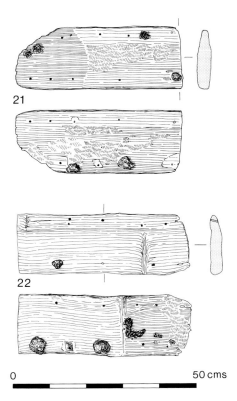

21

22

0   50 cms

Fig 180 Bethel Estate, 1988: no 21 context 785/419; no 22 context 784/380

Hays Wharf to Bethel Estate, Southwark, 1988 (site code BTH 88)

Some boat planking was found reused in the waterfront of a watercourse and a possible part of a moat for a late medieval and sixteenth-century house (Figs 178–81). Tree-ring dates were: context 312-741; context 784-380, dated 1467–1550; context 794-229, dated 1494–1548; context 711/3-420, dated 1464–1541; context 793-228, dated 1486–1543; context 1000/2-217/8, dated 1515–64; context 1005-221, dated 1474–1549; context 425-636/8, dated 1437–1575 sap; context 426-639, dated 1406–1559 sap; and context 93-639, dated 1470-1562 sap. They all indicate boatbuilding dates in the latter half of the sixteenth century (Fig 182).

All of this group were of oak, mostly radially cut, while four were radially or tangentially cut. The caulking was of hair, probably matted. Damage and repairs were evident, one plank having been split at the rivets and repaired with a thick deposit of tar (context 794-229), and in another were occasional extra rivets to strengthen the lap (context 53-488). The trenail in one plank (context 795-230) was 29mm in diameter, and at its outboard end a peg 10mm square had been driven into its centre (Fig 183). This planking also had a thick dressing of tar outboard (Fig 184). Note the lack of deformed wood around the square rivet hole, indicating that the rivet had been driven into a drilled hole.

245 Blackfriars Road, Southwark, 1987 (site code 245 BR)

A large north-south water channel was located with traces of a bridge and revetments of the late sixteenth to seventeenth centuries. From this several pieces of boat timbers were recovered (context 204/5-269). These were of radially-cut oak (Fig 185), with laps held by iron rivets. One lap had extra rivets, and there was a patch repair held by short iron nails.

Guys Hospital, Southwark, 1989 (site code GHL 89)

Pieces of boat planking (Fig 186) were found reused as the lining of a drain of the seventeenth century (context 160). The boat itself, therefore, was presumably built in the late sixteenth or early seventeenth centuries. The planking was of knotty wood, probably elm, which had been tangentially cut. There were iron rivets and matted hair caulking along the laps, and one lap had been repaired with extra rivets.

National Wharf, Southwark, 1990 (site code NAT 90)

This site lay immediately behind the present waterfront of the River Thames in the street named Bermondsey Wall East, Rotherhithe. A timber waterfront was found (context 027) containing reused ship timbers including probable carvel planking, and beside this were recovered two oak frames (Fig 187). The waterfront revetment was believed to date from at least the early seventeenth century, and had been sealed by dumped material. If the dating is correct the frames could be sixteenth-century.

One frame was curved, 180mm wide and between 135mm and 148mm thick, and in it were trenails about 30mm in diameter with wedges driven from inboard. These trenails no doubt originally held the planking to the frames, and in the the absence of

Fig 179 (opposite) Bethel Estate, 1988: no 11 contexts 636/8, 425; no 12 contexts 1005/221, 1007/233, 1008/224, 1009/225; no 13 context 488/53; no 14 context 712/421; no 15 context 53/488; no 16 context 713/422; no 17 context 639/426; no 18 context 795/230; no 19 context 93/639; no 20 context 40/475

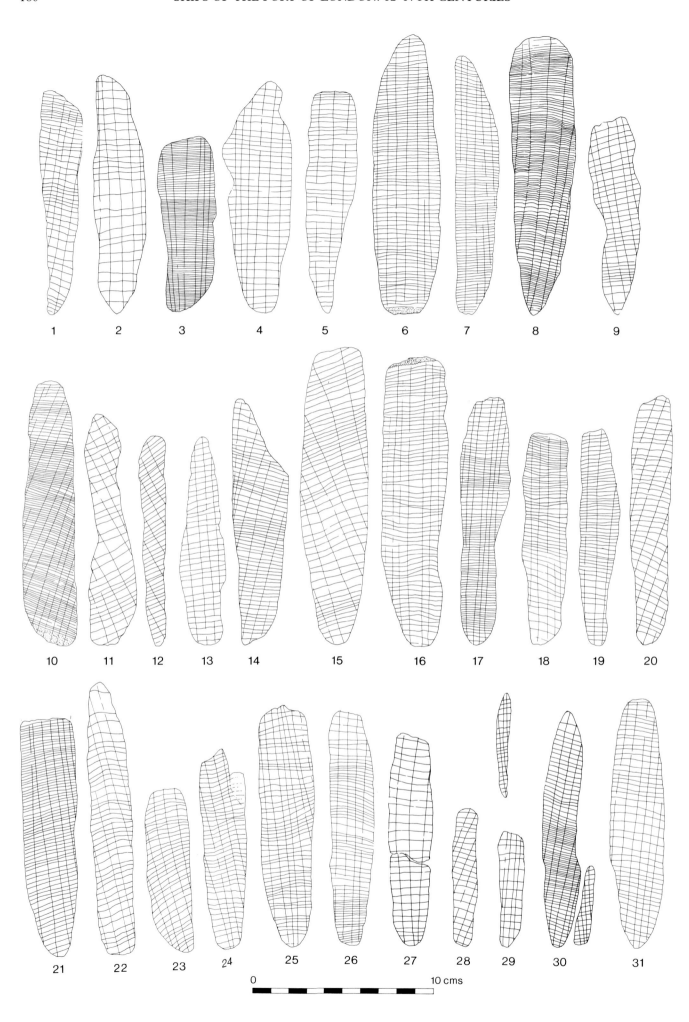

1 2 3 4 5 6 7 8 9

10 11 12 13 14 15 16 17 18 19 20

21 22 23 24 25 26 27 28 29 30 31

0 10 cms

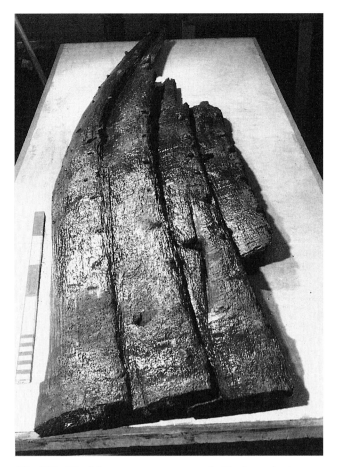

Fig 182 Planking cut to a curve, probably from the bottom of a boat, sixteenth century (BTH 88, context 1005/221, 1007/233, 1008/224, 1009/225) (metric scale)

joggling (ie steps) in the outboard face, and the association with carvel planking, it seems likely that the planking that was once attached to the frames was carvel-laid. On the outboard face were holes left by iron nails with shanks about 10mm square. These suggest that the trenails had become weak and that the plank fastenings were reinforced with iron nails. There were also two square holes about 25mm square passing laterally through the frame from side to side, as if a metal fastening to hold adjoining frames together in the ship had been removed.

The other frame was also of oak, about 180mm wide and 120–140mm thick. It had trenails 30mm in diameter which had been wedged inboard, and one had a secondary trenail which had been partly drilled through an earlier trenail. There was also a partly drilled trenail hole 30mm in diameter and 48mm deep, with a rounded bottom. This frame too had a lateral hole 25mm square, and on one side there were three iron nails 10mm square. One end of the frame had been sharpened roughly to a point, and contained axe cuts, as if to reuse it as a pile. These two frames seem to be from the same large vessel.

Conclusions

This study, mostly of sixteenth-century clinker-built boat and ship plank fragments, shows interesting changes from medieval shipbuilding practice. Firstly, many of the planks were of elm as well as oak, and,

Fig 183 Outboard end of a trenail with a tapering square peg driven into its centre to expand it, sixteenth century (BTH 88, context 795/230) (metric scale)

Fig 181 (opposite) Bethel Estate, 1988, tree-ring sections of planks: no 1 context 475/40; nos 2–5 context 53/488; no 6 context 93/639; no 7 context 312/741; no 8 contexts 636–638/425; no 9 contexts 636/425; 637/633; no 10 context 639/426; no 11 no context; no 12 contexts 711–713, 719–720, 420–42; no 13 context 712/421; no 14 context 713/422; no 15 context 758/419; no 16 context 784/380; no 17; context 793/228; no 18 and no 19 context 794/229; no 20–22 contexts 795–230; no 23 context 796/797/385; no 24 context 797/385; no 25 context 1000; no 26 context 1000/217; no 27–30 contexts 1005/221, 1007/223, 1009/225; no 31 context 1000/217.

Fig 184 *Tar dressing on the outboard face of a plank, except at the lap, sixteenth century (BTH 88, context 795–230)* *(metric scale)*

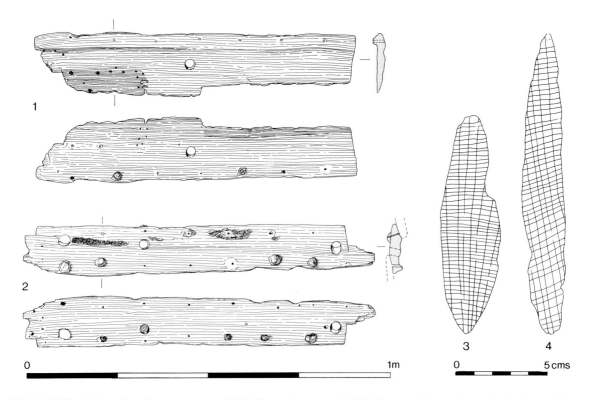

Fig 185 *245 Blackfriars Road: no 1 context 205/269; no 2 context 266/269, tree-ring sections of planks; no 3 contexts 204/269; no 4 context 205/269*

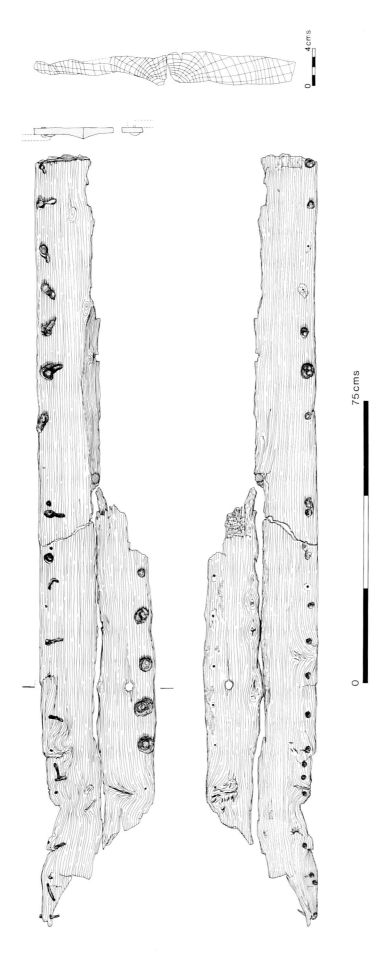

Fig 186 Guy's Hospital, 1989: context 160

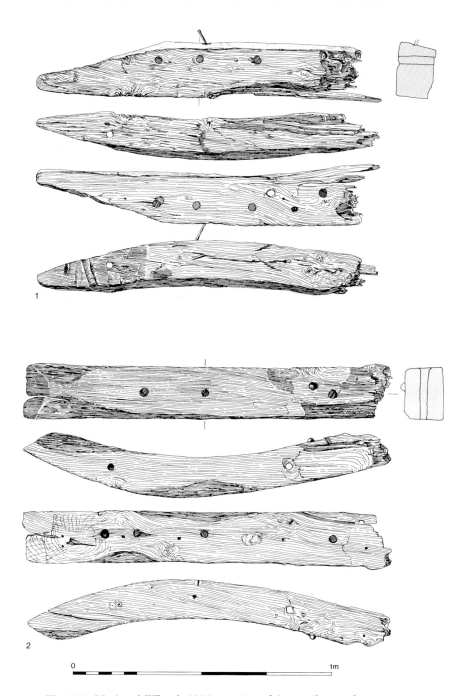

Fig 187 National Wharf, 1990: nos 1 and 2; two frames from context 027

secondly, many planks had been tangentially cut, with occasional saw marks indicating how they were fashioned, while others were radially cut. This indicates that although the traditional medieval shipbuilding methods remained, the sawn planks suggest that there was a ready supply of pre-cut timber available to shipbuilders. Also, the use of elm suggests that oak was not so readily available now as it had been in previous centuries. In general the elm was more knotty, had a wider grain, and was inferior to the oak, suggesting a decline in the quality of the building materials for smaller vessels.

The proportions or guiding rules used by shipwrights in clinker shipbuilding varied considerably (*see Appendix 1, Table 7*), but shared the following averages:

- plank thickness:maximum plank width, 1:4.99 (38 examples)
- plank thickness:lap width, 1:1.78 (57 examples)
- lap width:plank width, 1:3.19 (39 examples)
- maximum plank thickness:maximum rivet spacing, 1:5.25 (49 examples)
- maximum plank thickness:scarf length, 1:7.3 (26 examples)

Appendix 1   Dendrochronology of shipping from London, twelfth to seventeenth centuries

by Ian Tyers

Summary

This Appendix summarises the tree-ring analyses carried out upon the ship and boat timbers described in this volume.

A total of 192 samples were analysed during this study. Ninety one of them dated successfully and provided dates for nineteen groups of vessel timbers. A further six groups failed to date. The main results have been discussed within chapters 2 to 8. Additional timber details are provided by Peter Marsden in Tables 6 and 7 below, and a summary of the results presented in Table 8 and Fig 188, is in the same order as in Chapters 2 to 8. Then follows comment on the value of the results, a review of the methods employed, and an indication of the various aspects of wider interest that may be forthcoming from future work. A great deal of additional information is lodged in reports stored with the project archives (Tyers 1990, 1992).

Dendrochronology, or tree-ring dating, has been routinely carried out on excavated timbers in Britain for 20 years (for more details see Baillie 1982, Schweingruber 1988). It is independent of all other dating methods. Thus in the event of suitable timbers being found and dated in a rigorous fashion the tree-ring date produced can be relied upon to be correct. The technique involves the precise measurement of the sequence of annual ring widths within a timber and then the matching of this pattern of wide and narrow rings to dated reference sequences. These reference sequences have been built up by starting with old living trees, thus fixing the chronology absolutely. They have then been extended backwards by matching successively older ring series on to the sequence

Types of information provided

Tree-ring analysis of boat timbers can provide information of five types. It gives a date during or after which the tree or trees were cut down, and therefore an indication of the date of construction. The dated wood may provide some indication of the source area of the timbers. Analysis may show how many timbers are derived from the same trees, which, in combination with structural analyses, may provide information about the techniques employed to manufacture the vessel. It may provide information about either the selection of the trees used in shipbuilding or of the availability of certain types of timbers chosen by shipbuilders. Lastly, it may be possible to identify the useful life span of the vessels reported here, when the date of sinking or subsequent re-use can be established. However, tree-ring analysis of vessel samples is different from routine analyses of other types of timber structures.

To obtain an absolute date reference chronologies for the appropriate period, area, and species must be available for comparison. There are many oak (*Quercus* spp) sequences from northern, western, and central Europe covering the period represented in this volume. It must be noted, however, that the geographical and temporal coverage of reference chronologies is incomplete and of variable quality. Even within this European region there are areas whose timbers are at present undatable, and one effect of trade expansion in the twelfth to seventeenth centuries could have been to bring many foreign timbers or ships into London that cannot yet be dated by tree-ring analysis. In Table 8 the term 'local' may be taken to exclude areas such as Ireland, Scotland, Wales, Northern England, and Germany. It is likely to include all the areas that were exploited for timber in the Thames basin, for example the Wealden and Essex woods. Unfortunately the inability to be more precise in such interpretations leads to the probable inclusion of at least the areas within 100km of London, and does not necessarily exclude areas further away.

In the cases reported here the timbers do not retain all the outermost (ie the sapwood or most recent) rings of the original tree. Thus the end of the tree-ring sequences was not the date of the felling of the trees and additional years have to be added to the date of the last surviving ring to allow for these missing rings. Occasionally the edge of the sapwood had survived and a range of possible dates could be calculated. If no sapwood survived only a *terminus post quem* was produced. The sapwood estimate used here for the local material is a range of 10–55 rings, used as 95% confidence limits (Hillam *et al* 1987), a range of 7–36 is used for the Baltic material, and a range of 8–40 is used for the single identified German timber.

The identification of timbers from the same tree was based on high correlations between the samples and an unusually good visual match reflecting very similar medium-term growth trends in the sequences. These qualified identifications could have assistedin estimating the number of trees consumed in the building of different boats.

Table 6 Medieval *compiled* by *Peter Marsden*

site context	wood	radial or tangential	plank max thick	width	lap width	caulking	rivet spacing	shank	length	scarf rivets	caulking	diam	trenail spacing	wood
Custom House, 1987														
212	O	R	20	–	51	hair	77–107	7×7	c150	–	–	23	–	–
211	O	R	18	–	40	hair	35–74	6×6	–	–	–	–	–	–
19	O	R	20	240+	30	hair	89–106	5×5	–	–	–	–	–	–
5	O	R	26	238+	34	hair-string	109–33	6×7	–	–	–	23 27	–	–
210	O	R	19	170+	45	–	83–95	7×7	c160	–	–	24	–	–
91–2	O	R	21	–	48	–	69–110	–	–	–	–	–	–	–
52	O	R	17	–	42	hair-string	110–37	–	176	2 out	–	23	–	–
51	O	R	23	234	40	hair-2 string	92–117	7×7	200	2 out	–	–	–	–
44	O	R	21	–	40	hair-string	–	7×7	201	1 out	hair	–	–	–
103	O	R	20 26	210+	40	hair-string	76–142	6×6	170	–	–	24	–	–
45	O	R	20	269	48	hair-3 string	115–21	8×8	–	–	–	–	–	–
133	O	R	21	–	40	hair-3 string	85–110	6×6 7×7	–	2 out 1 mid	–	–	–	–
121	O	R	20	–	45	hair	–	6×6	–	–	–	–	–	–
46/47	O	R	17+	–	–	–	–	–	185	–	–	23	–	–
58	O	R	30	177	42	–	63–124	–	–	–	–	–	–	–
81	O	R	32	–	44	hair-2 string	148–54	7×7	–	–	–	24 27	317	–
Billingsgate, 1982														
4924–3058	O	R	36	285	49 47	hair	150–73	7×7	–	–	–	26	–	w/p
3058/9–4923/4	O	R	38 26	287	50	hair	115–62	7×8	260	–	–	–	606	O
5047–3534	O	R	43	387	–	–	108–64	–	–	–	–	24	–	–
6281–3578	O	R	41	293	60	hair-2 string	179–88 234–40	–	–	–	–	32 35	566	–
2606	O	R	30	266+	–	–	76–139	7×7	–	–	–	30	–	–
4445–3065	O	R	30 18	183+ 210+	–	?caulking groove	138 125–47	7×7 6×6	–	–	–	22	–	–
6794–3579	O	R	–	–	–	–	121–32	–	–	–	–	–	–	–
4925–3056	O	R	30	–	50	hair	100–184	7×7	–	–	–	–	–	–
6373–3582	O	R	45	320	60	–	157	7×7	300	–	–	29 30 31	255 267 340	–
?2724	O	R	14	–	45	caulking groove	103–52 53–130	4×4	170	–	hair strings	–	–	–
Blackfriars ship 3, 1970														
10	O	R	53	250	60	hair matted	95–192	–	300 300	1 in 1 out	–	30	–	–
Next 20	O	R	50	230	60	hair matted	110–200	–	440 400	1 in 1 mid	–	–	–	–
12	O	R	44	240	70	hair	130–200	–	280	1 in 1 out	–	32	560 570	–
4	O	R	36	230	70	hair	120–90	–	320	1 in 1 out	–	30	660 600	–
9	O	R	45?	260	80	hair	150–90	–	300	1 in 1 out	–	–	–	–
8	O	R	45	220+	80	hair	150–80	–	330	1 in 1 out	–	30	–	–
6	O	R	50	230	50	hair	160–80	7×7	360 330	1 in 1 in 1 out	–	30	–	–
15	O	R	45	250	90	hair	170–95	–	330	1 in 1 out	–	30	–	–
16	O	R	40?	250	60	hair	170–90	–	330	1 in 1 out	–	30	–	–

Notes: all measurements are in millimetres: O = oak; w/p = willow/poplar

Table 6 Medieval continued

site context	last ring date	dendro boat date	repairs	plank thick: plank width	lap width: plank thick	proportions lap width: plank width	max rivet spacing: plank thick	scarf length: plank thick
Custom House, 1987								
212	–		–	–	1:2.55	–	1:5.35	1:7.50
211	–		Patch over split at trenail. Hair	–	1:2.22	–	1:4.11	–
19	–		Patches in & outboard	–	1:1.50	–	1:5.30	–
5	–		None. Plank split at trenail	–	1:3.0	–	1:5.11	–
210	–		Patch over split at trenail inboard	–	1:2.36	–	1:5.0	1:8.42
91–2	–		–	–	1:2.28	–	1:5.23	–
52	–	16 samples 1160–90	–	–	1:2.47	–	1:8.05	1:10.35
51	–		–	1:10.56	1:1.73	1:5.85	1:5.08	1:8.69
44	–		–	–	1:1.9	–	–	1:9.57
103	–		–	–	1:1.53	–	1:7.1 1:5.46	1:6.53
45	–		1 extra rivet	1:13.45	1:2.4	1:5.60	1:6.05	–
133	–		–	–	1:1.9	–	1:5.23	1:9.52
121	1143		Extra rivets	–	1:2.25	–	–	–
46/47	–		–	–	–	–	–	1:10.88
58	1132		–	1:5.9	1:1.4	1:4.21	1:4.13	–
81	1141		–	–	1:3.75	–	1:4.81	1:4.53
Billingsgate								
4924–3058	–	same tree undated	–	1:7.91	1:1.36	1:5.81	1:4.8	–
3058/9–1923/4	–		–	1:7.55	1:1.31	1:5.74	1:4.26 1:6.23	1:10.0
5047–3534	–	same tree undated	–	1:9.0	–	–	1:3.81	–
6281–3578	–		–	1:7.14	1:1.46	1:4.88	1:4.58 1:5.85	–
2606	1183		New rivet line Patch. Oak peg filled					
		1193+	rivet hole	–	–	–	1:4.63	–
4445–3065	1181		Extra lap rivets or nails	–	–	–	1:4.60 1:8.16	–
6794–3579	1115	1125+	–	–	–	–	–	–
4925–3056	–	–	–	–	1:1.66	–	1:6.13	–
6373–3582	–	–	–	1:7.11	1:1.33	1:5.33	1:3.48	1:6.66
?2724	–	–	Split along nail line. Patch	–	–	–	1:10.85	1:12.14
Blackfriars ship 3, 1970								
10	–	–	–	1:4.71	1:1.13	1:4.16	1:3.62	1:5.66 1:5.66
Next 20	–	–	–	1:4.6	1:1.2	1:3.83	1:4.0	1:8.80 1:8.80
12	–	–	Pegged rivet hole	1:5.45	1:1.59	1:3.42	1:4.54	1:6.36
4	–	–	Patch over lap & trenail hole Peg lap rivet hole	1:6.38	1:1.94	1:3.28	1:5.27	1:8.88
9	–	–	Patch over lap & trenail hole	1:5.77	1:1.77	1:3.25	1:4.22	1:6.66
8	–	–	–	–	1:1.77	–	1:40	1:7.33
6	–	–	–	1:4.6	1:1.0	1:4.6	1:3.6	1:7.2 1:6.6
15	–	–	Patch over lap	1:5.55	1:1.2	1:2.77	1:4.33	1:7.33
16	–	–	–	1:6.25	1:1.5	1:4.16	1:4.75	1:8.25

Table 6 Medieval continued

site context	wood	plank radial or tangential	plank max thick	width	width	lap caulking	rivet spacing	rivet shank	length	scarf rivets	scarf caulking	trenail diam	trenail spacing	wood
Hays Wharf to Symonds Wharf, 1988														
141–168	O Baltic	R	58	298	40	hair 4 string	189–209	10×10	400	1 in 1 out	–	33 35	247, 423, 337, 407, 314, 400	O
168	O Baltic	R	55	–	60	hair 2 string	167–92	9×9	–	–	–	–	–	–
168	O Baltic	R	55	–	50	–	200–210	8×9	–	–	–	–	373	–
175–164	O Baltic	R	55	188+	–	–	195–225 186–212	7×12 9×9 10×10	–	–	–	32	322 450 285	O
194–136	O	R	–	168	33	hair	122–71	5×5	100+	–	–	17 19 18	144 61 406	–
196–120	O Baltic	R	35	253+	87	moss	160–86	8×9	485	?1 in 2 out	moss	34 35 37	404 368	–
Trig Lane, 1974														
1384/5–1134/6	O	R	25	198+	44	hair	–	6×7	240	1 out	–	21	76	–
1382	O	R	24	153+	58	hair & tar	107–202	6×6	250	–	–	18 20	355	–
1383–1136/1	O	R	24	179+	60	hair	123–202	10×10 8×7	165	–	hair	17	462	–
1381	O	R	26 25	116+ 114+	30	hair	–	7×7 6×6	–	–	–	26 20	340 338	–
1353–1136/1	O	R	25	243	66	hair	134–70	7×7	–	1 in 1 out	–	22	385 360	–
NL 10	O	R	27	195+	32	–	–	7×7	230	1 out	–	20 21	393	–
NL 11	O	R	21 16	140	78	hair felt	165–205	7×7	190 240	–	–	23	–	–
5–15 Bankside, 1987														
3163–84	O	R	28 26	268+ 220+	–	–	115–23	7×7 8×8	–	–	–	30 26 35	465 473 485+	–
Hays Wharf to Abbots Lane, 1987														
205–86	O	R	25	170+	44	–	232	8×8	–	–	–	–	–	–
187–66	O	R	–	–	–	–	–	–	–	–	–	–	–	–
185–64 237/8–155/6	O German	R	30	150+	–	–	–	–	–	–	–	25	115, 240, 135, 255	w/p
358–157	O	R	45	163+	56	hair	120–80	7×7	150	–	–	31	440	–
199 cont	O	R	23	–	63	–	–	11×10	225	–	–	23	–	–
236–154	O	R	41 30+	165+	57	hair across lap	112–98	–	170 190 180	–	–	– 25	407, 417	–
154/5–151/2 155–150	O	R	45	230	55	hair	118–82	6×6	144	1 out	hair	26 30 31	441, 407, 443	w/p
175–53	–	–	–	–	56	hair	–	8×8	–	–	–	–	–	–
199–78	O	R	23	67+	26+	hair across lap	122–57	–	220	–	–	23 26	–	–
189–68a	O	R	24	160+	–	–	–	–	155	–	–	–	–	–
b	O	R	18	100+	–	–	–	–	113	–	–	26	–	–
206–87	O	R	24	–	42+	hair	–	8×8	c200	–	hair	–	–	–
201–81	O	R	29	200+	50	hair	125–80	8×8	–	–	hair	25	–	–
201 cont	O	R	25	140+	–	–	–	–	250	–	–	–	–	–
176–54 178–56	O	R	26	222	53	hair	157–60	8×8	–	–	hair	25 25	486	–
195 cont	O Baltic	R	15	–	42	hair	–	7×7	190+	–	–	24	–	–
216–99 184–63, 186–65,	O	R	–	–	–	–	–	–	–	–	–	25	–	–
190–69	O	–	–	–	–	–	–	–	–	–	–	–	–	–
213–95/6	O	–	–	–	–	–	–	–	–	–	–	–	–	–
195–74	O Baltic	–	–	–	–	–	–	–	–	–	–	–	–	–
Hays Wharf to Gun and Shot Wharf, 1988														
449–53–158/60	O Baltic	R	54 60	350 360	73 77 94	moss	185	10×10	c400	–	–	35	–	O
149–274	O Baltic	R	40	155+	106	hair strings	170–74	10×10	–	–	–	–	–	–

Notes: all measurements are in millimetres: O = oak; w/p = willow/poplar

Table 6 Medieval continued

site context	last ring date	dendro boat date	repairs	plank thick: plank width	lap width: plank thick	proportions lap width: plank width	max rivet spacing: plank thick	scarf length: plank thick
Hays Wharf to Symonds Wharf, 1988								
141–168	1332		–	1:5.13	1:0.69	1:7.45	1:3.60	1:6.90
168	1325		–	–	1:1.09	–	1:3.49	–
168	1327	1340+	–	–	1:0.90	–	1:3.81	–
175–164	1333		Patch	–	–	–	1:4.09	–
194–136	–		Extra trenail	1:8.4	1:1.65	1:5.09	1:5.18	–
196–120	1307		–	–	1:2.48	–	1:5.31	1:13.85
Trig Lane, 1974								
1384/5–1134/6	–	–	Patch & hair caulking by rivets 6mm drilled hole in lap	–	1:1.76	–	–	1:9.3
1382	–	–		–	1:2.41	–	1:8.41	1:10.41
1383–1136/1	–	–	–	–	1:2.50	–	1:8.41	1:6.87
1381	–	–	–	–	1:1.15	–	–	–
1353–1136/1	–	–	Patch prob over scarf & trenails inboard	1:9.72	1:2.64	1:3.68	1:6.80	–
NI 10	–	–	–	–	1:1.18	–	–	1:8.51
NI 11	–	–	–	1:6.66	1:3.71	1:1.79	1:9.76	–
5–15 Bankside, 1987								
3165–84	1137	1147+	Plank split at trenails. Patch and hair over	–	–	–	1:4.39 1:5.00	–
Hays Wharf to Abbots Lane, 1987								
205–86	1352		Patch held by rivets. Hair caulking	–	1:1.76	–	1:9.28	
187–66	1333	?1362+	Patch held by rivet. Hair caulking	–	–	–	–	–
185–64	1344		Nails in end of trenail	–	–	–	–	–
237/8–155/6			Burnt surface inboard					
358–157	–	–		–	1:1.24	–	1:4.0	1:3.33
199 cont	–	–	Patch over scarf. ?Teredo	–	1:2.73	–	–	1:9.78
236–154	–	–	–	–	1:1.39	–	1:4.82	1:4.14
154/5–151/2 155–150	–	–	Patch Pegged rivet hole	1:5.11	1:1.22	1:4.18	1:4.04	1:3.2
175–3	–	–	Patch with rivet. Hair caulking Plank broken at rivet line.	–	–	–	–	–
199–78	–	–	2 adjacent trenails	–	–	–	1:6.82	
189–68a	–	–		–	–	–	–	1:6.45
b	–	–	?Teredo	–	–	–	–	1:6.27
206–87	–	–	–	–	1:1.75	–	–	1:8.33
201–81	–	–	–	–	1:1.72	–	1:6.20	–
201 cont	–	–	?Teredo	–	–	–	–	1:10.0
176–54								
178–56	–	–	–	1:8.53	1:2.03	1:4.18	1:6.15	–
195 cont	–	–	Pegged rivet hole	–	1:2.80	–	–	–
216–99	–	–	Patch. Hair caulking	–	–	–	–	–
184–63, 186–65								
190–69	–	–	–	–	–	–	–	–
213–95/6	–	–	–	–	–	–	–	–
195–74	1368	–	–	–	–	–	–	–
Hays Wharf to Gun and Shot Wharf, 1988								
449–53–158/60	1370 sap	1370–1400	–	1:6.48 1:6.00	1:1.35 1:1.56	1:4.79 1:3.83	–	1:6.66
149–274	1197		Extra rivet	–	1:2.65	1:4.35	–	–

Table 7 Post-medieval *compiled* by *Peter Marsden*

site context	wood	plank radial or tangential	plank max thick	width	lap width	caulking	rivet spacing	rivet shank	rivet length	scarf rivets	scarf caulking	diam	trenail spacing	trenail wood
Hays Wharf to Gun and Shot Wharf, 1988														
116–30	O	R	23	185	52	Hair felt	110–27	–	–	?1 in 1 out	–	–	–	–
117–41	O	R	23	193	43	Hair	85–125	5×5	240	1 in 1 out	–	22	500+	–
118–40 One boat	O	R	30	163	50	Hair felt	50–139	5×5	275	1 in 1 out	–	–	–	–
119–38a	O	R	27	170	40	Hair	73–134	5×5	180	–	–	24	–	O
119–38b	O	R	–	165	45 48	–	106–39 64–117	5×5 4×4	160	–	–	–	–	O
120–39	–	–	25	123	45	Hair	102–46	5×5	220	–	Hair	–	945+ 880+	–
138–36	E	T	29	257	55	Hair	80–155	6×6	–	–	–	–	–	–
139–37a	E	T	29	233+	45	–	105–21	5×5	310	–	–	–	–	O
139–37b	E	T	28	230+	60	Hair	115–57	5×5	–	–	–	24	–	–
Hays Wharf to Bethel Estate, 1988														
784–380	O	R	35	154	–	–	51–120 65–103	5×5	200	None	Hair & tar	–	–	–
785–419	O	R/T	36	157	52	Hair	54–148 77–115	4×4	193	?None	–	–	–	–
794–229	O	R	23	114	24	–	103–18 95–120	–	–	–	–	–	–	–
794–229	O	R	23	121	38	–	57–142 111–31	5×6		–	–	31	–	–
795–230	O	R/T	20	150	50	Hair	–	4×5	–	–	–	29	254 548+	–
795–230	O	R	22	165	–	–	58–140	5×5	208	None	Hair	24	–	–
793–228	O	R	24	127	35	–	103–20	–	190	None	–	–	–	–
711/3–420 719/20	O	R/T	–	115 143+	–	Hair	61–149	5×5	–	–	–	–	–	–
796/7–385	O	R	26	107+	–	–	75–115	5×5	218	1 out	Hair & tar	–	–	–
1000/2–217/8	O	R	28 24	140	35	–	104–132 70–127	5×5	180	None	–	25 24	–	O
1005/9–221/5	O	R	19 20	–	40– 45	Hair	100–134 94–154 99–124	–	170 143	1 mid	–	22 22 24 29	–	–
53–488a	O	R	24 24	137+ 110	40	Hair	87–107 120–29	–	–	–	–	32	–	–
53–488	O	R	–	124	40	–	97–160	4×4	165	–	Hair	–	–	–
53–488c	O	R	29	120	40	–	58–185	4×4	160	–	Hair	23	594 577 515	O
312–741	O	R	25+	140+	–	–	166–79	6×6	–	–	–	–	–	–
40–475	O	R	34 28	140	–	–	122–46	5×5	–	–	–	–	–	–
425–636/8	O	R	25 29	152	50	Hair	91–138	4×4	230 205	–	–	22 23	1120	–
426–639	O	T	30	151	49	Hair	92–136 69–145	4×4	180	?None	–	–	–	–
93–639	O	R	36	148	36	Hair	92–140	4×4	c158	?None	Hair	–	–	–
712–421	O	R	25+	–	–	–	63–195 85–153	5×5	–	–	–	–	–	O
713–422	O	R	30	142+	30+	–	96–143	5×4	–	–	–	33	–	–

Notes: all measurements are in millimetres: O = oak; E = elm

Table 7 Post-medieval continued

site context	dendro last ring date	boat date	repairs	plank thick: plank width	lap width: plank thick	lap width: plank width	max rivet spacing: plank thick	scarf length: plank thick
Hays Wharf to Gun and Shot Wharf, 1988								
116–30	–		Tacks at scarf edge	1:8.04	1:2.26	1:3.55	1:5.52	–
117–41	1549		Tacks at scarf edge	1:8.69	1:1.87	1:4.49	1:5.43	1:10.43
118–40 One boat	1568	1578+	Extra lap rivets. Tacks at scarf edge	1:5.43	1:1.66	1:3.26	1:4.63	1:9.16
119–38a	1550		–	1:6.29	1:1.48	1:4.25	1:4.96	1:6.66
119–38b	1514		Re-riveted lap	–	–	1:3.43	–	–
120–39			Patch & tar & hair over split plank. Tacks at scarf edge	1:4.92	1:1.80	1:2.73	1:5.84	1:8.80
138–36	–	–	–	1:8.86	1:1.90	1:4.67	1:5.34	–
139–37a	–	–	Tacks at scarf edge	–	1:1.55	–	1:4.17	1:10.69
139–37b	–	–	Tacks at scarf edge	–	1:2.14	–	1:5.60	–
Hays Wharf to Bethel Estate, 1988								
784–380	1550		Tacks at scarf edge inboard	1:4.4	–	–	1:3.42	1:5.71
785–419	–		–	1:4.36	1:1.44	1:3.01	1:4.11	1:5.36
794–229	1541		Split plank at rivets, ?tar repair	1:4.95	1:1.04	1:4.75	1:5.21	–
794–229	1548		–	1:5.26	1:1.65	1:3.18	1:6.17	–
795–230	–		–	1:7.50	1:2.50	1:3.00	–	–
795–230	–		–	1:7.50	–	–	1:6.36	1:9.45
793–228	1543	if one boat built 1584–1603	Tacks at scarf edge inboard	1:5.29	1:1.45	1:3.62	1:5.0	1:7.91
711/3–420 719/20	1541		–	–	–	–	–	–
796/7–385	–		Tacks at scarf edge inboard. Peg in rivet hole	–	–	–	1:4.42	1:8.38
1000/2–217/8	1574		–	1:5.00	1:1.25	1:4.0	1:4.71	1:7.2
				1:5.00	1:1.45		1:5.29	
1005/9–221/5	1549		–	–	1:2.25	–	1:7.70	1:8.94
								1:7.15
53–488a	–		–	1:4.58	1:1.66	1:2.75	1:5.37	–
53–488	–		Extra lap rivets. Tacks at scarf edge	–	–	1:3.10	–	–
53–488c	–		–	1:4.13	1:1.38	1:3.00	1:6.38	1:5.51
312–741	1490		–	1:4.11	–	–	1:4.29	–
				1:5.00			1:5.21	
40–475	–		–	–	–	–	–	–
425–636/8	1575 8 sap		–	1:5.24	1:2.00	–	1:5.52	1:9.2
					1:1.72	1:3.04	1:4.75	1:7.06
426–639	1559 11 sap		Tacks at inboard edge of scarf	1:5.03	1:1.63	1:3.08	1:4.83	1:6.0
93–639	1562 3 sap		Tacks at outboard edge of scarf	1:4.11	–	–	1:3.88	–
712–421	–		–	–	–	–	–	–
713–422	1575 8 sap		Plank split at rivet line	–	–	–	1:4.76	–

Table 7 Post-medieval continued

site context	wood	plank radial or tangential	max thick	width	lap width	caulking	rivet spacing	shank	length	scarf rivets	caulking	diam	trenail spacing	wood
37–46 Bankside, 1987														
267–266 revet 21	O	R	20 16	–	40	Hair & tar	127–90	6×6	200 230	–	Hair	18	503 510	O
194–165 revet 21	O	R	27	163	55 40	Hair	190–210 193–240	6×7	280	–	–	–	–	–
202 revet 21	O	R	20+	143+	32	Hair across lap	171–95	5×6	–	–	–	–	550	–
184 revet 21	O	R	24	190	40	–	142–80 188–90	5×5	230	–	–	23	–	–
180 revet 21	O	R	15	–	28	–	222–25	6×6	–	–	–	–	–	–
193 revet 21	O	R	18	144+	–	–	–	–	172+	–	–	–	–	–
298–299 revet 21	O	R	20+	–	24+	Hair across lap	172–82	6×6	–	–	–	–	–	–
196 revet 21	O	R	30	140	30	Hair	190–210	6×6	240	–	Hair	–	395	–
185 revet 21	O	R	–	–	32+	Hair	193	–	150	–	Hair	–	–	–
187–296 revet 21	O	R	23	132 162	41 42 30	Hair	135–237 193–255 175–85	– 5×6	–	–	–	– 17	530 560	Cork
183 revet 21	O	R	23	158	40 45	Hair across lap	168–216 179–93	5×5	220	–	–	–	495+ 480+	–
188–197 revet 21	O	R/T	16	167	45	Hair	76–172 193–96	–	140	None	Hair	17	520+ 480+	O
205–268	O	R/T	12+	145+	–	–	151–208	5×5	–	–	–	18	287 350 570+	– O
785–419	O	R	36	157	42 52	Hair	54–148	4×4	193	1 in	Hair	–	–	–
200–199	O	R/T	–	140+	40	–	160–73	–	–	–	–	6 7 19	555 263 230	–
Hays Wharf to Abbots Lane, 1988														
039–2	O	R	20	185	35 48	–	93–135 69–136	5×5	180	–	–	30	690 600 693	–
038–1	O	T	15	244+	45	–	105–10	6×6	–	–	–	29 31 15 6	–	–
040–3	O	R	23	149 170	35 45	Hair	95–152 98–129	4×4	190	– 1 out	Hair	29	–	–
Hays Wharf to Morgans Lane, 1987														
735–123	O	R	23	241	40	Hair	116–77	5×5	280?	1 mid	–	20	–	–
659–35	O	T	26	245+	50	Hair felt	45–145	–	–	–	–	22 25	527	–
625–13	E	T	28	–	–	–	87–125	4×4	–	–	–	–	–	–
632/4–32/4	O	T	30 36	182+ 255	60 40	Hair	93–112	–	286	2 in 2 out	–	18 19 23 26	510 520	O
837–50	O	R & T	25 18	–	37	Hair	87–115 101–36 111–18	– 5×5	180	–	–	24	–	–

Notes: all measurements are in millimetres; O = oak; E = elm

Table 7 Post-medieval continued

site context	dendro		repairs	plank thick: plank width	lap width: plank thick	lap width: plank width	max rivet spacing: plank thick	scarf length: plank thick
	last ring date	boat date						
37–46 Bankside, 1987								
267–266 revet 21	1434	1444+	–	–	1:2.00 1:2.50	–	1:9.5	1:10.00 1:14.37
194–165 revet 21	–	–	–	1:6.03	–	1:4.07	1:8.88	1:10.37
202 revet 21	1416	1426+	–	–	–	–	–	–
184 revet 21	1437	1447+	?*Teredo*	1:7.91	1:1.66	1:4.75	1:7.91	1:9.58
180 revet 21	–	–	–	–	1:1.86	–	1:15.00	–
193 revet 21	1474	1484+	–	–	–	–	–	–
298–299 revet 21	–	–	–	–	–	–	–	–
196 revet 21	–	–	–	–	–	–	–	–
185 revet 21	–	–	–	1:4.66	1:1.00	1:4.66	1:7.00	1:8.00
187–296 revet 21	1448	1458+	Pegs in rivet holes. New rivets	1:5.73 1:7.04	1:1.78 1:1.82 1:1.30	1:3.21 1:5.40	1:11.08	–
183 revet 21	1456	1466+	Pegs in rivet holes	1:6.87	1:1.74 1:1.95	1:3.95 1:3.51	1:9.39	1:9.56
188–197 revet 21	1476	1486+	–	1:10.43	1:2.81	1:3.71	1:12.25	1:8.75
205–268	–	–	Patch set in plank	–	–	–	–	–
785–419	–	–	–	1:4.36	1:1.16 1:1.44	1:3.73 1:3.01	1:4.11	1:5.36
200–199	1451	1461+	?*Teredo*	–	–	–		–
Hays Wharf to Abbots Lane, 1988								
039–2	1571	1581+	Burnt outboard	1:9.25	1:1.75 1:2.40	1:5.28 1:3.85	1:6.75	1:9.00
038–1	–	–	–	–	1:3.00	–	1:9.33	–
040–3	–	–	Tacks at outboard edge of scarf	1:7.39	1:1.52 1:1.95	1:3.77	1:8.26	1:8.26
Hays Wharf to Morgans Lane, 1987								
735–123	1480	1490+	–	1:10.47	1:1.74	1:6.02	1:7.69	–
659–35	–	–	–	–	1:1.92	–	1:5.57	1:12.85
625–13	–	–	Re-riveted	–	–	–	1:4.46	–
632/4–32/4	–	–	Patch & hair caulking over trenail & lap	1:7.08	1:2.0 1:1.11	1:6.37	1:3.73	1:9.53
837–50	–	–	Refaced with elm outboard	–	1:1.48 2:2.05	–	1:5.44	1:7.2

Table 7 Post-medieval continued

site context	wood	plank radial or tangential	plank max thick	width	lap width	lap caulking	rivet spacing	rivet shank	rivet length	scarf rivets	scarf caulking	diam	trenail spacing	trenail wood
Hays Wharf to Morgans Lane, 1988														
101–84 104/6–87/89	O	R/T	22 25	170	40	–	19–118	4×4	165 194	1 in 1 out	Hair	23 24	594 530 574	–
030/1–23/4	E	T	28	182+	60	–	99–155	–	360	1 in 1 out	–	23?	520	–
033–26	E	T	30	344	52	–	98–143	5×5	430	2 in 1 out	–	22	550 543 547	–
107–90	O	R	27	114+	45	–	40–93	5×5	167	–	Hair	23 24	106 484 80	–
102–85	E	T	30	207	42	Hair	113–48 97–143	5×5	230	–	Hair	–	–	–
101–84	O	R	25	161+	40	–	45–156	5×5	222 200	1 in 1 out 1 in 1 out	Hair	22	615	–
103–86	O	R	25	170	40	–	70–138 60–133	4×4	160	1 in	–	–	–	–
028–21	E	T	26	152+	60	–	94–118	5×5	230	1 in 1 out	Hair	–	–	–
025–83	E	T	26	154+	55	Hair	120–35	5×5	180	–	–	22	–	–
029–22	O	T	26	–	50 46	–	72–137	4×4	–	–	–	–	–	–
034–27	E	T	30	–	45	Hair felt	97–135	–	450	?1 in 1 out	–	22	565	–
040–033	–	T	–	–	56	Hair	95–143	–	180	–	–	–	–	–
Hays Wharf to Morgans Lane, 1987 (reverse clinker boat)														
723/4–87/8	O	R	30 25	186 187	50 37	–	90–125 85–150 70–165	–	–	–	–	20	–	–
722–89	O	R	25	145	37	–	115–78	5×5	–	–	–	–	–	–
726/7–85	O	R	20	184	55	–	75–125	–	185	1 in 1 out	Hair	–	–	–
727–67	O	R	25	137	40 42	–	80–120	–	–	–	–	19	–	–
725–86	O	R	25	187	40 50	–	90–140	–	–	–	–	–	–	–
Guys Hospital, 1989														
160	E?	T	24 29	292	50	Hair	108–32 25–144	5×5	–	–	–	25	545	O
245 Blackfriars Road, 1987														
269–205	O	R	22+	630+	42	–	112–20	5×5	–	–	–	27	–	–
269–204	O	R	34	132	54	Hair	38–122	4×4	–	–	–	25 27 26	–	–
Bridewell, 1978														
190–3	O	R	20 20	170 213	40	Hair	81–104 130–40 122–28	4×4	–	–	–	20	–	–
190–1	O	R	20	180	50	Hair	116	4×4	230	–	–	22	–	–
Hays Wharf to Butter Factory South, 1988														
158–150/4	O	R	30	262+	50	Hair	112–85	–	–	–	–	–	1334+	–
118–49	O	R	32	360	50	Hair	108–82	7×7	–	–	–	–	–	–
Cherry Garden Street, 1987														
2–6, 7–32	O	R	32	450+	28+	Hair	–	–	210	–	–	25	–	–
84–46	O	R	43	110+	–	–	–	4×4	–	–	–	35	–	–
3–8	O	R	18	–	42	–	103–32	6×6	–	–	–	25	–	–

Notes: all measurements are in millimetres; O = oak; E = elm

Table 7 Post-medieval continued

site context	dendro last ring date	boat date	repairs	plank thick: plank width	lap width: plank thick	lap width: plank width	max rivet spacing: plank thick	scarf length: plank thick
Hays Wharf to Morgans Lane, 1988								
101–84	–	–	2 rows of rivets	1:7.72	1:1.81	1:4.25	1:5.36	1:7.50
104/6–87/89			in lap	1:6.80	1:1.60		1:4.72	1:7.76
030/1–23/4	–	–	Extra nails in lap. Tacks in scarf cage	–	1:2.14	–	1:5.53	–
033–26	–	–	Tacks at edge of scarf	1:11.46	1:1.73	1:6.61	1:4.76	1:14.33
107–90	–	–	Patch over trenails	–	1:1.66	–	1:3.44	1:6.18
102–85	–	–	Tacks at scarf edge outboard	1:6.90	1:1.40	1:4.92	1:4.93	1:7.66
101–84	1568 8 sap	1570– 1615	Re-riveted	–	1:1.60	–	1:6.24	1:8.88 1:8.0
103–86	–	–	Extra lap rivets. Tacks at scarf edge	1:6.80	1:1.60	1:4.25	1:5.52	1:6.40
028–21	–	–	Tacks at scarf edge	–	1:2.3	–	1:4.53	1:8.84
025–83	–	–	Tacks at scarf edge outboard	–	1:2.11	–	1:5.19	1:6.92
029–22	–	–	–	–	1:1.92 1:1.77	–	1:5.27	–
034–27	–	–	Tacks at scarf edge. Many extra scarf fastenings	–	1:1.5	–	1:4.5	1:15.0
040–033	–	–	–	–	–	–	–	–
Hays Wharf to Morgans Lane, 1987 (reverse clinker boat)								
723/4–87/8	–		Plank E	1:1.6	1:1.66	1:3.72	1:5.5	–
			Plank D	1:7.48	1:1.48	1:5.05		
722–89	1567		Plank F	1:5.80	1:1.48	1:3.91	1:7.0	–
726/7–85	–	1577+	Plank B	1:9.2	1:2.75	1:3.34	1:6.25	1:9.25
727–67	–		Plank A	1:5.48	1:1.60 1:1.68	1:3.42 1:3.26	1:4.8	–
725–86	1555		Plank C	1:7.48	1:1.60 1:2.00	1:4.67 1:3.74	1:5.6	–
Guys Hospital								
160	–	–	Extra lap rivets	1:10.06	1:2.08 1:1.72	1:5.84	1:4.96	–
245 Blackfriars Road, 1987								
269–205	–	–	Patch held by tacks	–	1:1.56	–	–	–
269–204	–	–	Extra lap rivets	1:3.88	1:1.58	1:2.44	1:3.58	–
Bridewell, 1978								
190–3	–	–	Plank split at trenails. Patch over	1:8.50 1:10.65	1:2.00	1:4.25 1:5.32	1:7.00	–
190–1	–	–	Plank split at trenail. Patch over	1:9.00	1:2.50	1:3.60	1:5.80	1:11.50
Hays Wharf to Butter Factory South, 1988								
158–150/4	1531	1541+	–	–	–	–	1:6.16	–
118–49	–	–	–	1:11.25	1:1.66	1:7.20	1:5.68	–
Cherry Garden Street, 1987								
2–6, 7–32	–	–	–	–	–	–	–	1:6.56
84–46	1554	1564+	–	–	–	–	–	–
3–8	–	–	–	–	–	–	1:7.33	–

Table 8 Summary results of all the material studied

site name	group	wood	total no samples	too short	not dated	dated	years	date of chronology	date of group	origin
Custom House	1	oak	19	-	3	16	235	AD922-1156	AD1160-1190	local
	2	oak	1	-	1	-	-	-	-	-
Blackfriars	3	oak	11	4	-	7	103	AD1267-1380	AD1380-1415	local
Abbots Lane (87)	A	oak	16	8	4	1	68	AD1266-1333	AD1343++	local
						2	91	AD1278-1368	AD1375++	Baltic
						1	149	AD1196-1344	AD1352++	German
	B	oak	3	1	2	-	-	-	-	-
	C	oak	2	-	1	1	57	AD1296-1352	AD1362++	local
	D	oak	2	1	-	1	73	AD1279-1351	AD1353-1398	local
5-15 Bankside		oak	2	-	1	1	110	AD1028-1137	AD1147++	local
Billingsgate		oak	11	1	6	4	157	AD1027-1183	AD1183++	local
Symonds Wharf	1	oak	9	-	-	9	201	AD1133-1333	AD1340++	Baltic
	2	oak	1	1	-	-	-	-	-	-
	3	oak	2	1	-	1	115	AD1193-1307	AD1314++	Baltic
Gun and Shot	1	oak	10	-	-	10	319	AD1052-1370	AD1370-1397	Baltic
Trig Lane		oak	6	4	2	-	-	-	-	-
Morgans Lane (87)	reverse	oak	5	1	2	2	74	AD1494-1567	AD1577++	local
37 Bankside		oak	18	6	2	10	164	AD1313-1476	AD1486++	local
Gun and Shot	2	oak	12	2	5	5	128	AD1441-1568	AD1578++	local
		elm	3	3	-	-	-	-	-	-
Morgans Lane (87)	others	oak	3	-	1	2	139	AD1387-1525	AD1535++	local
		elm	2	2	-	-	-	-	-	-
Morgans Lane (88)		oak	3	1	-	2	98	AD1471-1568	AD1570-1615	local
		elm	5	5	-	-	-	-	-	-
Abbots Lane (88)		oak	4	1	2	1	71	AD1501-1571	AD1581++	local
Butter Factory		oak	3	1	1	1	90	AD1442-1531	AD1541++	local
Cherry Garden		oak	3	1	1	1	67	AD1488-1554	AD1564-1609	local
Bethel Estate		oak	32	14	5	13	181	AD1395-1575	AD1584-1603	local
Guys Hospital		elm	2	2	-	-	-	-	-	-
245 Blackfriars Rd		oak	1	1	-	-	-	-	-	-

However, the bulk of the same tree links made during this study were subsequently found to be multiple samples of the same piece of timber. In no case was enough material recovered and sampled to indicate the methods or order of construction.

Many fragmentary parts of vessels were found reused in other structures, some of which were not necessarily related. In these cases converting the tree-ring dates into useful archaeological information was complicated by a lack of hard information about which planks belonged together. Some problems may also have arisen with insecure identification of patches and other repairs. Further problems may have arisen where samples have become mis-labelled between excavation and analysis. The use of relatively freshly felled timber for the construction of the vessels is assumed in any interpretation.

When using the results from this volume the following three rules should be noted:

- Only oak samples were analysed. The only non-oak material was elm, all of which had too few rings for dating purposes. No softwood timbers were recovered.

- The samples had to contain enough rings to enable a reliable cross-match with another sequence to be found. 50 rings was regarded as the absolute minimum necessary.

- Since many timbers were incomplete or potentially fragmentary the most reliance can be placed on those vessels or fragments from which more than one datable sample was obtained. Multiple dates having a similar range lends more confidence to a suggested construction date. For those groups, although reliably dated, from which only a single dated sample was obtained, the sample may have lost many outer rings and thus indicate a date somewhat earlier than the real date.

The method of analysis

The samples consisted of 30–50mm-thick sections cut across the grain of a timber to maximise the number of rings, or to include any surviving sapwood. The samples were not necessarily considered representative of the entire construction.

Examination using a low magnification binocular microscope was usually enough to distinguish the wood type concerned. If not, the methodology outlined for the pegs, etc in Appendix 2 was adopted. The primary hardwood species (oak, ash, elm, and beech) were easily distinguished in this quick fashion, and in this case all the tree-ring samples reported here are of oak (*Quercus* spp), and elm (*Ulmus* spp).

Prior to tree-ring measurement, the samples were cleaned so that the entire ring sequence was clearly visible. The beginning and ending of each ring along a radius or series of connected sub-radii was identified. The samples were processed by freezing them until they were solid, and the surfaces were cut using surforms and razor blades until the ring sequence was completely visible. They were then left to thaw out.

The sequence of rings in each tree-ring sample was measured using a low-power binocular microscope and a travelling stage connected to a computer that enabled the ring-widths to be recorded automatically. Measure-ment was carried out to an accuracy of 0.01mm and the resulting computer file also recorded the site and context information for the timber and a number of other details. In some cases more than one radius was measured.

The sequence resulting from each sample was then plotted out, either by hand onto standard semi-log roll paper, or by the computer using a plotter. These enabled visual checks of the ring-sequence matches to be made and errors in the sequences to be recognised.

When all the timber samples from each boat had been measured and plotted, cross-matching between individual timbers was carried out using computer programs and checked for validity using the graphs. Where acceptable matches were found a new 'mean' series was built by averaging the patterns at the appropriate relative positions. The timbers not in the new mean were compared with the new mean and the process repeated until as many of the timbers as possible were incorporated into the working mean sequence. All the individual timbers and the working means were then compared with reference sequences from London and elsewhere in order to find significant correlations for each of these sequences. These positions were again checked by comparing the graphs and where acceptable resulted in a tree-ring date for the individual timbers. After interpretation for missing rings, etc a date for the boat was produced.

Discussion

There are a number of points ensuing from the tree-ring analysis that should be noted here. Neither the available material nor the sampling strategy adopted supports any interpretation based on the assumption that the data produced is representative of the wood assemblage used in vessels of this period. Thus no

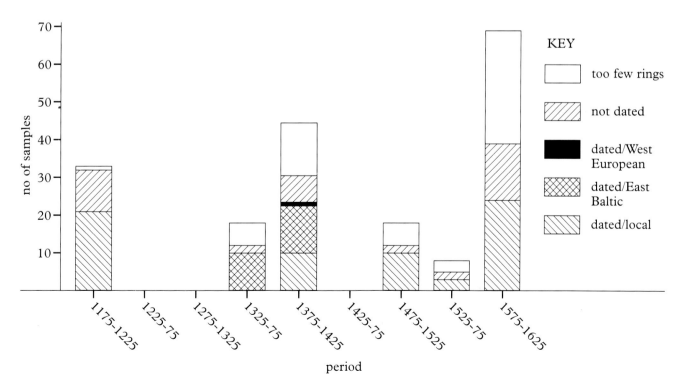

Fig 188 Summary of variations in timber origins

Table 9 Dating of vessel fragments

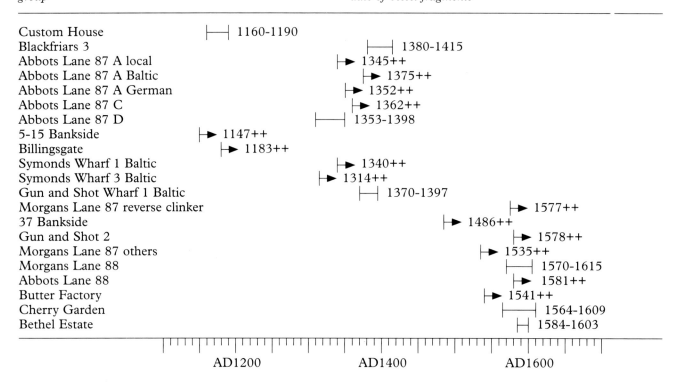

group	date of vessel fragments
Custom House	⊢—⊣ 1160-1190
Blackfriars 3	⊢—⊣ 1380-1415
Abbots Lane 87 A local	⊢▶ 1345++
Abbots Lane 87 A Baltic	⊢▶ 1375++
Abbots Lane 87 A German	⊢▶ 1352++
Abbots Lane 87 C	⊢▶ 1362++
Abbots Lane 87 D	⊢—⊣ 1353-1398
5-15 Bankside	⊢▶ 1147++
Billingsgate	⊢▶ 1183++
Symonds Wharf 1 Baltic	⊢▶ 1340++
Symonds Wharf 3 Baltic	⊢▶ 1314++
Gun and Shot Wharf 1 Baltic	⊢—⊣ 1370-1397
Morgans Lane 87 reverse clinker	⊢▶ 1577++
37 Bankside	⊢▶ 1486++
Gun and Shot 2	⊢▶ 1578++
Morgans Lane 87 others	⊢▶ 1535++
Morgans Lane 88	⊢—⊣ 1570-1615
Abbots Lane 88	⊢▶ 1581++
Butter Factory	⊢▶ 1541++
Cherry Garden	⊢—⊣ 1564-1609
Bethel Estate	⊢—⊣ 1584-1603

AD1200   AD1400   AD1600

generalised reconstructions of, for example, the local wooded landscape or of the local market in timber can be reliably made from the data.

An approximate depiction of the date of the various groups of the data shows convincingly that the data set lacks material of the thirteenth and mid fifteenth centuries (Table 9). The apparent trend away from the use of local timber and then back again over the period needs further investigation, especially as the majority of the foreign timbers are derived from more substantial vessels than those built of local timber.

The presence of imported timbers in the fourteenth century of eastern Baltic origin has many parallels with other archaeological and art-historical tree-ring studies (Bonde 1992, Wazny 1992). These and other studies have shown convincingly that an extensive trade in eastern Baltic timbers existed from the early fourteenth to mid seventeenth centuries. The single piece of German timber also has many comparable

findings since several buckets and barrels excavated within London of contemporaneous date are derived from the same source. Thus, although rather less common than the Baltic timbers, the German material nevertheless represents a persistent component of the later-medieval timber assemblages so far studied (author's unpublished information).

There are two groups of undated samples from the Billingsgate vessel timbers that seem likely to represent a group of timbers undatable by our current geographic range of reference chronologies. It would be of great interest to compare the temporal spread of imported material within the entire assemblage reported here to the patterns derived for other objects such as medieval boards or panelling. However, this aspect is outside the scope of this volume. At the time of writing this data represents the first major assemblage of tree-ring dated boat timbers to be analysed. There are therefore no other assemblages with which to compare or contrast the data.

Appendix 2 Wood identifications, twelfth to seventeenth centuries
by Ian Tyers

This appendix summarises the wood identifications carried out upon the ship and boat timbers described in this volume. Reference should be made to Appendix 1 for the plank identifications made during the tree-ring analyses.

In addition to the 192 plank samples submitted for tree-ring analysis, a further 58 samples of pegs, trenails, and plank fragments were submitted for timber identification. These identifications are reported in chapters 2 to 8 and in Tables 6 and 7: only summary details are provided in Table 10. The summary results use the common names of the timber species. Full details of the analyses are lodged with the project archives (Tyers 1990, 1992).

The identifications were carried out by making microscope slides of radial, tangential, and longitudinal sections. These were then compared with reference slides and appropriate identification keys (Schweingruber 1982, Wilson and White 1986, and Schweingruber 1990) using high-magnification microscopes. A very restricted range of wood-types was identified during the study. There are two marked trends that require further investigation from similar groups of material. At around AD 1200 the use of willow/poplar (*Populus/Salix* gen and spp *indet*) for trenails appears to be superseded by the use of oak (*Quercus* spp). During the sixteenth century the use of elm (*Ulmus* spp) for planking becomes common.

Table 10 Summary of wood identifications in the same order as the separate groups of vessel fragments in the main text. Group codes and descriptions are also those used in the main text

group	sample type	species type
Custom House	2 trenails	1 oak/ 1 ?willow/poplar
Blackfriars 3	1 trenail	willow/poplar
	1 wedge	oak
Abbots Lane (87) A-D	2 trenails	2 willow/poplar
	2 pegs	2 oak
	3 planks/patches	3 oak
Billingsgate	3 trenails	3 willow/poplar
	1 peg	oak
	1 wedge	oak
Symonds Wharf 1-3	2 trenails	2 oak
Gun and Shot 1	2 trenails	2 oak
	2 pegs in trenails	2 oak
Morgans Lane (87) reverse clinker	1 peg	oak
37 Bankside	3 trenails	3 oak
	2 pegs	2 oak
	1 bung	cork
Gun and Shot 2	2 trenails	2 oak
	6 planks/patches	4 elm/2 oak
Morgans Lane (87) others	1 trenail	oak
	1 peg	oak
	8 planks/patches	3 elm/5 oak
Morgans Lane (88)	1 trenail	oak
	7 planks/patches	5 elm/1 oak/1 unidentified
Bethel Estate	2 trenails	2 oak
Guys Hospital	1 trenail	oak

This table is in the same order as the separate groups of vessel fragments in the main text. Group codes and descriptions are also those used in the main text

Appendix 3 Hair in the boat caulking
by Michael L Ryder

Introduction

This investigation follows earlier ones on caulking from boats of the Roman period found in London (Cutler 1994) and of the Saxon period (Ryder 1994). The constraints of funding and time, which restricted this investigation to the qualitative identification of species, means a lack of detail. The usual quantitative study would not only have thrown light on the breed types and husbandry practices involved with the livestock from which the hair came (Ryder 1969; 1983), but would have allowed the matching of caulking samples, for instance. Hopefully a more detailed investigation of this material will be possible before long. The same approach could be followed with any plant fibres such as flax or hemp used as caulking.

Previous findings

All the Roman caulking studied was plant material. Cutler (1994) showed that the caulking of two Romano-Celtic vessels from London were made from shavings of hazel wood, but on the other hand some material described as 'hull covering' from Roman ships on Lake Nemi, Italy, was fine wool (measurements of Ucelli 1950, quoted by Ryder 1969). The caulking of an eleventh-century boat excavated at Fennings Wharf, London, in 1984 comprised two samples of cattle hair and two of wool (Ryder 1994).

Although animal hair caulking is well known, few detailed studies of the material have been made. The hair in the late Saxon Graveney boat was identified as sheep's wool by Hunt (1978). The wool was identified as a long-wooled breed from the surface scale pattern, but the two fibres illustrated having diameters of only 22 and 26 microns appear to be too fine for this type, the existence of which at that date is doubtful. In order to define fleece type, fibre diameter distribution can be obtained by measuring 100 fibres.

Fibrous remains in the form of 73 flattened rolls or pads from Queen Street waterfront site in Newcastle were investigated by Walton (1988). These were dated to the thirteenth century and were thought to represent caulking although they were no longer associated with timbers either in the original boat or the revetment from which they had come. The rolls were ropes of twisted fibres and in eight of the finds two or more rolls had been plied to make a thicker cord.

Identification of the hair in a random sample of 25 finds from the Queen Street site showed that 13 were cattle hair, two possibly goat hair, and ten were wool. Measurement of the wool samples showed that they were predominantly of Hairy-medium type, the coarser variety of the common medieval wool type. Three of the samples had natural pigmentation and another had been dyed blue with indigotin from woad. This compares with one sample from the Fennings Wharf wool, which was of Hairy-medium type and also dyed, possibly green rather than blue (Ryder 1994, Fennings Wharf). It also compares with several wool samples in the present collection, which were dyed blue.

A study of caulking from Bergen, Norway, quoted by Walton (1988) indicated a gradual change from the use of wool in the twelfth century to the use of cattle and goat hair in the fifteenth century, mostly as plied cords. A survey of English reused boat timbers by Walton (*ibid*) showed the use of mainly single twisted cords, all of wool in twelfth-century Hartlepool, 40% of wool in thirteenth-century Newcastle (above), wool, cattle, and goat hair in fourteenth to fifteenth-century Hull, and cattle hair and wool on a medieval site in York that had not been firmly dated.

Walton (1989) described another 130 rolls and pads of thirteenth and fourteenth-century date from Crown Court waterfront site in Newcastle. All were made from hair except one of unidentified plant fibre, another of cotton grass, and one of hair moss, although it is not certain that the last two examples were caulking material. A sample group gave the following identifications: wool 10, cattle 3, goat 2, dog 1, human head 1, and one mixture of goat hair and wool. The proportion of wool fell from 71% in the thirteenth century to 38% in the fourteenth. Five of the wool samples were measured for fleece type and three were primitive Hairy-medium wools, typical of the medieval period. The other two were modern types, one was a true Medium fleece and the other a Semi-fine (shortwool). Like the single dyed sample from Queen Street (Walton 1988), two of these had been dyed with indigotin (woad) and the identification of these as wool waste was confirmed by the remains of spun threads in one of the samples.

More recent and modern caulking seems to have been mainly plant, flax and hemp fibre. Hemp and tar were used to caulk the reconstruction ship built in Barcelona to commemorate the five hundredth anniversary of Columbus's voyage. It is not clear whether this represents the authentic caulking material of late fifteenth-century Spain, or is a modern type.

Materials and methods

There were over 200 samples of caulking from an uncertain number of boats. As with other British sites, most of the material investigated did not come from intact boats, but from boat timbers that had been reused as revetments. The hair was, however, still *in situ* between overlapping planks (the lap), between plank joints (the scarf), and in repair patches.

As before, the present fibrous material had been preserved by waterlogging and was mostly received in a dirty, wet condition so it had to be either air-dried and cleaned, or washed and dehydrated with surgical spirit before whole mount preparations in Euparal could be made for microscopic examination. Some hairs showed partial degredation (under the microscope) otherwise the material was in good condition.

Result and discussion

Eye examination

The gross appearance of the material is recorded in Tables 11–16, giving the species identifications. Since most samples comprised an irregular mass of hairs or fibres it was difficult to give a meaningful description that would distinguish one sample from another. Most samples had the clear tufts or locks of hair seen in the coat of animals. Some that turned out to be cattle had tufts 30mm or 40mm long, others that turned out to be goat had longer tufts, in one instance as long as 0.1m. This provided evidence that hair of different species had in general not been mixed. The tuft lengths are shown in the tables, but discussion of these in relation to coat type follows discussion of the hair diameter measurements.

Table 11 Hair identifications in twelfth-century caulking

Context and sample no	location	description	species
Custom House: late twelfth century (1157–1190)			
0	plank	felted mass	cattle
1/15a		mass	cattle
1/15b	patch	sub-rect. mass	cattle
1/16a	lap	band	cattle
1/16b	scarf	small mass	cattle
1/16c	repair	large mass	cattle
5		sub-rect. mass	cattle
7		long mass	cattle
13		band	cattle
19a		small mass	cattle
19b	patch B	mass	cattle
21/14	lap	1 cm-thick rope	cattle
25	scarf	mass	cattle
41		1.5 cm-wide band	cattle
44/11a		1.5 cm-wide band	cattle
44/11b		mass	cattle
45/10		broad band	cattle
50a	lap	broad band	cattle & some wool
50b	scarf	mass	cattle & some wool
51a/12	lap	band	cattle
51b/12	scarf	mass	cattle
81a	scarf	irregular mass	cattle
81b	lap	felted band	cattle
91/14	lap	felted band	cattle
103	lap	felted band in tar	cattle & dyed wool
121	lap	felted band in tar	cattle
133/3a		tarred band	cattle
133/3b	lap	mass	cattle
138	scarf	long band	cattle
212	lap	band	cattle & some wool
212	scarf	irregular mass	cattle & some wool
5–15, Bankside: late twelfth century			
5BS87/3163	patch	small mass	cattle & wool

Table 12   Hair identifications in fourteenth-century caulking

Context and no	location	description	species
Trig Lane: ?fourteenth century			
10	lap	mass 4cm locks	goat
10	scarf	mass 4cm locks	goat
11	lap	felted band, muddy	goat
11	scarf A	felted band, muddy	goat & cattle
11	scarf B	mass with hair locks	goat
1353	intact lap		goat
1353	open lap		goat & cattle
1353	patch		goat
1381	luting	small mass	goat
1382	lap	band	goat
1382	scarf	mass, 10cm locks	goat & cattle
1383	lap	4cm felted band	goat
1383	scarf	6cm felted band	goat
1384	lap	felted band	goat
1384	scarf	small matt	goat & cattle
1384	tingle	mass, some plant	goat
Blackfriars 3: fifteenth century			
BL3/17c/0	repair A	felt with black tufts to 7 cm	goat
BL3/0 Dendro A	scarf	black mass with tufts	goat
BL3/0 stem/heel	scarf	black mass with tufts	goat
BL3/0 rabbet	scarf	felted mass	goat
BL3/0/10	repair	tufts to 8cm, pointed tips	goat
BL3/0/11	patch	felted band	goat
BL3/0/12	patch	felted band	goat
BL3/0/13	lap	mass w tufts to 6cm	goat
BL3/0/14	lap	felted band cut long edge	goat
BL3/0/15	lap	felted band cut short edge	goat
BL3/0/20	scarf	felted band cut long edge	goat
BL3/0/21	lap	mass adhering to wood flakes	goat
BL3	patch	small tufts	goat
BL3	garboard/keel	few tufts to 5cm	goat
BL3/0/22	lap	mass of tufts	goat
BL3/16 Dendro A	lap	mass of tufts	goat
Hays Wharf, Gun and Shot Wharf: late fourteenth century			
160/452	between planks	unmatted tufts	goat cattle wool
274/149	no location		cattle
Hays Wharf, Symonds Wharf (boat not local); late fourteenth century			
168	lap	thick matted band	cattle
168/141	no location	thick matted band	cattle
194/136	outboard lap	band	cattle, few goat
196/120	lap	irregular mass	cattle
196/120	scarf	plant	plant, few cattle

There was virtually no evidence that the material had been prepared in any way before use; a single 10mm rope was recorded in CUS73, fragments 14 and 21. Other samples (ie from laps) comprised slightly-felted bands, the width of which (shown in the tables) indicated the extent of overlap of the planks. There was no evidence that the material had been made into a felt before use. Much of that identified as wool was in the raw state, while other examples had been dyed. The term 'wool' is here used to indicate fibres from sheep (Ryder 1983).

As with the Fenning's Wharf dyed wool, there was no evidence of weave in these and so the fibres are unlikely to have come from woven rags. Neither was there any evidence of the twist found in spun yarns. One source of such dyed wool is spinners waste that

Context and no	location	description	species
Hays Wharf, Abbots Lane; late fourteenth century +			
155/152a	large lap	irregular mass	wool
155/152b	small lap	irregular mass	goat
155/152c	scarf	irregular mass	goat
155/152d	patch	irregular mass	wool
155/152e	NOT FOUND		
175/53a	lap	band	goat
175/53b	scarf	matted with 3cm locks	cattle
175/53c	patch	felted	goat
178/54	lap	irregular mass	cattle
178/54	scarf	locks evident	cattle
183/62a	scarf A	small mass	goat
183/62b	lap	irregular mass	goat
183/62c	scarf B	rectangular felt 3cm locks	goat
183/62d	scarf C	2–3cm locks	goat
183/62e	scarf E	as above	goat
183/62f	hole	small tufts	goat
183/62g	? patch	large felted mass	goat
187/66	patch	irregular mass with tufts	goat
189/68	fragment A	loose 2–3cm locks	cattle
195	lap	felted 3cm band	goat
195/74	lap	a few tufts	goat
195/74	scarf	mass with 3–4cm locks	goat
199a	scarf	small mass, 3cm tufts	cattle
199b	repair	mass of tufts, at least 3cm	goat
199c	lap	5cm tufts in mass	cattle
199/78	lap	mass of tufts	cattle
199/78	scarf	tufts, with 3cm pointed staples	cattle
201	scarf	felt with tufts to 3cm	cattle
201/81	scarf	as above but shorter tufts	cattle
201/81	lap	mass of tufts up to 4cm	cattle
206/87	lap	similar tufts up to 4cm	cattle
206/87	scarf	mass of tufts length not clear	goat
209/91	patch	felted	goat
213/95	no location	felt with some tufts	goat
216/99a	lap	felt with some tufts	goat
216/99b	scarf	tufts up to 3cm	cattle
236/154a	lap	felted band	cattle
236/154b	scarf	tufts	cattle
238/156a	lap	felt	cattle
238/156b	scarf	tufts	cattle
238/156c	lap	4cm tufts, pointed tips	cattle
238/156d	scarf	debris only, not sampled	–

had been 'dyed-in-the-wool'. This contrasts with a single sample reported by Walton (1989) as having a spinning twist, and the fifteenth-century historical record quoted by Marsden (*see chapter 1*) of the supply for caulking of thrums, which are warp-ends left when the cloth is cut from the loom. Some types of wool readily lose their spinning twist, which would be hastened by the handling involved in the caulking

process, and so most of the dyed examples could be thrums.

During the preparation for mounting, the surgical spirit used to wash the hair often acquired a dark brown colour that is assumed to have come from tar. This provided the main evidence for the use of tar, since it was rarely evident to the eye and few globules on the hairs were observed under the microscope.

Microscopic examination

Microscopic examination was carried out in date order and confirmed that no true felt had been made before the use of the fibrous material. The felting almost certainly had been caused by movement of the planks under wet conditions during normal use of the boat (*cf* Ryder and Gabra-Sanders 1984).

Cattle and goat hair as well as wool was identified under the microscope. As in the earlier investigation of Ryder (1994) more than one type of cattle coat appeared to be represented, and also possibly calf. Details of coat type and age differences can be obtained only by detailed fibre diameter measurements (Ryder 1969; 1984). The goat hair accords with the fifteenth-century record quoted by Marsden (*see chapter 1*) of the supply of goat hair for caulking. It was used in its entirety with no separation of the underwool (Ryder 1986). The most likely source of the cattle and goat hair is from skins before their use in leather making. Fibre measurements would be particularly valuable here since little is known about medieval goat hair (Ryder 1987). The hair identifications in the caulking from individual boats are shown by species and by century in Tables 11 to 15. These are summarised in Table 16 to show how the species represented changed with time.

During the twelfth century cattle hair predominated with 78%, the remainder (7 examples) containing cattle hair and wool (see discussion on mixtures below). By the fourteenth century goat hair had become predominant with 65%, cattle coming next with 28%, while 3% (two examples) were wool and 4% (three examples) were apparently mixtures, two of which were cattle and goat, and one of cattle, goat, and wool. In the single fifteenth-century boat (37–46 Bankside) 94% of the samples were goat and the remainder (one sample) was cattle. The use of goat hair had declined by the sixteenth century, forming only 3%, and wool predominated with 49%, although there were nearly as many examples of cattle hair (46%). One example of a 'mixture' of cattle hair and wool accounted for 2% of the total.

These results are quite different from the pattern at Bergen in Norway, where there was a gradual increase in the use of hair in place of wool from the twelfth to the fifteenth century. Walton (1988; 1989) saw evidence of a similar increase in the use of wool in northern English sites.

In this study all samples with hair from more than one species observed under the microscope were at first regarded as mixtures. Then it was realised that this did not necessarily mean conscious mixing; some had so few hairs from another species that the different hairs could be explained by contamination perhaps at the boatyard, which is not uncommon. The presence

Table 13   Hair identifications in fifteenth-century caulking

context and no	location	description	species
37–46 Bankside; late fifteenth century			
165	lap	irregular mass	goat
165	scarf	tufts to 4cm	goat
183	lap	felted band	goat
183	scarf	2 by 0.5cm fragment	goat
185	lap	few hairs, much earth	cattle
185	scarf	felted band, much earth	goat
187	lap	irregular felt	goat
188	lap	irregular felt	goat
188	scarf	irregular mass	goat
196	scarf	felt band, tufts to 3cm	goat
196	lap	wavy tufts to 3cm	goat
202	lap	felted band	goat
266	lap	felted band with tufts	goat
266	scarf	separate masses with tufts	goat
266	scarf 2	sparse mass	goat
298	B	felted band	goat

of a small proportion of different hairs could mean the use of different hair at different times, so that a new batch of hair from a different species might have been contaminated with hair left lying about from previous operations. The fibre diameter measurements proposed, in which a count of fibres is made automatically, would indicate the proportion of alien fibres in such samples, from which it might be decided which are truly mixtures. One mixture involved plant material.

No animal hair appears to provide what can be regarded as 'normal' caulking. The species of hair varied between and within boats as well as between centuries. Despite the large number of examples, the overall sample was too small to reveal whether one period showed more variation than another. It was also too small to show whether variation between boats was more important than variations between centuries.

Regarding possible variation with the lap-/scarf/patch location, during the twelfth century (one boat, Table 11) all the laps, associated scarfs, and patches contained hair from the same species. By the fourteenth century (Table 12), 20 laps and scarfs had the same hair, compared with seven in which the hair was different. Where one lap had two scarfs there were two examples in which one scarf had the same hair as the lap and the other had a different hair from the lap. Surprisingly, considering that patches must have been made later than the original construction, nine had the same hair as the associated lap and scarf, compared with only one that was different. This is probably chance rather than a conscious matching of the original caulking.

Table 14 Hair identifications in sixteenth-century caulking

context and no	location	description	species
245 Blackfriars Road; undated, ?sixteenth century			
269/204	lap	few hairs among earth/wood	cattle
Bethel Estate; late sixteenth century			
488/53	lap A	few small tufts	cattle
488/53	lap C	irregular mass with tufts	cattle
488/53	scarf C	separate lumps	wool
636/425	lap	few felted lumps	cattle
639/426	lap	irregular mass	cattle
639/93	lap	small mass in earth	cattle
639/93	scarf	small mass in earth	wool
711/420	lap	few small tufts	cattle
711/420	scarf	few matted fragments	wool
712/421	scarf	few small tufts	wool
784/380	scarf	very matted, few hairs	wool
785/419	lap	small, dust only	no hairs
785/419	scarf	two felted fragments	cattle & wool
795/230	lap	felted band	wool
795/230	scarf	irregular mass	wool
796/385	scarf 1	few fragments only	wool
796/385	scarf 2	small irregular mass	cattle
1001/231	lap	two felted fragments	wool
1001/231	scarf	few felted fragments	wool
1005/221	lap B-C	irregular felted mass	cattle
1005/221	scarf A	irregular 2–3cm tufts	cattle
Hays Wharf, Abbots Lane; late sixteenth century +			
39	scarf	small, felted fragments	wool
40/3	inboard lap	short, narrow band	blue wool
40/3	outboard lap	small, felted mass	blue wool
40/3	outboard scarf	rectangular, felted mass	blue wool
Hays Wharf, Butter Factor, South; late sixteenth century +			
158	lap A	irregular tufts	cattle
158	scarf A	few fragments only	cattle
158	scarf C	irregular mass	cattle
Hays Wharf, Gun and Shot Wharf; late sixteenth century +			
116/30	lap	little hair in caked earth	cattle
116/30	scarf	several small, masses	blue wool
117/41	scarf	mass with 6cm pointed staple	wool
117/41	lap	felted fragments, few hairs	blue wool
118/40	lap joint	felted fragments, few hairs	blue wool
NB The dyed samples look similar; measurements would elucidate			
118/40	scarf	felted fragments, few hairs	blue wool
119/38	lap	wood flakes	no hair
119/38	no location	felted mass	blue wool
120/39	lap (a)	wood flakes	no hair
120/39	lap (b)	small felted fragments	blue wool
120/39	patch	long felted masses	blue and red wool
138/36	lap	wood flakes	no hair
138/36	no location	small felted fragments	wool
139/37	scarf	several hair tufts	wool
NB This is similar to 138/36; measurements would confirm			
139/37	lap	wood flakes	no hair
137/37	lap joint	wood flakes	no hair
149/274	no location		cattle
Morgans Lane, 1987; late sixteenth century +			
632/32	lap	wood flakes, some hair	cattle
632/32	scarf	felted mass	cattle
632/32	patch	felted fragments, some tufts	wool
639/35	no location	small fragments earth	no hairs
735/123	scarf	mass with black tufts	goat
837/50	lap B/E	fibres matted with mud	wool
837/50	lap A/E	mud-caked tufts	cattle
837/50	scarf	few tiny tufts	cattle
Morgans Lane, 1988; late sixteenth century +			
25/83	no location	caked mass of wool	wool
28/21	scarf	felted mass	cattle
29/22	NOT FOUND		
29/22		plant, not supplied	
30/23		plant, not supplied	
30/23	no location	few tiny masses of wool	wool
33/26	lap	wood flakes, protruding hairs	wool
34/27 (two)		plant, not supplied	
40/33	lap	short, matted band	CATTLE contam. wool
40/33	scarf	few, tiny fragments	dyed WOOL contam. cattle
101/84	scarf A	mass with tufts	cattle
102/85	lap	small mass	cattle
102/85	scarf	mass with tufts (?not same as lap)	cattle
103/86	scarf	black tufted mass	cattle
104/87	scarf A	black tufts (?not same as 86)	cattle
104/87	scarf B	black tufts (?not same as A)	cattle
104/87		plant, not supplied	
107/90		plant, not supplied	
107/90	scarf	felted mass	cattle
Cherry Garden, 1987; ? late sixteenth century, boat not local			
32/2	lap	felted band	goat
32/2	scarf	tufted mass	cattle

Table 15 Hair identifications in seventeenth-century caulking

context and no	location	description	species
BL2	NOT FOUND		

Guys Hospital 1989

160	no location; wood flakes, too few hairs

In the single fifteenth-century boat (Table 13) nine scarfs had the same hair as the laps, compared with only one that had different hair. There was much less uniformity in the sixteenth-century boats (Table 14) in that whereas eight laps and scarfs had the same hair, seven had different hair. There was one example of two adjacent strakes each with a scarf, one of which had the same hair as the lap between them and the other different hair. One patch had the same hair as its associated lap and scarf, while another had different hair. Finally, a pair of laps in one fragment had different hair, and a pair of scarfs in another also had different hair.

Regarding the possibility of associating or linking boat fragments by the similarity of their caulking, the hair in the lap and scarf sometimes appeared so similar that the caulking was probably carried out with the same material, perhaps at the same time. One cannot be sure of this, however, without making fibre measurements. The same approach, with greater knowledge, might be used to suggest the origin of the boat. Similar blue-dyed wool in CUS73, fragment 103, and FW84, fragment 2124a (Ryder 1994) at first sight suggested that the boats had been built in the same yard. The use of dyed wool in boats found in Newcastle (Wyder 1988; 1989) might appear to support such a conclusion. But the Customs House and Fennings Wharf boats are separated in date by 100 years, and the present investigation shows that the use of dyed wool waste as caulking is not unique.

Sample BTH88, fragments 796 and 385 that turned out to be wool, was seen to contain plant material at the time of mounting. But this did not necessarily mean a conscious mixture of plant material with wool since a fragment removed was a burr of the kind that becomes attached to the fleeces of sheep during life and constitutes a wool fault. Although no attempt was made to identify the plant species, this adds a new dimension to the study of medieval sheep husbandry.

Summary and conclusions

Most of the hair and wool investigated still had its staple form, as if it had come straight from the animal. There was therefore virtually no evidence of any preparation, eg into cords, before use, and any felting was almost certainly caused by movement of the boat timbers during sailing.

Table 16 Proportion of different species by boat and by century

	cattle	goat	wool	'mixture'	plant
Twelfth-century total/mean	25 (78%)	–	–	7 (22%)	–
Custom House	25 (81%)	–	–	6 (19%)	–
Bankside	–	–	–	1 (100%)	–
Fourteenth-century total/mean	22 (29%)	50 (64%)	2 (3%)	3 (4%)	–
Trig Lane	–	14 (88%)	–	2 (12%)	–
Blackfriars 3	–	16 (100%)	–	–	–
Gun and Shot Wharf	1 (50%)	–	–	1 (50%)	–
Symonds Wharf	1 (100%)	–	–	–	1
Abbots Lane	18 (45%)	20 (50%)	2 (5%)	–	–
Fifteenth-century total/mean					
Bankside	1 (6%)	15 (94%)	–	–	–
Sixteenth-century total/mean	28 (46%)	2 (3%)	30 (49%)	1 (2%)	–
Blackfriars Road	1 (100%)	–	–	–	–
Bethel Estate	9 (45%)	–	10 (50%)	1 (5%)	–
Abbots Lane	–	–	4 (100%)	–	–
Butter Factory	3 (100%)	–	–	–	–
Gun and Shot	1 (9%)	–	10 (91%)	–	–
Morgan's Lane 1987	4 (57%)	1 (14%)	2 (29%)	–	–
Morgan's Lane 1988	9 (69%)	–	4 (31%)	–	5
Cherry Garden	1 (50%)	1 (50%)	–	–	–

Cattle and goat hair were identified as well as sheep wool; some of the wool had been dyed and was therefore textile waste. Some samples had more than one kind of hair, but one cannot be sure without hair counts whether this was due to conscious mixing or to contemporary contamination.

Cattle hair predominated in the twelfth century, goat hair in the fourteenth and fifteenth centuries, and wool in the sixteenth century, although cattle hair was still important. The number of samples was insufficient to show whether this variation with time was real or whether it was really due to differences between boats.

The hair species varied within as well as between boats, but the number of samples was insufficient to show any pattern.

The scarfs, and even the patches, were more often than not of the same hair species as the laps, although by the sixteenth century these showed more variation.

The measurement of fibres to give a fibre diameter distribution would provide information not only on breed types and husbandry practices, but also details that might allow the matching of timbers from the similarity of associated caulking where the location is not known. The same approach could eventually indicate the source of boats.

Appendix 4 Analysis of resin and tar samples
by John Evans

Table 17   Site of tar resin samples

site	context	sample
Medieval		
ABB 87	199	Inboard plank face (2)
Post-medieval		
37BS87	185	Outboard face of scarf
	194/165/264/297	Outboard plank face
	196	Outboard plank face
	266–267	At edge of planks inboard
G&S 88	118–40	Inboard plank face
	118–40	Outboard plank face
	119–38	Inboard plank face
	120–39	Under repair patch
	139–37	Inboard plank face
	139–37	Outboard plank face
	Next to 160	In angle of lap inboard
MOR 87	723–88	Inboard plank face
	723–88	Outboard plank face
	724–87	Inboard plank face
	724–87	Hair caulking at upper lap
	726/7–85	Outboard plank face
	727–85	In scarf
	659–35	Inboard plank face
	659–35	Outboard plank face
MOR 88	033–26	Outboard plank face
	034–27	Inboard plank face
	101–84	Inboard plank face
	101–84	Outboard plank face
	103–86	Inboard plank face
	103–86	Outboard plank face
	104/5–87/8	Inboard plank face
	104/5–87/8	Outboard plank face
BTH 88	53–488a	Inboard plank face
	53–488c	Inboard plank face
	636/8–425	Outboard plank face
	639–93	Inboard plank face
	639–93	Outboard plank face
	639–93	With hair in scarf
	639–426	Inboard plank face
	711/3,719/20–420	Inboard plank face
	712–421	Inboard plank face
	713–422	Inboard plank face
	784–380	Outboard plank face
	784–380	With hair caulking in scarf
	785–419	Inboard plank face
	785–419	Outboard plank face
	793–228	Inboard plank face
	794–229	Inboard plank face
	794–229	Outboard plank face
	795–230	Inboard plank face
	795–230	Outboard plank face
	795–230	With hair caulking in scarf
	796/7–385	With hair caulking in lap
	1002–218	Inboard plank face
	1002–218	Outboard plank face
	1005–221	Outboard plank face D
ABB 88	039–2	Inboard face B
	039–2	Outboard plank face
	039–2	Outboard face A over scarf
	040–3	Outboard face, plank 1

A comprehensive range of samples from various sites (listed below) was submitted for analysis. Initially the samples were subjected to infrared spectroscopy followed by both thin-layer and gas chromatography, in order to establish their chemical identities. Next the samples were investigated by X-ray fluorescence spectroscopy to identify the suite of elements present. This information served a two-fold purpose. Firstly, it would establish the use of additives such as lime or clay. Secondly, it would detect the use of mineral bitumens that tend to have a characteristic metal presence. Finally, the samples were examined by differential scanning calorimetry to determine their melting/softening temperatures and possible presence of secondary organic additives.

The data obtained showed that all of the samples had traces of resin of a very similar nature. None involved the use of mineral additives or bituminous materials; all were of a wood origin. All were soft wood tars derived from the *Pinus* species. All showed the presence of abeitic acid and palustric/isopimaric acid as well as the expected dehydroabeitic acid. In all cases the latter substance was the major component. However, the presence of the former substances suggests the use of a relatively low-heated resin. Possibly the resin was mixed with a wood tar to make the latter thinner and therefore more easy to work. Alternatively a relatively low-heated resin could have been used directly. The identifications of tar resin is described in Table 17.

Comment
by Peter Marsden

The samples were taken mostly from plank faces, and occasionally from hair caulking, but only from positions where there were noticeable deposits that resembled tar. This shows that far more tar was apparently used in the sixteenth century than in the medieval period, unless of course the earlier tar had decayed away. This seems to be unlikely, though is possible. However, the study of the hair caulking (*see Appendix 3*) showed that the hair too had a thin coating of tar, but because the great quantity of material involved it was not possible to undertake the tar analysis of the caulking. The guideline was that only those pieces of timber that appeared to have traces of tar were sampled.

Appendix 5 Expenditure on ship building and repair by London Bridge, 1382–98

by Brian Spencer

The following extracts are taken from the earliest surviving administrative records of London Bridge, fifteen bridgewardens' account rolls covering the years 1382 to 1398. The accounts, which are in the Corporation of London's Guildhall Record Office, provide a detailed record of the cost, week by week, of maintaining London Bridge and its extensive endowments of property. By the fourteenth century, if not before, the bridge was a major going concern, running a considerable works department and supply depot. Even at slack times it had about fifty men on its payroll, half of them skilled in the building trades.

A boatman was a member of the permanent staff and he organised some part of the bridge's transport requirements. Receiving 2s 6d a week, with modest bonuses at Christmas and Easter, he was better paid than the bridge's chaplains or carter, for example, but received appreciably less than the masons and carpenters. Sometimes the boatman was supported by casual labour. On 15 March, 1382, for instance, labourers were hired to 'unload piles from the boat at the Bridge House'. The Bridge House stood at the foot of the bridge in Southwark and it was here that the boatman and his fellow-workers had their headquarters. Here, too, the bridge's boats were moored. As the extracts below demonstrate, the boats required regular repair and replacement. Thus shipwrights were brought in to build new boats in 1382, 1383, and again in 1386 and they returned in strength as early as 1389 to undertake a general overhaul.

At least one of the bridge's boats seems to have been largely committed to pile-driving operations. The 'great and little rams' were powered by teams of 23 and 15 tidemen and were used to repair or bolster the bridge's massive starlings, or foundations. This was an almost daily procedure at low tide, except during the winter and early spring, and involved a continuous programme of maintenance on the pile-drivers themselves. The frequent scrubbing of the starlings was another operation that must have involved boats. The bridge's boats, however, seem to have been principally used for the transportation of chalk (up to 30 boatloads a year), Kentish ragstone (*see Appendix 6*), and timber. The bridge was ideally situated to take full advantage of water-transport. When bridge officials rode out in search of suitable standing timber, their searches were concentrated on woodland accessible to the Thames. Even so carriage by water, when not undertaken by the bridge's own boats, added to the cost of bulky timber by about half. Thus in March 1385 the bridge bought 39 elms for 67s at Windsor. It

paid a local carpenter to fell and lop them, sent bridge horses to haul them to the Thames and then paid 44s 2d to have them taken downstream to London Bridge.

The following extracts include only those disbursements that specifically mention the bridge's boats. It is possible that some other supplies of timber, rope, pitch, etc, bought by the bridge for unspecified purposes or implements like the long rod bought in 1391 for sounding the water under the bridge, could have been employed in the building, repair or navigation of the bridge's boats. In some entries the original text has been slightly abbreviated.

1382

8 February: Paid to two carpenters called shipwrights working on one new boat for six days at 8d apiece daily, 8s; to two other shipwrights for six days, and each drawing 7d a day, 7s.

15 February: Paid to two carpenters called shipwrights working on the said boat for six days, 8s; to two other shipwrights for the same period, 7s; one piece of curved timber to make two stems for a new boat, 15d; a wiveling for the said boat, 15d.

22 February: Paid to two shipwrights working on the above-mentioned boat for four days, 5s 4d; to two other shipwrights for four days, 4s 8d.

1 March: Paid to four shipwrights working on the above-mentioned boat for six days, 15s.

15 March: Paid to four shipwrights working on the above-mentioned boat for six days, 15s; 300 wooden pegs for the aforesaid boat, 3s; four pieces of curved timber to make knees for the aforesaid boat, 16d; other timber for the same boat, 4s; oil and resin for the same boat, 2s 1d; 1000 clench-nails for the same, 15s; 300 spiking-nails for the same, 2s 3d; one great iron tie for the said boat weighing 38 pounds, at 2d a pound, 6s 4d.

2 August: Two oars for the Bridge House boat, 2s 4d.

15 November: Paid to a certain shipwright for mending various defects in the Bridge House boats, 6s 3d; tilts for covering the Bridge House boat, 6s 6d; four sprits of alder, 5d; four oars for the Bridge House boat, 6s 2d.

1383

18 April: Paid to two carpenters called shipwrights working on a new boat for six days, drawing 15$^{1}/_{2}$d daily between them, 7s 9d; to another shipwright for the same period, drawing 5d a day, 2s 6d; a wiveling for the same boat, 6d.

25 April: Paid to two shipwrights working on the said boat for six days, drawing per day wages as above, 7s 9d; to another shipwright for the same period, 2s 6d; a wiveling for the said boat, 3d.

2 May: Paid to two shipwrights for five days, drawing per day wages as above, 6s 5½d; to another shipwright for five days, 2s 1d; curved timber for the same boat, 22d; 200 wrong-nails for the aforesaid boat, 16d.

9 May: Paid to five shipwrights working on the aforesaid boat for six days, and drawing between them 3s 0½d a day, 18s 3d; 4½ gallons of tar, at 6d a gallon, 2s 3d; oil for the said boat, 5½d; curved timber for the said boat, 12d; 12 pounds of resin for the said boat, 9d; four oars for the Bridge House boat, 5s 4d.

16 May: Paid to one shipwright working on the aforesaid boat for two days, 16d.

13 June: Clench-nails and other nails, together with divers other iron fittings, for making a new boat, 16s 10d.

1384
20 February: Paid to four carpenters called shipwrights, for mending one boat belonging to the Bridge House, for one week drawing 4s apiece weekly, 16s; to a certain 'tentor' for the same week, 2s 6d.

27 February: Paid to four shipwrights working on the above-mentioned boat for one week, 16s; to a tentor working for the same period on the same boat, 2s 6d; a barrel of pitch, 4s 6d; one long piece of timber and curved timber for the same boat, 5s 0½d; 26 ship-boards for the same boat, 14s.

5 March: Paid to four shipwrights for one week, 16s; to one tentor for the same period, 2s 6d.

12 March: Paid to four shipwrights for one week, 16s; to a tentor for the same period, 2s 6d; curved timber for the said boat, 8d; wooden nails and a wiveling for the same, 4s 8d; canvas for the said boat, namely for caulking, 12d.

2 April: Two oars for the Bridge House boat, 2s 4d.

10 July: Two oars for the Bridge House boat, 2s 2d.

29 October: Tanned hide for covering the sword [part of a pile-driver] in the Bridge House boat, 5d.

1385
19 August: Two oars, 2s.

1386
14 June: Four oars for the Bridge House boat, 7s 4d.

29 September: Paid to William Talworthe and Walter Sakyn, shipwrights, working on one new boat belonging to the Bridge House called a *shoute*, for four days, at 8d apiece

daily, 5s 4d; to another shipwright working on the same boat for two days, 16d; to another shipwright for three days, 2s; to another shipwright for four days, 2s; to another shipwright for two days, 8d.

6 October: Paid to William Talworthe and John Stokflete, shipwrights, working on the aforesaid boat for five days, at 8d a day each, 6s 8d; to another shipwright working on the same boat for six days, 4s; to another shipwright for six days, 3s; to another shipwright for three days, 12d.

13 October: Paid to William Talworthe, shipwright, working on the aforesaid boat for six days, 4s; to two other shipwrights working on the same boat for four days, at 8d a day each, 5s 4d; to another shipwright for six days, 3s; to another man working on the aforesaid boat for four days, 16d; 300 wrong-nails for the same boats [sic], 3s.

20 October: Paid to one shipwright working on the aforesaid boat for one day, 8d.

1387
30 March: One mast for the Bridge House boat, 18d.

1388
26 September: Two oars for the bridge boat, 2s 9d.

1389
23 January: Paid to one carpenter called a shipwright working on mending the Bridge House boats for three days and a half, at 8d a day, 2s 4d; to two other shipwrights working on the same boats for six days, each drawing 8d a day, 8s; to another shipwright for five days, at 8d a day, 3s 4d; to another shipwright for five days, at 7d a day, 2s 11d; to another shipwright working on the said boats, drawing 6d a day, 3s.

30 January: Paid to three shipwrights working on the aforesaid boats for five days, at 8d a day each, 10s; to one shipwright for five days at 7d a day, 2s 11d; to another shipwright for five days at 6d a day, 2s 6d.

6 February: Paid to three shipwrights working on the aforesaid boats for five and a half days, at 8d each, 11s; to another shipwright for the same period, drawing 7d a day, 3s 2½d; to another shipwright for the same period, at 6d a day, 2s 9d.

13 February: Paid to four shipwrights working on the aforesaid boats for six days, at 8d a day each, 16s; to another shipwright for the same period, at 7d a day, 3s 6d; to another shipwright for the same period, 2s.

20 February: Paid to four shipwrights working on the aforesaid boats for six days, 16s; to one shipwright for the same period, 3s 6d; to another shipwright for the aforesaid period, 3s; to another shipwright for the aforesaid period, 2s.

27 February: Paid to four shipwrights working on the aforesaid boats for six days, 16s; to one shipwright for the same period, 3s 6d; to another shipwright for the same

period, 3s; to one workman called a shipwright for the same period, 2s; curved timber and wivelings for the aforesaid boats, 8s 10d; four shipboards for the same boats, 4s 6d.

6 March: Paid to two shipwrights working on the aforesaid boats for six days, 8s; to two other shipwrights for the same period, 6s 6d; one barrel of pitch, 5s; linen cloth called canvas for caulking a certain boat belonging to the Bridge House, 15d.

13 March: Paid to one shipwright working on the said boats for six days, 4s; to another shipwright for five days, 3s 4d; to another shipwright for six days, 3s 6d; to another shipwright for three and a half days, 21d.

20 March: Paid to two shipwrights working on the aforesaid boats for one week, 7s 6d; to another shipwright for four days, 6s 8d.

27 March: Paid to two shipwrights working on the aforesaid boats for one week, 7s 6d; 800 wooden wrong-nails for the same boats, 7s; curved timber for the said boats, 3s.

7 August: Two oars called 'ores' (*remis dictis ores*) for the Bridge House boat, 3s.

1390
12 February: Two sculls, 5s.
9 July: Four oars for the bridge boat, 5s 8d.

10 September: One sailyard for a certain Bridge House boat, 4d.

1391
28 October: Four tilts for covering the Bridge House boat, 6s 8d.

25 November: Four oars called 'ores' for the Bridge House boats, 5s.

1392
27 April: Tallow, bitumen, and canvas for mending the Bridge House boat, 11d; wrong-nails for the said boat, 18d; paid to one carpenter called a shipwright, and his two mates, for one day, for repairing the said boat, 18d.

3 August: Three oars called 'ores' for the bridge boat, 3s.

1393
10 May: Paid to one shipwright working on the Bridge House boat for six days, 4s; paid to two other shipwrights working on the same boat for the same period, 7s; paid to another shipwright for five days, 2s 11; paid to another shipwright for six days, 3s; paid for a wiveling and one earthenware pot for melting pitch, 8d; 40 shipboards purchased at Croydon for the boat aforesaid, at 4½d each, 11s 8d [sic].

17 May: Paid to a shipwright working on the aforesaid boat for one week, 4s; paid to another shipwright working on the said boat for five days, 3s 4d; paid to three other shipwrights for five days, each at 7d a day, 8s 9d; paid to another shipwright for five days, 2s 6d; a wiveling for the same boat, 5d; thick oak boards purchased for the same boat, 7s 5d.

24 May: Paid to three shipwrights working on the aforesaid boat for six days, 12s; to four other shipwrights for the same period, at 7d a day each, 14s; to one other shipwright for the said period, 3s; a wiveling for the said boat, 5d; curved timber for the said boat, 3s 11d; earthenware pots and scoops for melting pitch, 10d.

31 May: Paid to three shipwrights working on the aforesaid boat for three days, 6s; to three other shipwrights for three days, 5s 3d; to one other shipwright for three days, 18d; one barrel of pitch for the boat aforesaid, 3s 1d; to William Smith, for clench-nails and iron rivets for the said boats, and for other articles for bridge rents ....; one rope weighing six pounds for the Bridge House boat, 12d.

7 June: Paid to three shipwrights working on the above-named boat for one week, 12s; to three other shipwrights for one week, 10s 6d; to two other shipwrights for the said week, 6s; earthenware pots for melting pitch, 6d; tow for caulking the same boat, 7d; curved timber for making knees for the said boat, 14d; 300 wrong-nails for the same boat, at 16d a hundred, 4s; nails for the said boat, 9d; three ells of canvas for caulking the said boat, 13d.

14 June: Shipboards for the aforesaid boat, 2s 1d.

23 October: Four oars called 'ores' for the bridge boats, 9s 4d.

1396
4 March: Paid to four shipwrights working on the bridge boats for one week, each at 4s a week, 16s; to four other shipwrights for the same period, each at 3s 6d, 14s; curved timber for the same boats, 9d; a wiveling for the same, 6d; earthenware pots for melting pitch in, 5d; one and three quarter hundred shipboards for melting pitch in, 5d; one and three quarter hundred shipboards for making a certain new boat for the bridge, 48s 2d.

11 March: Paid to four shipwrights working on the aforesaid boats for one week, at 4s each, 16s; to four other shipwrights for one week, each at 3s 6d, 14s; to another shipwright for five days, 3s 4d; curved timber for the aforesaid boats, 3s; six shipboards for the same, 22d.

18 March: Paid to four shipwrights working on the aforesaid boat [sic] for one week, 16s; to four other shipwrights working on the same boat for the said week, 14s; to one shipwright working on the same for three days, 2s; wooden nails for the same boat, 12d; rope for binding the mast of the said boats [sic], 8d; curved timber for the aforesaid boat, 18d; iron nails and wivelings for the same boats, 7d.

25 March: Paid to three shipwrights working on the said boats for one week, 12s; to three other shipwrights working on the said boats for the said period, 10s 6d; resin for putting on the same boats, 11d; wivelings for the same boats, 5d; one bottle of oil for the said boats, 4½d.

1 April: Paid to three shipwrights working on the aforesaid boats for one week, 12s; to three other shipwrights for the same period, 10s 6d; to one shipwright for three days, 2s; wrong-nails for the same boats, 2s 8d; curved timber for the said boats, 11d; earthenware pots for melting pitch in, 5d.

8 April: Twelve ells of canvas for making a certain sail for a bridge boat, 4s 6d; a small rope for the same sail, 7d.

6 May: One mast for a bridge boat, 14d; paid to three shipwrights working on the aforesaid boats for five days, each at 8d a day, 10s; curved timber for the same boats, 12d.

13 May: Paid to three shipwrights working on the aforesaid boats for one week, 12s; to one shipwright for five days, 3s 4d; earthenware pots for pitch, 3d; oil for putting on the said boats, 2½d.

20 May: Paid to two shipwrights working on the aforesaid boats for one week, 8s; to one shipwright for three and a half days, 2s 4d; curved timber for the same boats, 12d; half a last of pitch and bitumen, 15s; earthenware pots and tow for the aforesaid boats, 4½d; rope for binding the masts of the said boats and nails for the same purpose, 17d.

27 May: Paid to two shipwrights working on the aforesaid boats for three days, 4s.

3 June: Paid to two shipwrights for six days, 8s.

17 June: Two oars for the bridge boat, 5s 5d.

1397
4 August: Bails of wood for the bridge boat, 16d.

1398
15 June: Paid to two shipwrights for three days, 4s 10d; one barrel of pitch for the boats of the said bridge, 10d; nails for the said boats, 10d; earthenware pots for melting pitch, 9d; packthread, 2d; wooden nails for the said boat and a wiveling, 10d.

Appendix 6   Expenditure on cargoes of stone by London Bridge, 1381–98

by Brian Spencer

Table 18 has been compiled from the bridge records cited in Appendix 5. Cargoes of similar size but from different areas invite comparison. A cargo of 29 tunstight of Northern (Yorkshire) stone cost £13 1s, including freightage, on 5 July, 1382. On 12 March, 1390, a cargo of 24 tunstight of Kentish ragstone, presumably transported from the Maidstone area cost only 22s. Cargoes of chalk (costing 8s or 9s in 1381, 10s or 12s from 1386, and 13s 4d or 14s from 1397) are omitted from the list, and during the period covered by the account rolls several hundred loads of freestone and freestone mouldings were brought to the bridge by cart, mainly from Reigate, Surrey. Stone from more distant quarries, such as Portland, and many other requirements of prepared stone such as ashlar or corbels seem to have been transported by road.

Table 18 Quantities and costs of cargoes to London Bridge, 1381–98

date	cargo	quantity	cost
1381			
5 Oct	Rag	1 boatload	18s
12 Oct	Rag	1 boatload	15s
21 Dec	Rag	1 boatload	18s
1382			
11 Jan	Rag	1 boatload	18s
25 Jan	Rag	1 boatload	18s
1 Feb	Rag	1 boatload	15s
21 Jun	Rag	1 boatload	17s
5 Jul	Northern	29 tunstight with freightage	£13 1s
30 Aug	Rag	a large boatload	24s
30 Aug	Rag	1 boatload	22s
13 Sep	Rag	1 boatload	20s
20 Sep	Rag	1 boatload	16s
27 Sep	Rag	2 boatloads	36s 4d
1383			
14 Mar	Rag	1 boatload	16s
11 Apr	Rag	1 boatload	15s
27 Jun	Rag	1 boatload	15s 6d
11 Jul	Rag	1 boatload	15s 6d
1384			
19 Mar	Rag	1 boatload	16s
14 May	Rag	1 boatload	18s
20 Aug	Rag	1 boatload	18s
10 Sep	Rag	1 boatload	22s
17 Sep	Rag	1 boatload	14s
5 Nov	Rag	1 boatload	24s
1385			
20 May	Rag	1 boatload	14s
28 Jul	Rag	1 boatload	13s 4d
2 Sep	Rag	2 boatloads	40s
9 Sep	Rag	1 boatload	12s
23 Sep	Northern	60 tunstight at 8s a tuntight	£24 0s
30 Sep	Rag	1 boatload	13s 4d
21 Oct	Rag	1 boatload	19s 6d
23 Dec	Rag	1 boatload	15s
1386			
29 Sep	Rag	1 boatload	15s
1387			
13 Apr	Rag	1 boatload	18s
17 Aug	Northern	17 tunstight & 3 weys at 8s 6d a tuntight	£ 7 6s 7d
1388			
18 Apr	Rag	1 boatload	17s
4 Jul	Northern	26 tunstight, 1 pipe bought from Robert Gamelstone	£11 5s 3d
15 Aug	Rag	2 boatloads	44s
29 Aug	Rag	1 boatload	20s
29 Aug	Rag	1 boatload	17s 6d
5 Sep	Rag	1 boatload	21s
5 Sep	Rag	1 boatload	17s
12 Sep	Rag	1 boatload	16s
12 Sep	Rag	1 boatload	19s
19 Sep	Rag	1 boatload	18s 6d
19 Sep	Rag	2 boatloads	40s
26 Sep	Northern	20 tunstight	£ 8 10s
3 Oct	Rag	1 boatload	17s
10 Oct	Rag	1 boatload bought from Stephen Charles of Hoo	16s
10 Oct	Rag	1 boatload bought from Simon Sherman of Gillingham	13s 4d
17 Oct	Rag	1 boatload bought from John Hoo, mariner	20s
17 Oct	Rag	1 boatload bought from Sampson Gladwyne	17s
24 Oct	Rag	3 boatloads	60s
7 Nov	Rag	1 boatload	13s 4d
14 Nov	Rag	1 boatload	16s
5 Dec	Rag	1 boatload	20s
1389			
27 Feb	Rag	1 boatload	19s
10 Apr	Rag	1 boatload	20s
10 Apr	Rag	1 boatload	15s
17 Apr	Rag	1 boatload	20s
1 May	Rag	1 boatload	20s
15 May	Rag	2 boatloads	40s
29 May	Rag	1 boatload	20s
29 May	Rag	1 boatload	13s 4d
19 Jun	Rag	1 boatload	18s
26 Jun	Rag	2 boatloads	38s
3 Jul	Rag	1 boatload	22s
4 Sep	Northern	16 1/2 tunstight	£ 7 0s 3d

date	cargo	quantity	cost
11 Sep	Rag	2 boatloads	40s
18 Sep	Rag	Wharfage & carriage of 7 boatloads of chalk & rag from Dibbleswharf to Paternoster Row at 3s 8d a boatload	25s 8d
25 Sep	Rag	1 boatload	20s
16 Oct	Rag	1 boatload	15s
13 Nov	Rag	1 boatload	19s
1390			
1 Jan	Rag	1 boatload	14s
12 Feb	Rag	1 boatload	18s 1d
12 Mar	Rag	1 boatload of 24 tunstight	22s
19 Mar	Rag	2 boatloads	36s
30 Apr	Rag	1 boatload	19s
28 May	Rag	1 boatload	17s 8d
4 Jun	Rag	1 boatload	14s 6d
4 Jun	Rag	1 boatload	20s
23 Jun	Rag	1 boatload	14s
10 Sep	Rag	1 boatload	14s
8 Oct	Rag	1 boatload	20s
1391			
11 Feb	Rag	1 boatload	18s
11 Feb	Rag	1 boatload	22s
29 Apr	Rag	1 boatload	14s
29 Apr	Rag	2 boatloads	36s
15 Jul	Rag	2 boatloads	36s
22 Jul	Northern	14 tunstight & 1 third of a dole bought from Robert Gamelstone	£ 6 1s 0d
23 Sep	Rag	1 boatload	20s
25 Nov	Rag	2 boatloads	36s
2 Dec	Rag	1 boatload	18s
23 Dec	Rag	1 boatload	18s
1392			
17 Feb	Rag	2 boatloads	36s
23 Mar	Rag	1 boatload	18s
30 Mar	Rag	1 boatload	18s
20 Apr	Rag	1 boatload	18s
27 Apr	Rag	1 boatload	18s
25 May	Rag	1 boatload	15s
15 Jun	Rag	1 boatload	16s 8d
20 Jul	Beer	41 tunstight at 6s 8d a tunstight	£13 13s 4d
27 Jul	Rag	1 boatload	14s
10 Aug	Rag	1 boatload	14s
17 Aug	Rag	1 boatload	15s
24 Aug	Rag	1 boatload	19s
5 Oct	Rag	1 boatload	15s
9 Nov	Rag	2 boatloads	30s
23 Nov	Rag	1 boatload	15s
7 Dec	Rag	1 boatload	14s
1393			
26 Apr	Rag	2 boatloads	30s
14 Jun	Rag	1 boatload	15s
21 Jun	Rag	1 boatload	15s
6 Sep	Rag	1 boatload	18s
1395			
25 Dec	Rag	1 boatload	14s 6d
1396			
22 Jan	Rag	1 boatload	14s
29 Jan	Rag	1 boatload	16s
5 Feb	Rag	3 boatloads	54s
26 Feb	Rag	1 boatload	14s
8 Apr	Rag	1 boatload	18s
29 Apr	Rag	1 boatload	18s
27 May	Rag	1 boatload	16s
31 Sep	Rag	1 boatload	17s
30 Dec	Rag	1 boatload	20s
1397			
13 Jan	Rag	1 boatload	20s
10 Feb	Rag	1 boatload	20s
3 Mar	Rag	2 boatloads	37s
10 Mar	Rag	1 boatload	20s
28 Apr	Rag	1 boatload	19s
16 Jun	Rag	2 boatloads	40s
7 Jul	Rag	1 boatload	19s
28 Jul	Rag	1 boatload	18s
4 Aug	Rag	1 boatload	18s
1 Sep	Rag	1 boatload	20s
13 Oct	Rag	1 large boatload	26s 8d
1 Dec	Rag	1 boatload	26s 8d
1398			
11 May	Rag	1 boatload	15s
8 Jun	Rag	1 boatload	26s 8d
29 Jun	Rag	1 boatload	26s 8d
17 Aug	Rag	2 boatloads	52s 8d

Appendix 7 Three medieval London shipbuilders
by Tony Dyson

In the excerpts from the Bridge House account rolls for February 1382 to June 1398, printed in Appendix 5, there occur the names of three shipwrights, William Talworth, John de Stokflete, and Walter Sakyn, who were recorded in September and October 1386 as working together on 'a new boat belonging to the Bridge House called a shoute' (*see Appendix 5*). All three shipwrights are also recorded, in the property deeds collected for the waterfront parishes of medieval London, as residents of the parish of All Hallows Barking at the eastern extremity of the City, adjoining the Tower of London. In two instances the properties which they occupied can be identified.

William Talworth

On 7 May 1391 William Capelyn called Talworth shipwright granted to Hugh Sprot and William Palmer all his tenement with adjacent quay in the street of Petywales (Little Wales) in the parish of All Hallows Barking, between the tenement lately of Matthew Broun on the E and the tenement of the same William Capelyn on the W, and extending from the street to the Thames. And also the tenement in which the grantor dwells in parva Wallia (Little Wales) between the tenement of John Smart junior on the W and the tenement lately of Adam Gylle and wife Elena on the E, extending from the street towards the N as far as the Thames towards the S. The list of witnesses includes Walter Saykyn (City of London Record Office, Husting Roll 119/110).

'Little Wales' was the name given to Thames Street in the parishes of All Hallows and also of St Dunstan in the East. Talworth, subsequently Tolworth, is in Surrey, between Chessington and the Thames. These two adjacent tenements represent the sixth and seventh of the twelve that comprised the Thames frontage of All Hallows parish (and are designated as W6 and W7 in the documentary reconstruction of the medieval parish). W6 lay three doors along to the east from the lane which continued across Thames Street to the river from the foot of Bear Lane.

William Capelyn of Talworth married the widow of William son of Richard of Talworth some time before 1352, and had presumably been an employee or associate of the deceased. He witnessed deeds of fellow parishioners in All Hallows between 1350 and 1392, a period closely corresponding with his occupation of these tenements. Richard of Talworth had first acquired one of these tenements, probably W7, in 1316, adding W6 to it some time before his death, which occurred between 1336 and 1338. All male members of the family recorded here were shipwrights.

John De Stokflete

Stokflete, another shipwright, held the freehold of Tenement A8 at the far E end of the north side of Thames Street before disposing of it in November 1383 (*ibid*, HR 112/40). He had acquired the tenement at some date between 1368 and 1374 (*ibid*, 99/106). He had also leased the adjoining property to the W (A7) by 1377, and continued to hold it until at least May 1390, after he had disposed of A8. He died between that date and October 1391, having witnessed neighbours' deeds between June 1353 and May 1386.

In contrast with Talworth, there is no specific evidence that Stokflete held property on the south side of Thames Street, as would certainly be expected of a shipwright. This may simply be because, as will be seen, occupants of properties on the north side of Thames Street in the parishes of All Hallows and St Dunstan in the East tended also to occupy the corresponding riverfront tenement on the south side. It may be therefore that the documentation of A7 also took account of of W7 opposite, but in the present context it is rather more likely that Stokflete occupied W7 as tenant and immediate neighbour of his colleague Talworth, who also also held W6. It is worth noting that Talworth disposed of W7 in 1391, the year of Stokflete's death.

Walter Sakyn

There is no evidence to associate Sakyn with the ownership or tenancy of any specific property in the immediate area, and he appears to have witnessed local deeds only twice, in May 1391 (Talworth's deed, as above) and January 1392 (*ibid*, 120/94). It is likely that Sakyn was a short-term resident, probably a tenant, who passed unrecorded in the surviving deeds of the relevant property.

Some general points arise from these references in the Bridge House accounts and title deeds. One is the striking fact that although there are innumerable other references to unspecified shipwrights in the Bridge House accounts of this period, Talworth, Stokflete, and Sakyn were the only ones to be mentioned by name, and even they were mentioned only in connection with a single commission. It is difficult to know what significance (if any) to attach to this, though it could be that the ordering of a new shout was a major and comparatively rare venture on the part of the Bridge House, one that might well have involved the drawing up of a formal contract. If so, the other disbursements to unnamed craftsmen may have concerned mere routine maintenance and labour, arranged on a casual, piece-work basis. At any rate, it seems reasonable to see in the contrast an indication that Talworth, Stokflete and Sakyn enjoyed some special status, perhaps as specialist shout builders.

As collaborators in a single project it is hardly a coincidence that the three shipwrights were near neighbours, nor is it coincidental that they were resident in the parish of All Hallows. From the late thirteenth century onwards, when surviving records are first available in adequate quantity, shipwrights are exclusively recorded in the adjoining parishes of All Hallows and St Dunstan in the East, where they were particularly numerous up to the early fourteenth century. Their concentration in this area, and their absence elsewhere on the City waterfront, presumably had some specific explanation, and may well have arisen from a distinctive local pattern of foreshore occupation. Until the end of the thirteenth century, as the Custom House excavations showed, the available space between Thames Street and the river was much more confined than it was on the rest of the waterfront, and only from that date did it begin to be enlarged by means of the revetments that had been commonplace elsewhere since at least the twelfth century (Tatton-Brown 1974, 128). Moreover, property deeds of the late thirteenth and early fourteenth century show that tenements facing each other across Thames Street in these parishes were usually in single ownership (Dyson 1975), a feature virtually unknown elsewhere on the London waterfront, and one that was still in evidence, though to a much lesser degree, at the end of the fourteenth century.

The most obvious explanation of this unique arrangement is that the limitation of space on the south side of the street obliged the occupants to place their main premises on the north side. Since however it would have been perfectly possible to extend the frontages here in the same way that they had been extended elsewhere, it must be that the apparently inconvenient layout was justified by some useful and specialised purpose. On the evidence of the local concentration of shipwrights in the early medieval period, it would seem that the natural, gently inclining foreshore, unimpeded by vertical revetments, had proved particularly well suited to the repair and building of ships, the more so perhaps in a remote and hitherto underdeveloped area close to the Tower and clearly demarcated from the rest of the waterfront. By 1400, however, no doubt as a result of the installation of revetments and the intensive commercial development of this sector of the waterfront downstream of the bridge during the fourteenth century, the range of local trades and activities had become much more varied. The concentration of shipwrights in these parishes, like the tendency for properties facing each other across Thames Street to be held by the same occupant, was in consequence now much less apparent.

Appendix 8   A thirteenth-century Thames tide table
by Tony Dyson

The tide table printed below as Table 19 is to be found in BL Cotton Julius D vii. It appears in a section of the MS which consists of a miscellany of historical and other material collected together by John of Wallingford, who was a monk at St Albans Abbey from at least 1231 until his death in 1258, and infirmarer there by 1250 (Vaughan 1958, 66–7). The table (folio 45v) precedes a 'Description of the climates of the world' (folio 46r), the final item in the first section of the book, which is followed on folio 46v by historical matter preliminary to John's chronicle of England on folios 61–110. All this material is written in a single hand which can conclusively be shown to be John's, and to date from the period of his infirmarership in the 1250s (*ibid*, 67). There can therefore be no doubt of the antiquity of the existing text.

Nor is there much doubt about the immediate source, at least, of the table and of John's other material: almost certainly it was copied, or was otherwise derived, from the collections of his contemporary and close associate at St Albans, the rather more celebrated Mathew Paris, and includes two of Mathew's drawings and one of his well-known maps of England (*ibid*, 67–9). John evidently enjoyed unrestricted access to Mathew's writings, not all of which have survived independently. The tide table, in all probability, had been previously acquired by Paris some time during the first half of the thirteenth century.

How Mathew himself came by the table is a matter for speculation. In the opinion of one commentator, it is the work of a scholar rather than of a sailor, and shows that theory rather than observation was the rule in the learned world of Mathew's day (Taylor 1956, 136–7). On the other hand, the table can hardly be a wholly scholastical exercise, and is very likely to have had some basis in practical reality, as well as some actual connexion with London Bridge. Indeed, the vernacular 'Flood[tide] at London Bridge' itself makes an odd contrast with the Latin of the other rubrics, and it is difficult to see why this phraseology should

have been favoured if it had not already been a feature of some pre-existing source. Similarly, the use of Arabic, rather than Roman, numerals can hardly be regarded as a hallmark of scholasticism, or indeed as ordinary clerical usage, in the thirteenth century. The Arabic system, however, could well have proved more serviceable to mariners, who were also more likely than monks to have come into close contact with it.

Table 19   A thirteenth-century Thames tide table

fflod at London brigge			*Quantum luna lucet in nocte*[1]		
Estas lune[2]	*hore*	*minuta*	*Estas lune*	*hore*	*minuta*
1	3	48	1	0	48
2	4	36	2	1	36
3	5	24	3	2	24
4	6	12	4	3	12
5	7	0	5	4	0
6	7	48	6	4	48
7	8	36	7	5	36
8	9	24	8	6	24
9	10	12	9	7	12
10	11	0	10	8	0
11	11	48	11	8	48
12	12	36	12	9	36
13	1	24	13	10	24
14	2	12	14	11	12
15	3	0	15	12	0
16	3	48	16	11	12
17	4	36	17	10	24
18	5	24	18	9	36
19	6	12	19	8	48
20	7	0	20	8	0
21	7	48	21	7	12
22	8	36	22	6	24
23	9	24	23	5	36
24	10	12	24	4	48
25	11	0	25	4	0
26	11	48	26	3	12
27	12	36	27	2	24
28	1	24	28	1	36
29	2	12	29	0	48
30	3	0	30	0	0

[1] 'How much the moon shines at night'
[2] 'The age of the moon'

216

Appendix 9   Gazetteer of ships and boats, from the seventeenth century and earlier, in the Lower Thames Valley

by Peter Marsden

The potential wealth of knowledge about early shipping on the River Thames and its tributaries, much of which is related to the port of London, is best illustrated by summarising the many plank-built ship and boat finds of all periods down to the seventeenth century, some of which are not dated (see *Figs 1 and 9*). The list, which extends to the estuary of the river, has been compiled by the author over the past thirty years whenever published references to discoveries were encountered, and these are given below. It is only concerned with plank-built vessels, though it is important to remember that at least twenty dugout canoes have also been found (*see Appendix 10*).

1 Woolwich Power Station, 1912

The remains of a ship were found in 1912 during the construction of Woolwich Power Station, and were recorded by officials from London County Council. It lay at a depth of 5.5m and at a right angle to the Thames only a few metres away. It was apparently lying in an old creek or inlet as there was no evidence of revetments around the vessel. The ship was about 13m broad and had a keel probably about 36m long. It was carvel-built on frames containing traces of notches, which indicated that when first built it had clinker planking. The seams in the outboard planking were covered outboard with laths of timber, and the planks were fastened to the frames by trenails, the frames themselves being 0.35m broad, 0.2m deep, and 0.13m apart. Inboard of the frames was a ceiling of planking covered by heavy transverse riders on which were fastened stringers lying fore-and-aft. Near amidships was the base of a mast 1.32m in diameter made from an assembly of timbers held by iron bands. Five stone 'cannon balls' were found in and around the ship.

The construction and the stone shot show that the ship probably dated from the early sixteenth century. It seems most likely that was the English warship *Sovereign*, built in 1488 and rebuilt in 1509–10. In 1521 she was reported to be lying in 'a dock at Woolwich', and was in such a state that 'she must be new made from the keel upwards'. Her repair was urged because 'the form of which ship is so marvellously goodly that great pity it were she should die.' (Salisbury 1961, 81–90).

2 Deptford, before 1667

Pepys in his Diary entry for 28 April, 1667 writes:

'And so by water, the tide being with me again, down to Deptford, and there I walked down the Yard, Shish [Jonas Shish, master builder at Deptford Dockyard] and Cox [Captain John Cox, master attendant at Deptford] with me, and discoursed about cleaning of the wet docke, and heard, which I had before, how, when the dock was made, a ship of near 500 tons was there found; a ship supposed of Queen Elizabeth's time, and well wrought, with a great deal of stone shot in her, of eighteen inches [0.45m] diameter, which was shot then in use.'

The identity of this ship is unknown. Although it lay close to the site of the Golden Hind, it cannot be identified with that famous vessel for the tonnage of the Golden Hind was only 100–150 tons (Naish 1948, 42–5).

3 Cherry Garden Street, Southwark, 1987

Clinker boat planking was recovered from this site, one fragment producing a tree-ring date of 1554 at the heartwood-sapwood boundary, suggesting a later sixteenth-century building date (*see chapter 8*).

4 National Wharf, Bermondsey Wall East, Rotherhithe, 1990

Carvel planking and two frames were found reused in a river waterfront, probably from the seventeenth century. The ship timbers may therefore date from the sixteenth century (*see chapter 8*).

5 Southwark Park Road (?Grange Road), Bermondsey, *c* 1882

During the construction of a sewer between Ernest Street and Alfred Street various geological features were recorded by a Mr J Grant of the Metropolitan Board of Works. He wrote that:

'a little west of this spot the excavators have come across what appears to be the oak timber of some vessel, from 7 to 8 feet (2.13m to 2.43m) below the surface, at the bottom of the dark, superficial gravel, etc, and on top of the bright sand and gravel.'
(Whitaker 1889, 331).

6 Abbots Lane, Southwark, 1987–8

A large slab of clinker boat planking from the bottom of a boat was found reused in a waterfront dating probably from the latter half of the fourteenth century. There were other pieces of fourteenth-century clinker planking, some of local oak, and others of Baltic oak (*see chapter 5*). In 1988 two pieces of other clinker planking were found with tree-rings in the heartwood suggesting a boatbuilding date of these fragments of *c* 1600 (*see chapter 8; Goodburn 1988, 427*).

7 Morgans Lane, Southwark, 1987–8

Many pieces of sixteenth-century clinker boat planking, including part of the stern of a boat built in 'reverse clinker', were found reused in the revetment of a moat (*chapter 6*).

Others, probably of normal clinker construction, and with a boatbuilding date of *c* 1580, were found in the dumped fill of the moat (*see chapter 8*).

8 Bethel Estate, Southwark 1988

Clinker boat timbers of the sixteenth century were found reused in a revetment on this site where a watercourse and possibly part of a moat were recorded (*see chapter 8*).

9 Gun and Shot Wharf, Southwark 1988

A small fragment of a substantial ship, possibly built about 1400, was found reused in a revetment of an inlet from the River Thames. It was clinker-built of Baltic oak, and had iron rivets, and a caulking of hair and moss (*see chapter 5*). Other fragments of clinker planking dating from the sixteenth century were found reused in the revetment of a moat (*see chapter 8*).

10 Butter Factory South, Hays Wharf, Southwark 1988

Part of a clinker-built boat probably built in the middle or latter half of the sixteenth century was found in the revetment of a pond or watercourse dating from the fifteenth to eighteenth centuries (*see chapter 8*).

11 Symonds Wharf, Southwark 1988

Clinker planks of Baltic and local oak were found reused in a fourteenth-century revetment (*see chapter 5*).

12 New Guys House, Southwark, 1958

Part of a Romano-Celtic barge of the second century AD was found during building operations in 1958 and subsequently its north end was archaeologically excavated. It was about 4.25m wide, 1m deep amidships, and although a length of only 6.7m at the north end was found, its minimum possible length is estimated at 16m. Its carvel-laid oak planks were fastened to oak frames by hooked iron nails, and between some planks was a caulking of hazel wood shavings set in pine resin. Its outboard face was coated in similar resin. It had been abandoned in a former marshland creek. The site is now protected as a Scheduled Ancient Monument (Marsden 1994).

13 Maze Pond, Southwark, before 1889

During the construction of the new College for Guy's Hospital in 1888 there were found

'what were evidently old breakwaters. Some years ago, in digging for the foundation of an adjacent warehouse, an old barge was found embedded in mud deposits below.'

(Guy's Hospital Gazette 1889)

Since this lay slightly north of New Guy's House, where a Roman barge was found in a creek (Marsden 1994) in 1958, it is possible that the nineteenth-century find was another Roman vessel, and that the 'breakwater' was part of a Roman timber revetment of the creek found on site 14.

14 Guys Hospital, Tooley Street, Southwark, 1989

Fragments of clinker boat planking were found reused in a seventeenth-century drain (*see chapter 8*).

15 Fennings Wharf, Southwark, 1984

Clinker planking of oak with iron rivets, a flat plank-like keel, and a probable ship's wale, were found reused mostly in waterfronts of the eleventh century (Marsden 1994).

16 Park Street, Southwark, 1867

In December 1867, in Park Street at the corner of Clink Street, at a depth of 4.87m from the roadway,

'navvies came upon an ancient wooden structure formed of stout piles set about two feet [0.6m] apart, and supporting beams and joists overlaid with planking rabbeted and fastened together by broad-headed, four-sided nails of iron; their points passing through and spread on rhombic pieces of the same metal, such as in boatbuilding are denominated *burrs* or *roves*.' This was thought to be a Roman landing stage

(J British Archaeol Assoc **25**, 1869, 79–81)

A few of the nails with roves attached are preserved in the British Museum, and are clearly typical ship rivets from a post-Roman clinker-built vessel. They are not of Roman date as has been suggested (Manning 1985, 134), but it seems likely that this find was a medieval or later waterfront revetment in which part of the hull of an old boat had been reused.

17 5–15 Bankside, 1987

Clinker planks of oak were found reused in a riverside revetment of the fourteenth century. Tree-ring dating suggests a late twelfth to thirteenth-century boatbuilding date (*see chapter 8*).

18 37–46 Bankside, 1987

Clinker boat timbers of oak were found reused in a riverside revetment of the Thames, and their tree-ring dating suggests a date of *c* 1500 for the vessel's construction (*see chapter 8*).

19 Bankside Power Station, Southwark, 1948

Parts of two clinker-built boats were found while Bankside Power Station was being built. They lay immediately east of the former Fletcher Lane, and the remains of one may have been reused in a timber jetty. The other was found about 120m from the river at a depth of 3.6m. It had overlapping planks held with rivets, and from this Adrian Oswald of the Guildhall Museum, who studied the site, estimated that the boat was more than 9m long. The boat lay in the ooze which covered the site for a depth of between 0.9m to 1.8m above the natural sand. Above this was 1.8m of mixed seventeenth-century composition. From within the boat a decorated buckle of Tudor style, a slipped-in-the-stalk spoon of *c* 1600, and a *guisarme* of *c* 1500 were recovered. The wooden jetty or pier lay about 12.8m inland, and as the deposits above this were identical with those above the boat, it was believed that the boat and jetty might be contemporary. Dendrochronological examination of timber by A W Lowther suggested a date not earlier than the end of the fourteenth century, but not later than 1600. No part of either vessel has survived, though other finds are in the Museum of London. (Oswald 1949, 4; Mss records of A Oswald in the Museum of London).

20 245 Blackfriars Road, Southwark, 1987

A large watercourse with revetments of the late sixteenth to seventeenth centuries was found, and with it were pieces of clinker boat planking (*see chapter 8*).

21 County Hall site, Lambeth, 1910

A substantial portion of a Roman ship 13m long and 5.5m wide, including its collapsed side, was found while building County Hall. Dating of tree-rings and coins indicates that it was built about AD 300. The ship is reconstructed as having had a beam of about 5m wide, and a gunwale height of about 2m. The collapsed side contained the ends of beams for a deck which originally lay 1.3m above the top of the lowest frames. Its original length is estimated at at least 19.1m. It was carvel-built with mortice-and-tenon joints in the Mediterranean tradition, though a recent tree-ring study shows that it was locally built. An excellent report was published in 1912, but considerably more information has been recovered and published from a study of the preserved timbers (Marsden 1994).

22 Storey's Gate, Westminster, 1913

'The oaken ribs of a ship, found in 1913 at a depth of 20 feet (6m), on sand below peat at Storey's Gate, Westminster, and now in the London Museum, may be of Roman date; but this cannot be stated with certainty.'

(Vulliamy 1930, 219)

No trace of the timbers can be found in the Museum of London.

23 9–11 Bridewell Place, City, 1978

Fragments of a clinker-built boat were found beneath the palace of Bridewell built 1515–23 and must pre-date that period. It may have been reused in a waterfront of the River Fleet during the medieval period (*see chapter 5*).

24 River Thames, Blackfriars, City of London, 1962–3

Blackfriars ship 1 was found during building operations to construct a new riverside embankment wall in the bed of the Thames. It was a Romano-Celtic carvel-built sailing ship, and a tree-ring study shows that it was locally built, probably about the middle of the second century AD. *Teredo* and *Limnoria* borings show that it was a seagoing ship, even though its cargo when wrecked was of Kentish ragstone from the Maidstone region of north Kent. Its final voyage at least

was mostly in the fresh water of the Rivers Medway and Thames. The ship had two broad thick keel-planks forming a flat bottom, and the planks were attached to massive oak frames by hooked iron nails with cone-shaped heads in which was a caulking of hazelwood shavings and pine resin. The same caulking lay between the planks. Finds from within the wrecked ship suggest that it was sunk in the mid second century, possibly in a collision. It is estimated that the ship had a beam of about 6.12m, a length of about 18.5m, and a height amidships of about 2.86m. The mast was stepped just forward of the hold. It is not clear if it once had a deck (Marsden 1994).

25 River Thames, Blackfriars, City of London, 1969

Blackfriars ship 2 was a clinker-built vessel sunk in the River Thames while carrying a cargo of bricks, c 1670. Its planks were of oak and its plank-like keel was of elm. It is estimated that the vessel was a river barge or lighter with a beam of 3–4m, and a length of 12–16m (*see chapter 7*).

26 River Thames, Blackfriars, City of London, 1970

Blackfriars ship 3 was an almost complete clinker-built sailing river barge that tree-ring studies show was built about 1400. It had been sunk during the fifteenth century in the bed of the River Thames. It was about 14.64m long, 4.3m wide, and 0.88m high amidships. A mast-step amidships indicated that it once had a square sail, and there was reason to believe that it had a steering oar. In the wreck were over a thousand lead weights from a fishing net that had presumably been caught after the vessel had sunk (*see chapter 3*).

27 River Thames, Blackfriars, City of London, 1970

Blackfriars ship 4 was a clinker-built vessel of the fifteenth century which had sunk with a cargo of Kentish ragstone, just a few metres from Blackfriars ship 3. Only the bottom had survived, suggesting a vessel about 3.4m wide at the point investigated. (*see chapter 4*).

28 Baynards Castle, City, 1972

Part of an oak frame that had probably been reused in a revetment was found dumped with fourteenth-century rubbish at the entrance to a dock, the East Watergate, on the west side of Baynards Castle. It was joggled for clinker planking, and was originally from a flat-bottomed vessel more than 3.5m wide (*see chapter 5*).

29 Upper Thames Street, before 1890

'A mysterious ship...reposes beneath the basement-floor of the new building [of Messrs Pilkington, close to the site of Baynards Castle], and by the side of which lay a clench bolt.'

(Macmichael 1890, 177)

The 'clench bolt' probably indicates that this boat was medieval. No part of the vessel is known to have survived.

30 Trig Lane, City, 1974

Clinker boat planks were reused in a fourteenth-century timber revetment of the River Thames (*see chapter 5;* Milne and Milne 1982, 26–7)

31 Thames Exchange, Upper Thames Street, City, 1989

Fragments of ships and boats were found with waterfront structures of the eleventh century. They included clinker planking with rivets and pegs, part of a flat keel 5m long, the stem of a boat, a mast support, a frame, and part of a side rudder (Milne and Goodburn 1990, 629–36)

32 Thames Street, 1870

Excavations in Upper or Lower Thames Street, City, revealed part of a clinker-built boat. There is no known documentary record of the discovery, but some iron rivets and a small piece of planking with three nails in position were acquired by the Guildhall Museum, now the Museum of London. A note with the pieces states that they were found in 1870 on an unspecified site in Thames Street (Marsden 1963, 144–5).

The fragment, 26.5cm long by 7.5cm broad, consists of three pieces of oak planking, two forming a scarf joint, from two overlapping strakes. They were held together by iron rivets with square shanks and diamond-shaped roves, and although the thickness of the planking had shrunk, the rivets show that the total thickness of the overlapping clinker planks was originally about 50mm. There was a caulking in the lap joint and in the scarf, of twisted mammalian hair, probably from a cow or horse. There was a trace of pitch on the plank face with the roves.

According to the 'rules' of clinker construction (*see chapter 1*) the roves should have been on the inboard side of the boat, and the scarf and clinker lap joint indicate that the fragment is probably from the starboard side. The vessel is presumably of medieval or later date.

33 New Fresh Wharf, Lower Thames Street, City, 1974

Broken pieces of oak clinker planking were recovered from an eleventh-century foreshore. They indicate a tree felling date of AD 920–955. The planks had been pegged together, with a caulking of moss. Knee and frame fragments were also found (Marsden 1994).

34 Billingsgate, City, 1982

Oak planks from several clinker-built vessels were found associated with waterfronts of the eleventh to thirteenth centuries. They included eleventh-century pegged and riveted clinker planking (Steedman *et al* 1992, 51, 61, 68; Marsden 1994), and riveted clinker planking of the twelfth to thirteenth centuries (*see chapter 5*).

35 Custom House, Lower Thames Street, City, 1973

Slabs of oak clinker planking from a boat (Boat 1) were found reused in a waterfront of the late thirteenth to fourteenth centuries. Tree-ring dating indicates a boat-building date of *c* 1160–90. The surviving length of the slabs was 4.3m, and it is estimated that the minimum width of the vessel was 3.5m and its minimum length was 9.75m. There was also the frame from another flat-bottomed vessel, Boat 2 (*see chapter 2*).

36 City of London Boys School, Carmelite Street, 1987

Hundreds of pieces of carved timber from several ships of the seventeenth to eighteenth centuries were found reused in the foundations of a building. They included painted decorative timbers, parts of deck structure, and knees and frames. Also found were small fragments of a clinker-built boat (Goodburn 1988, 427; 1991, 112–5).

37 Hackney Marsh, 1830

The partly decayed remains of a clinker-built boat were found at a depth of 1.22m in Hackney Marsh. They lay below a stratum of black clay with shells, and under a layer of yellow clay which were thought to be an old bed of the River Lea. The boat was resting on its keel, and is said to have measured 6m long from stem to stern, 1.8m across the beam, and 0.45m deep. Between its clinker planks was a caulking of cow hair (Robinson 1842, I, 24; Vulliamy 1930, 250).

38 Walthamstow, 1900

A clinker-built boat was found during the excavation for the Lockwood Resevoir in the valley of the River Lea between Tottenham and Walthamstow. It lay upside down on the former bank of the river, and was about 12.2m long. Its clinker planks were fastened by iron rivets, and had a caulking of cow hair. It was thought to be possibly Viking, but has now been dated by ^{14}C to AD 1604 ± 54 (Vulliamy 1930, 249–50; Marsden 1964, 2–6; Fenwick 1978a, 187–94).

39 Old Bridge Wharf, Thames Side, Kingston, 1986

Large slabs, 9.3m, 13m, and 6m long, of clinker-built boats were found reused in medieval waterfronts close to the medieval bridge crossing the Thames. The earliest revetment was provisionally dated to about 1300, but the later was undated. However, it is likely that the boats were of thirteenth and fourteenth-century date (Goodburn 1988, 425–6; 1991, 108–11; Potter 1991, 143–6).

40 1 Wheatfield Way, Kingston, 1989

Pieces of boat planking were found in a revetment, probably of the early eighteenth century, of the Hogsmill River. Some were of clinker planking held by iron rivets, and others were 'flush-lapped' planks held by hooked nails, and with hair caulking (Potter and Marsden forthcoming).

41 Benfleet Creek, before 1890

Ships possibly destroyed in 893–4 were found in Benfleet Creek during the nineteenth century.

'That the ships lay there I had curious evidence some years ago. An old gentleman ... told me that when the railway bridge across the fleet [ie the stream] was being built, the navvies came upon many ships deep in the mud, several of which on exposure had evidently been burnt, as their charred remains showed. Indeed, about them lay numerous human skeletons.'

(Essex Naturalist, IV, 1890, 153)

The site of this potentially very important discovery can be fixed precisely as only one pier of the railway bridge goes into the creek.

42 Graveney, north Kent, 1970

The lower part of a late Saxon boat was found in Graveney Marsh, and was raised and preserved at the National Maritime Museum. One end and much of the midships area had survived. It was of oak and had a plank-like keel, and up to eight strakes were held together by iron rivets. Much of the stern had survived, but the bow was destroyed. It is estimated to have had eleven strakes and to have been about 13m long, 4m wide and 1m deep amidships. There was no clear evidence for its steering or method of propulsion. Hop seeds were found in the bottom of the boat, and fragments of a cooking pot perhaps imported from Belgium or France in the eighth to ninth centuries (Fenwick 1978a).

Appendix 10 The dugout canoes from the Thames valley

by Peter Marsden

The discovery of twenty dugout canoes in the Thames and its tributaries are recorded by McGrail (1978, nos 20, 26, 34–6, 48, 73, 81, 97–9, 116, 123, 125, 140–2, 158, 160, and 168). They were found by the River Thames at Brentford, Church Ferry (3 boats), Erith, Kew, Marlow, Molesey (2 boats), Mortlake, Putney, Shepperton, Weybridge, and Windsor. Others were found beside the River Wey at Byfleet, Walton, and Wisley, and beside the River Lea at Sewardstone, Waltham Cross, and Walthamstow.

Seán McGrail collected samples from the surviving canoes and these were carbon dated by Dr Roy Switsur of the Godwin Laboratory, Cambridge. The results, shown below, have been generously provided by Seán McGrail in advance of his publication.

In addition to this the fragments of the canoe Molesey 2 listed above have been found to have a latest tree-ring date of AD 870 in heartwood, suggesting a boat construction date in the late ninth or tenth centuries (information kindly supplied by Paul Hill of Kingston-upon-Thames Museum and Heritage Centre, and Ian Tyers of the Museum of London).

Another canoe found at Clapton in 1987, beside the River Lea, has given a latest tree-ring date of AD 932 in heartwood, suggesting a construction date of AD 950–1000 (Marsden 1989). The end of perhaps another canoe was found at Chamberlains Wharf, Southwark, in 1984, in the fill of a channel between sandbanks on the edge of the Thames with Roman and medieval material (Heal and Hutchinson 1986, 206–10).

Table 20 Dug-out canoes from the Thames valley

lab no	boat	date BP	calibrated range 68%	(cal AD) 95%
Q–3038AD	Kew	720+–40	1250–1270AD	1225–1335
Q–1453		770+–45	1220–1265	1170–1270
Q–3052	Sewardstone	1070+–45	905–1000	875–1025
Q–3040		1130+–45	875–965	805–990
Q–3041	Walthamstow	1255+–40	675–810	655–885
Q–1388		1335+–45	650–685	620–785
Q–3042	Walton	1585+–50	405–530	370–575
Q–1399	Wisley	1780+–45	195–255	110–345
Q–1389	Woolwich	1990+–50	45BC–55AD	110BC–105AD
Q–3039		2070+–45	145BC–35AD	205BC–10AD

Glossary of nautical terms

This glossary has been compiled with reference to a number of publications (Falconer 1815; Bradford 1954; McKee 1972; Greenhill 1976; Fenwick 1978a; Kemp 1979; Steffy 1982; Christensen 1985; McGrail 1987). For some terms, such as *carvel* there are various meanings, and in these cases the meaning intended in this study has been specified.

beam: (a) timber; transverse timbers supporting or resting on the sides of the ship, (b) measurement; the greatest breadth of a ship's hull.

bevel: The angled edge of a timber so formed as to make an angle with another.

bilge: The lowest part of the interior of a ship.

boat: A small vessel usually used in inland waters.

bulkhead: An internal cross-partition or wall in a ship.

carvel: In this study it means edge-to-edge planking to give a smooth-sided hull. This is the meaning given by Falconer (1815, 78), Bradford (1954, 52), and Kemp (1979, 143). However, others restrict its meaning to planking which is attached to a pre-erected skeleton of frames (McKee 1972, 26; Fenwick 1978a, 331; Christensen 1985, 270) and add that in the navy it refers to a vessel with a double skin whose inner layer lies at about 45 degrees to the keel and the other layer horizontal.

caulking: This is a wadding that has been driven into the seam between planks to make the hull watertight, but in this publication it refers to the wadding between the planks of a ship or boat, or in any repair. The term 'luting', sometimes used in other publications, seems to be not wholly appropriate to Romano-Celtic ships, even though the wadding was placed in position as the planking was being assembled. The term 'luting' is not used here.

ceiling: The planks lining the interior of a vessel inside the frames.

chine: An angle formed by two strakes, usually between the bottom and the side of a vessel.

clinker: A method of planking in which the lower edge of one strake normally overlaps the upper edge of the strake below.

displacement: The weight of water displaced by a floating ship. This is about equal to the weight of the vessel.

double-ended: A vessel which is of similar shape at both ends.

draught: The depth of water needed to float a vessel.

feather-heading: The thin commencement of a plank.

floor-timber: The lowest transverse frame in a ship.

frame: A transverse timber or rib, part of the skeleton structure of a ship. The lowest parts of frames are termed floor-timbers, and the separate ribs at the side of a ship are here termed side-frames.

freeboard: The distance between the waterline and the lowest part of the gunwale.

garboard strake: The strakes immediately next to the keel.

gunwale: The uppermost rail or timber of a ship's side.

heel: The lowest part of a mast. Also the list or inclination of a ship.

hooked nail: A nail whose shank has been bent at an angle of 90 degrees, and whose point has been bent through a further 90 degrees.

hull: The main body of a ship.

joggle: Outer face of a frame which has been stepped or otherwise shaped to fit overlapping clinker planking.

keel: The central longitudinal strengthening beam of the bottom of a ship, from which rise the frames and the stem and sternposts. Normally it projects below the bottom planking of a ship and helps to stop leeway.

keel-plank: A broad extra-thick plank instead of a keel, sometimes found in flat-bottomed ships and barges that sail in shallow waters and are beached at low tide.

keelson: A longitudinal strengthening timber, or stringer, overlying the keel inside a ship.

knee: A right-angled timber, usually carved from naturally angled tree growth, fastening the intersection of timbers such as the deck-beams and the frames of the ship's side. A 'hanging knee' is angled downwards below the deck-beam, a 'lodging knee' is angled horizontally to the beam, and a 'standing knee' is angled upwards above the beam.

lap: The overlap of two strakes fastened together clinkerwise.

leeway: The amount a ship is carried sideways to leeward by the force of the wind or current.

limber hole: Hole in the underside of a bottom frame or floor-timber which allows bilge-water to flow to the lowest part of a ship so that it can be pumped out.

mast-beam: Transverse beam immediately on the forward side of the mast to help support the mast.

mast-step: Socket to hold the foot of the mast.

metacentric height: Distance between the metacentre and the centre of gravity in a ship.

peg: A wooden nail less than 10mm in diameter.

plank: Flat lengths of wood normally forming the outer and inner skins of a ship, as well as the deck.

port: The left-hand side of a ship looking forward.

quarter rudder: A rudder hung on the side of the ship near the stern.

rabbet: Longitudinal recess cut in the face of a timber, particularly in the keel, stempost and sternpost.

reverse clinker: Clinker construction in which the lower strakes overlap the upper.

rivet: Wrought-iron fastening to hold overlapping planks together, formed from a nail whose 'pointed' end has been splayed or clenched over a diamond-shaped washer or rove.

scarf: The bevelling of the ends of two timbers, particularly planks and frames, in such a way that when fastened together they form one timber in appearance.

seam: The gap between two ship's planks. This is normally made watertight with a caulking.

sheer-strake: The upper line of planks in the side of a ship.

shell: The outer skin of planking of a ship.

shell-built: A vessel that has been built with its planks first, to which the frames have been added later to strengthen the 'shell'. Shell-building is only possible when there is a system of fastening planks to each other, as, for example, in Scandinavian clinker-built vessels which used rivets, and in classical ships of the Mediterranean which used mortice-and-tenon joints.

ship: A large vessel able to sail on voyages for considerable periods of time.

skeleton-built: A vessel that has been built first with a skeleton framework of keel, frames and endposts, to which the skin of planks has been added subsequently.

skin: The outer shell of planking in a ship.

side-frame: A frame not connected to floor-timbers which supports the side of a ship.

starboard: The right-hand side of a ship looking forward.

stanchion: An upright pillar often used to support a deck.

steering oar: A long oar used for steering, fastened over the stern of a vessel. Particularly used in inland waters.

stocks: The timber supports for a ship while it is being built.

strake: A line of planks of the outer skin running the length of a ship.

stringer: An internal longitudinal beam giving additional strength to a ship.

thole pin: A wooden pin inserted into the gunwale or sheer-strake of a boat to provide a fulcrum for an oar.

thwart: Transverse beam used as a seat.

trenail: A wooden nail used to fasten timbers together, normally more than 10mm in diameter

turned nail: A nail whose shank has been bent through an angle of 90 degrees.

wale: An extra-thick plank running fore-and-aft in the side of a ship. It provides additional longitudinal strength, and can help support cross-beams and a deck.

wash-strake: Thin movable boards above the gunwale which provide protection from spray entering a ship or boat.

yard: A horizontal spar located near the top of a mast from which a sail is set.

Bibliography

Akerlund, H, 1951 *Fartygsfynden i den forna hamnen i Kalmar*, Uppsala, Sweden

Aston, M, 1988 *Medieval fish, fisheries, and fishponds in England*, BAR Brit Ser, Oxford

Baillie, M, 1982 *Tree-ring dating and archaeology*, London

Barron, C, Coleman, C, and Gobbi, C, 1983 The London Journal of Alessandro Magno, in *London J* **9.2**, 137–52

Bateson, M, 1902 A London municipal collection, in *Engl Hist Rev* **17**, 430–511, 707–30

Beckmann, B, 1974 The main types of the first four production periods of Sieburg pottery, in V Evison and J Hurst (eds) *Medieval pottery from excavations*, London, 183–220

Bell, W, 1938 *A short history of the Worshipful ceremony of Tylers and Bricklayers of the City of London*, London

Blaeu, W, 1612, *Sea Mirrour*, London

Bonde, N, 1992 Dendrochronology and the timber trade in northern Europe from the fifteenth to the seventeenth century, in T Bartolin, B Berglund, D Eckstein, and F Schweingruber (eds) *Tree rings and environment: proceedings of the International Dendrochrononological Symposium 1990*, Lundqua Rep **34**, 53–5

Bradford, G, 1954 *A glossary of sea terms*, London

Bridge House Weekly Payments, 10 vols, Corporation of London Record Office

Brindley, H, 1938 *Impressions and casts of seals, coins, tokens, medals and other objects of art exhibited in the Seal Room, National Maritime Museum*, London

Brogger, A, and Shetelig, H, 1951 *The Viking ships, their ancestry and evolution*, Oslo

Broodbank, J, 1921 *History of the port of London*, 2 vols, London

Brooke, C, 1975 *London 800–1216: the shaping of a city*, London

Burwash, D, 1969 *English merchant shipping 1460–1540*, Newton Abbot

Calendar of Close Rolls, Henry IV, 25 Feb 1413, 428

Camden, W, 1610, *Britain*, London

Carr, F, 1989 *Sailing barges*, Lavenham

Chaucer, G, *The Canterbury Tales*, F N Robinson (ed), 1974, Oxford

Chew, H, and Kellaway, W (eds), 1973 *London Assize of Nuisance*, London

Christensen, A, 1985 Boat finds from Bryggen, in I Bergen *The Bryggen Papers*, 47–280

City of London Record Office, no date *Journal 10*, modern fo **257**

Clowes, G, 1959 *London sailing ships, their history and development*, London

Crumlin-Pedersen, O, 1979 Danish cog-finds, in S McGrail (ed) *Medieval ships and harbours in northern Europe*, BAR Int Ser **66**, 17–34

Cutler, D, 1994 Romano-Celtic ship caulking, in Marsden 1994, 189–90

Douglas, D, and Greenaway, G, 1953 *English historical documents 1042–1189*, London

Dunning, G, Hurst, J, and Tischler, F, 1959 Anglo-Saxon pottery: a symposium, *Med Arch* **3**, 1–78

Dyson, T, 1985 Early harbour regulations in London, in A Herteig (ed) *Conference on waterfront archaeology in north European towns*, **2**, Bergen 1983, 19–24

Egan, G, 1991 A fragment in time, *Municip J* **38**, 14–16

Ellmers, D, 1979 The cog of Bremen and related boats, in S McGrail (ed) *Medieval ships and harbours in northern Europe*, BAR Int Ser **66**, 1–15

Ellmers, C, and Werner, A, 1991 *Dockland life: a pictorial history of London's docks 1860–1970*, London

Falconer, W, 1815 *A new universal dictionary of the marine*, 1974, London

Fenwick, V, 1978a *The Graveney boat*, BAR Brit Ser **53**, Oxford

—, 1978b Was there a body beneath the Walthamstow boat?, *Int J Nautical Archaeol* **7**, 187–94

Findlay, A, 1885 *A handbook for the navigation of different channels of the Thames and Medway and the coast between Folkestone and Orfordness*, London

Fliedner, S, 1969 Kogge und Hulk, in *Die Bremer Hanse-Kogge*, Bremen, 39–121

Gadd, D, and Dyson, T, 1981 Bridewell Place. Excavations at 9–11 Bridewell Place and 1–3 Tudor Street, City of London 1978, *Post-Medieval Archaeol* **15**, 1–79

Goodburn, D, 1988 Recent finds of ancient boats from the London area, *London Archaeol* **5.16**, 423–8

—, 1991 New light on early ship and boatbuilding in the London area, in G Good, R Jones, and M Ponsford (eds) *Waterfront Archaeology*, CBA Res Rep **74**, 105–15

—, 1994 Anglo-Saxon boat finds from London, are they English?, in C Westerdahl (ed) *Crossroads in ancient shipbuilding*, Oxbow Monog **40**, Oxford, 97–104

Greenhill, B, 1976 *Archaeology of the boat*, London

Guy's Hospital Gazette, 1889, **3** new ser, 11

Harben, H, 1918 *A dictionary of London*, London

Harris, G, 1969 *The Trinity House of Deptford 1514–1660*, London

Heal, S, and Hutchinson, G Three recently found logboats, *Int J Nautical Archaeol* **15.3**, 205–13

Hillam, J, Morgan, R, and Tyers, I, 1987 Sapwood estimates and the dating of short ring sequences, in R Ward (ed) *Applications of tree-ring studies*, BAR Int Ser **333**, 165–85

Hind, J, 1982 *Stability and trim of fishing vessels and other small ships*, Farnham

Hunt, H, 1978 Report on fibrous samples, in Fenwick 1978a, 152–4

Hurst, J, Neal, D, and van Beuningen, H, 1986 *Pottery produced and traded in north-west Europe 1350–1650*, Rotterdam Papers **VI**, Rotterdam

Hutchinson, G, 1986 The southwold side rudders, *Antiquity* **60**, 219–21

Ingelman-Sundberg, C, 1985 *Marinarkeologi*, Wiken

James, M, 1971 *Studies in the medieval wine trade*, Oxford

Journal of the British Archaeological Association, 1846, ser 1, **2**, 361–2

—, 1869, ser 1, **25**, 79–81

Kemp, P, 1976 *The Oxford companion to ships and the sea*, Oxford

Kemp and Young, 1971 *Ship stability, notes and examples*, London

Larn, R, 1979 *Goodwin Sands shipwrecks*, Newton Abbot

Leather, J, 1987 *Clinker boatbuilding*, London

Liber Albus: the white book of the City of London, 1419, Carpenter, J, and Whittington, R (compilers), 1861, ed H Riley, London

Loomie, A, 1963 An Armada pilot's survey of the English coastline, October 1597, *Mar Mirror* **49**, 288–300

Loyn, H, 1962 *Anglo-Saxon England and the Norman conquest*, London

Manning, W, 1985 *Catalogue of the Romano-British iron tools, fittings, and weapons in the British Museum*, London

Marsden, P, 1963 Ancient ships in London, *Mar Mirror* **49**, 144–5

—, 1964 The Walthamstow boat, in *Mar Mirror* **50**, 2–6

—, 1971 A seventeenth-century boat found in London, *Post-Medieval Archaeol* **5**, 88–98

—, 1972 Archaeology at sea, *Antiquity* **46**, 198–202

—, 1989 A late Saxon logboat from Clapton, London Borough of Hackney, *Int J Nautical Archaeol* **18.2**, 89–111

—, 1994 *Ships of the port of London: First to twelfth centuries AD*, English Heritage Archaeol rep 3, London

McGrail, S, 1978 *Logboats of England and Wales with comparative material from European and other countries*, parts 1 and 2, BAR Brit Ser **51**, Oxford

—, 1987 *Ancient boats in north-west Europe*, London

—, 1993 *Medieval boat and ship timbers from Dublin*, Dublin

McGrail, S, and Denford, G, 1982 Boatbuilding techniques, technological change, and attribute analysis, in S McGrail (ed) *Woodworking techniques before AD 1500*, BAR Int Ser **129**, 25–72

McKee, E, 1972 *Clench lap or clinker*, London

Macmichael, J, 1890 Baynard Castle, and excavations on its site, *J Brit Archaeol Ass* 1st ser **46**, 173–85

Milne, G, and Goodburn, D, 1990 The early medieval port of London AD 700–1200, *Antiquity* **64**, 629–36

Milne, G, and Milne, C, 1982 *Medieval waterfront development at Trig Lane, London*, London Middlesex Archaeol Soc Spec Pap **5**, London

Moxon, J, 1703 *Mechanical exercises or the doctrine of handy-works*, 1979, Scarsdal, New York

Murray, J (ed), 1908, 1923 *A new English dictionary on historical principles*, Oxford

Naish, F Prideaux, 1948 The mystery of the tonnage and dimensions of the Pelican-Golden Hind, *Mar Mirror* **34**, 42–5

Nautical Archaeology Society, 1983 *Newsletter*, October, 3

Olsen, O, and Crumlin-Pedersen, O, 1967 The Skuldelev ships, *Acta Archaeologia* **38**, 73–174

Orton, C, 1979 Medieval pottery from a kiln site at Cheam: Part 2, *London Archaeol* **3.11**, 355–9

—, 1982 The excavation of a late medieval transitional pottery kiln at Cheam, Surrey, *Surrey Archaeol Collect* **73**, 492

Oswald, A, 1949 Finds from a London building site, *Archaeol Newsl* March, 4

Peterson, M, 1973 *History under the sea*, Alexandria, Virginia

Phillips-Birt, D, 1962 *Fore-and-aft sailing craft, and the developments of the modern yacht*, London

Potter, G, 1991 The medieval bridge and waterfront at Kingston-upon-Thames, in G Good, R Jones, and M Ponsford (eds) *Waterfront Archaeology*, CBA Res Rep **74**, 137–49

Pownall, T, 1779 Memoire on the Roman earthen ware fished up within the mouth of the River Thames, *Archaeologia* **5**, 282–90

Reddaway, T, 1951 *The rebuilding of London after the Great Fire*, London

Reinders, R, 1985 Cog finds from the Ijsselmeerpolders, *Flevobricht* **248**, Lelystad

Rotuli Parliamentorum, **1767**, J Strachey and others (ed), 6 vols, London

Rowse, A, 1974 *The Tower of London in the history of the nation*, London

Rule, M, 1983 *The Mary Rose: the excavation and raising of Henry VIII's flagship*, Leicester

Ryder, M L, 1969 Changes in the fleece of sheep following domestication (with a note on the coats of cattle), in P Ucko and G Dimbleby (eds) *The domestication and exploitation of plants and animals*, London, 495–521

—, 1983 *Sheep and man*, London

—, 1984 The first hair remains from an Aurochs (Bos primgenius) and some medieval domestic cattle hair, *J Arch Sci* **11**, 99–101

—, 1986 The goat, *Biologist* **33**, 131–9

—, 1987 Feral goats - their origin and history, *The Ark* **14** (9) 305–11, (10) 334–8

—, 1994 Hair in caulking from Fennings Wharf boat fragments, in Marsden 1994, 211

Ryder, M L, and Gabra-Sanders, T, 1984 A note on wook felting in sheep, *J Agric Sci* **103**, 369–71

Salisbury, W, 1961 The Woolwich ship, *Mar Mirror* **47**, 81–90

Salzman, L, 1931 *English trade in the Middle Ages*, Oxford

—, 1967 *Building in England down to 1540*, Oxford

Sandahl, B, 1951 *Middle English sea terms: I The ship's hull*, Uppsala, Sweden

—, 1958 *Middle English sea terms: II Masts, spars, and sails*, Uppsala, Sweden

Schweingruber, F, 1982, *Microscopic wood anatomy*, Teufen, Switzerland

—, 1988 *Tree-rings*, Doredrecht

—, 1990 *Anatomy of European woods*, Bern und Stuttgart

Sharpe, R (ed), 1899–1912 *Calendar of Letter Books of the City of London*, 10 vols

Sheldon, H, 1974 Excavations at Toppings and Sun Wharves, Southwark, 1970–2, *Trans London Middlesex Archaeol Soc* **25**, 1–116

Steedman, K, Dyson, T, and Schofield, J, 1992 Aspects of Saxo-Norman London: III The bridgehead and Billingsgate to 1200, *London Middlesex Archaeol Soc Spec Pap* **14**, London

Steffy, R, 1982 Shipbuilding glossary, in G Bass and F Van Doornick (eds) *Yassi Ada, vol 1. A seventh-century Byzantine shipwreck*, 333–4

Stow, J, 1603 *A survey of London*, 10 vols, introduction by C Kingsford, 1908, Oxford

Sturdy, D, 1977 Boat-archaeology of the Thames, in S McGrail (ed) *Sources and techniques in boat archaeology*, BAR Supp Ser **29**, London

Sutherland, W, 1711 *The ship-builders assistant: or, some essays towards completing the art of marine architecture*, London

Tatton-Brown, T, 1974 Excavations at the Custon House site, City of London, 1973, *Trans London Middlesex Archaeol Soc* **25**, 117–219

Taylor, E, 1956 *The haven-finding art*, London

Taylor, L, 1984 *The principles and practices of ship stability*, Glasgow

Tyers, I, 1990 *Southwark boats*, MoL Dendrochronology Report **3/90**

—, 1992 *City: early to late medieval boats*, MoLAS Dendrochronology Report **4/92**

Ucelli, G, 1950 *Le Navi de Nemi*, Rome

Vaughan, R, 1958 The chronicle of John of Wallingford, *Eng Hist Rev* **73**, 66–77

Vidler, L, 1935 The Rye river barges, *Mar Mirror* **21**, 21–37

Villain-Gandossi, C, 1979 Le navire medieval a travers led miniatures des manuscrits Francais, in S McGrail (ed) *Medieval ships and harbours in northern Europe*, BAR Int Ser **66**, 195–226

Vince, A, 1985 Saxon and medieval pottery in London: a review, *Med Arch* **29**, 25–93

—, 1990 *Saxon London: an archaeological investigation*, London

Vulliamy, C, 1930 *The archaeology of Middlesex and London*, London

Walton, W, 1832 Accompts of the Manor of the Savoy, temp Richard II, *Archaeologia* **24**, 299–316

—, P, 1988 Caulking, cordage and textiles, in C O'Brian, L Brown, S Dixon, and R Nicholson *The origins of the Newcastle Quayside*, Soc Antiq Newcastle Monog Ser **3**, 78–85

—, P, 1989 Caulking, textiles and cordage, in C O'Brian *et al* Excavations at Newcastle Quayside: The Crown Court site, *Archaeol Aeliana* 5th ser, **17**, 74–76

Wazny, T, 1992 Historical timber trade and its implications on dendrochronological dating, in T Bartolin, B Berglund, D Eckstein, and F Schweingruber (eds) *Tree rings and environment: proceedings of the International Dendrochrononological Symposium 1990*, Lundqua Rep **34**, 331–3

Whitaker, W, 1889 *The geology of London and of part of the Thames valley*, **2**, London

Williams, G, 1971 *The heraldry of the Cinque Ports*, Newton Abbot

Wilson, K, and White, D, 1986 *The anatomy of wood: its variability and diversity*, London

Wright, L, 1988 *Technical vocabulary to do with life on the River Thames in London c AD 1270–1500*, unpubl D Phil thesis, University of Oxford

Index
by Lesley and Roy Adkins

The main references are given in **bold**